WHO KILLED GEORGE?

WHO KILLED GEORGE?

The Ordeal of Olive Sternaman

Cheryl MacDonald

Natural Heritage/Natural History Inc.

This publication has been assisted by an Ontario Heritage Book Award from the Ontario Heritage Foundation, an agency of the Ministry of Tourism, Culture & Recreation.

Who Killed George?
Published by Natural Heritage/Natural History Inc.
P.O. Box 95, Station O
Toronto, Ontario M4A 2M8

Design: Derek Chung Tiam Fook
Printed and Bound in Canada by Hignell Printing Limited, Winnipeg, Manitoba
First Printing August 1994

Canadian Cataloguing in Publication Data
MacDonald, Cheryl, 1952 –
     Who killed George? : the ordeal of Olive Sternaman

ISBN 0–920474–90–X

1. Sternaman, George, d. 1896.
2. Sternaman, Olive Adele
3. Poisoning – Ontario – Haldimand – History – 19th century.
4. Poisoners – Ontario – Haldimand – Biography.
I. Title.

HV6555.C22H35 1994   364.1'523'092   C94–930611–8

This publication has been assisted by an Ontario Heritage Book Award from the Ontario Heritage Foundation, an agency of the Ministry of Tourism, Culture & Recreation.

Natural Heritage/Natural History Inc. gratefully acknowledges the assistance of the Canada Council, the Ontario Arts Council, and the Government of Ontario through the Ministry of Culture, Tourism & Recreation.

DEDICATION

For sisters everywhere
whether of blood or of spirit
and especially for mine
Sandra MacDonald

TABLE OF CONTENTS

ACKNOWLEDGEMENTS

Many individuals and organizations have helped in the preparation of this book. Thanks go to the following: Hamilton Public Library, Special Collections; Frank W. Anderson; Harold Averill, University of Toronto Archives; Gail Benjafield, St. Catharines Public Library; Pierre Berton; Margaret Boothe, Dodge Chemical Company; *Dunnville Chronicle*; Mohawk College Library; Seneca College; Stuart Cumming, Welland Historical Society; Christopher Dafoe, *The Beaver*; Dunnville District Heritage Association; Sam and Annemieke Gowling; North Erie Shore Historical Society; Professor Edward C. Johnson; Merle Knight, Haldimand County Museum; Jim Lewis, Archives of Ontario; Jean Lint, Cayuga United Church; Dana B. Stavinga, Wilson MacDonald Memorial School Museum; David McClung; Toronto Metropolitan Library; Lee-Ann Misetich, Supreme Court of Ontario; Roanne Mokhtar, National Archives of Canada; Fred Mudge, Rose-Le Studios; Debra Pass, National Funeral Directors Association; Estelle Pringle; Buffalo Public Library; Simcoe Public Library; Debbie A. Silverman, Bar Association of Erie County; Theresa Starkes, Law Society of Upper Canada; Lydia Thompson; United Church of Canada; McMaster University Library; Anne Unyi, Welland Historical Museum; Frederick G. Vogel, *American Funeral Director*; Mary Walker; Ken Wilson, Victoria University/United Church Archives; Wilf Wrigglesworth, Supreme Court of Ontario.

Thanks also go to Barry and Jane Penhale for their interest in and support of the project; to my patient and painstaking editor, Robert L. Fraser, and to Paul Bator of the Ontario Heritage Foundation.

Finally, extra special thanks also go to Harry E. Sweet of Lowbanks, Ontario, for providing photographs and family information; to Sharon Warring for a guided tour of the Haldimand County Jail, including the area where Olive was imprisoned. And, as always, the dedicated staff of the Selkirk (City of Nanticoke) public library, Pat Reidy, Gloria Logan and Marg Fearman, who go above and beyond the call of duty in getting material to me.

FOREWORD

The story of Olive Sternaman is one of many episodes in Canadian history which has been largely forgotten. Although her trial for murder made headlines in two countries during the 1890s, she never achieved the lasting notoriety of Lizzie Borden or Evelyn Dick. Some memory of the case survives in rural southern Haldimand, especially in the Rainham Township area, but the details have been lost in the mists of time. Olive is mentioned in John Wilson Murray's *Memoirs of a Great Detective* and Hector Charlesworth's *Candid Chronicles* – both treasure houses of information for the lover of Victorian history – but I confess that the references aroused little curiosity the first time I encountered them.

What finally sparked my interest was stumbling across a newspaper report of the case. I remember the circumstances vividly: it was 1985 and I was reading the *Hamilton Spectator* on microfilm on the third floor of the Hamilton Public Library. (Normally, I would have been reading in the Special Collections room, but all the microfilm readers were in use, so I was in the main area.) My research was for *Adelaide Hoodless; Domestic Crusader*, my biography of the founder of the Women's Institute. While looking for accounts of Adelaide's battles with the Hamilton Board of Education, I stumbled across a headline mentioning Cayuga. As a former resident, my interest was piqued. For the next couple of hours I followed the progress of the trial in the press. Before I was finished, I knew I wanted to do something with the story.

This book is the result. My purpose was neither to present a case history of a specific murder trial, nor to analyze the treatment of working–class women by the 1890s Canadian justice system. Although any writer of history must acquire some scholarly skills, I have never considered myself a scholar. My bias has always been in favour of storytelling, and I prefer to leave detailed analysis and interpretation to others.

Olive's story is sensational, a true Victorian melodrama filled with love, hate, passion and violence, all bubbling beneath the bland, conservative surface of respectable working class and farming communities.

It is just one of many, many fascinating stories from Canada's past, and I am thankful for my good fortune in rediscovering it and finding sufficient archival material to shape it into this book.

GLOSSARY OF MEDICAL TERMS

Addison's disease Named for British physician Thomas Addison (1793–1860). A disease of the suprarenal glands involving insufficient activity of the cortices of the adrenal glands. Anemia, weakness, pigmentation of the skin are symptoms. Addisonism is a syndrome similar to Addison's disease, often present in patients with pulmonary tuberculosis. Symptoms include weakness and pigmentation of the skin.

Arsenic poisoning In acute cases, symptoms include vomiting, diarrhea, difficulty swallowing, thirst. In chronic arsenic poisoning, the same symptoms may be present in a milder form, as well as neuritis, inflammation of the kidneys, irritation of the mucous membranes of the nose and changes in skin colour.

Desquamation Scaling or peeling of the top layers of the skin.

Duramater Tough outer membrane covering the brain.

Suprarenal glands Flattened triangular glands at the top part of each kidney.

Summer complaint *Cholera nostrus* – Not true cholera, but often fatal. Diarrhea and vomiting, frequently the result of salmonella food poisoning.

Multiple neuritis Also called peripheral neuritis. Inflammation of the nerves resulting in pain and tenderness, and reduced or lost sensation or motor power. Loss of motor power can be very slow, typically might

involve legs, arms, loss of voice. Causes
include inflammation, metallic or alco-
holic poisons, infectious disease, bacteria,
and lack of vitamins.

PROLOGUE

On the evening of August 13, 1896, a sad little group disembarked from a train at Cayuga, Ontario. Olive Sternaman, a tall slim woman in her late twenties, helped her two young sons off the train. Then, her grey eyes clouded with worry, she watched as Grand Trunk Railway brakeman Albert Cox and her two brothers-in-law lifted the cot, on which her husband George was lying, to the ground.

Nearby, George's mother watched grimly as 21-year-old Avery and 18-year-old Freeman lifted George, cot and all, into the high-sided wooden wagon. Eliza Sternaman greeted her daughter-in-law coolly, and Olive, worn out from the journey and from weeks of tending to George, was equally reserved. Then the group settled in for the eight-mile ride home. For George, who felt every bump and jolt, the journey over country roads from Cayuga to the third concession, Rainham Township, was agonizing. It was nearly as painful for the others, who could do nothing to make George's journey easier, and who were uncomfortably aware of the tension between the two women. As the wagon climbed the long hill out of the Grand River valley and turned southward toward Lake Erie, no one was in any mood to appreciate the quiet beauty of the summer evening.

Haldimand County stretches along the north shore of eastern Lake Erie just west of the Niagara Peninsula. Named for Sir Frederick Haldimand, the Swiss mercenary who served as governor of Quebec during the American Revolution, the county was opened up to settlement in the late 1790s. Among the first new arrivals were the Six Nations Iroquois under the leadership of Joseph Brant, who had been rewarded for their service as allies of the British crown with a huge land grant on either side of the Grand.

White settlers soon followed. At first, most made their homes along the banks of the river. Small communities emerged along its lower stretches – Caledonia, York, Indiana, Cayuga, Dunnville –buoyed by trade in lumber, farm produce and gypsum. The construction of the Welland Canal in the late 1820s improved transportation to and from Dunnville in the southeastern corner of the county and by the late 1800s the town was the largest in Haldimand. For a time, steamers plied the waters of the Grand as far north as Brantford, but the river was shallow and locks built to aid shipping quickly silted up. Eventually, railroads became the main link to

Hamilton, Toronto and Buffalo; to London and Windsor; and to the prairies beyond.

While the early settlers were clearing land along the Grand, other new arrivals took up residence near the shores of the lake. Among the first was Jakob Huber, a Swiss Mennonite from Pennsylvania, whose mill at Stoney Creek became the focal point of a settlement which was named Selkirk in 1855. Their name anglicized to Hoover, Huber's relatives and descendants married other new settlers in Walpole and Rainham townships. A large number of them were German–speaking Mennonites, whose parents had left the United States in search of new land. Many settled along Twenty Mile Creek in the Niagara Peninsula. When farmland in that area became scarce, their children moved into Haldimand County. If the heavy clay soil along the lake was difficult to work, it was fertile. In time, small villages grew up amid the farm fields. Even by the 1890s, however, few had populations of more than 100. Fisherville was the centre of Rainham's German settlement, a tidy crossroads village of some 150 residents, boasting two stores, a hotel, a blacksmith shop and a handful of other small businesses.

Olive and George Sternaman were both members of Rainham's community of sturdy German farmers and artisans. The daughter of a shoemaker, Olive Sevenpifer was born in Sweet's Corners in 1867 and lived there until the age of 12. Then, like many families seeking higher wages and a better way of life, the Sevenpifers moved to Port Colborne. Two years later, they moved again, this time to Buffalo. Soon afterwards, Olive found work as a domestic servant, a position she held until her marriage to Elon Chipman in 1886.

Meanwhile, George was growing up on the family farm just east of Fisherville and northwest of Sweet's Corners. The second child and first son of David and Eliza Sternaman, George descended from the Hoover family on his mother's side, and so was part of a countywide network of relatives. Like many young men in the late 1880s and 1890s, he was eager to escape the humdrum routine of rural life, anxious for a little excitement and better wages. By the time he was 20, his younger brothers were old enough to help their father on the farm, leaving George free to find work in Buffalo. And there he might have remained, joining thousands of other Canadians, if tragedy had not intervened.

It was dark long before the wagon reached the Sternaman house. With no scenery to distract her and Eliza's disapproving presence putting a damper on conversation, Olive had time to mull over the

events of the last two years. In that short period she had been widowed, remarried, and now she had lost her home. Her second husband was gravely ill, and she had been forced to live off the charity
of a woman who despised her. It was a bitter end to a chain of
events that had begun with a simple act of kindness.

PART ONE

SUSPICIOUS DEATHS

Shelter for a stranger

Three hundred thousand people lived in Buffalo in the 1890s. One-third were foreign-born and, of these, a significant number were Canadians who had crossed the Niagara River separating the two countries in hopes of a new and better life. The Irish were equally well-represented and there were a significant number of Poles, but it was the Germans who dominated the immigrant enclaves. Fully half of those listed as foreign born in the 1890 census were of German origin.

Buffalo was not only a significant Great Lakes' port, it was also a railway centre and the site of a huge cattle market. Immigrants generally found jobs working on the railroads or in steel foundries, in shipyards or mines. Some, particularly the Germans, set up small businesses, working as boot-makers, butchers, bakers or in other essential occupations. While some immigrants prospered, others struggled to survive. In working-class neighbourhoods, housing was stretched to its limits. In some areas, five families crowded into a single house. In others, the sight of a family with a few meagre possessions, trudging through the street, as they searched for shelter was commonplace.

Ezra Elon Chipman was among the more fortunate new Buffalonians. Born in St. Catharines, Ontario, he was a carpenter whose skill and hard work had paid off. He earned between $2.00 and $2.50 a day, about as high a rate as the average working man could expect. "A good, steady man," sober and industrious, he had a comfortable home in Black Rock (now a part of Buffalo), a working-class district from which a Fenian raid against Canada had been launched in 1866. Thanks to the hard work of his wife, Olive, the house was clean and nicely furnished, and their two sons well cared for. Moreover, the future looked promising: in 1890 Charles Young, the contractor who employed Elon, had promoted him to foreman.

In contrast to so many of his contemporaries, Elon was not a "drinking man." He was sociable enough, though, and respected by his co-workers. He was also kind-hearted. In 1893, he encountered George Sternaman, who was working on a construction project not far from Chipman's home. George had been in Buffalo about a year and, like Elon, was a hard worker who shunned alcohol. Whatever the reason –a shared nationality, a similarly sober approach to work, or a brotherly interest in a young man far from home, Elon decided to take George under his wing.

One night after work, he spoke to Olive. George needed a place to stay until his current job was finished, and he would be calling the next morning to arrange board for the next few weeks, until the job he was working on finished. Olive agreed, and George moved into the house. The extra money was naturally welcome although at first Olive had some reservations about a third adult in the household. Apparently those reservations evaporated when she learned George had grown up in Rainham Township, not far from her childhood home.

A few weeks later, when the nearby job ended, George showed no signs of moving out. Olive and Elon discussed the matter privately and told George he could stay if he wished. George stayed, fitting into the household routine as unobtrusively as possible. He and Elon remained friends, keeping each other company on week nights at home. On Sunday mornings, the two men cleaned out the lamp chimneys, one of the messier household tasks. George shrugged off protests that he needn't help, saying he had done the same while living with his parents. Sometimes, George would accompany Olive, Elon and their two sons on weekend outings, and one September George and the four Chipmans visited the Rainham agricultural fair.

For several decades, many Ontario communities had hosted annual or semi–annual agricultural fairs. Most were sponsored by local agricultural societies, partly as a forum for the latest innovations in equipment and livestock breeding. But the fairs were also great entertainment, with side shows, hucksters, horse races and games of chance. The Ontario Department of Agriculture, which provided some money for the fairs, might object to the fairs' unsavoury and uneducational features, but the public loved them.

Fair–goers also loved the chance to meet with absent friends and family. Railroads offered special discounts for those travelling to some fairs, making it relatively cheap to attend. And besides, fair day was a holiday, even for farmers exhibiting livestock, or their wives who brought quilts, dairy products and pies to competition.

Without a doubt, George and Olive ran into friends and family at the Rainham Fair. In addition, George took the Chipmans home to meet his family. If for appearance's sake Eliza Sternaman was polite, it seems she was not impressed with the young Mrs. Chipman. Was it the easy familiarity between her son and his friend's wife that annoyed Eliza – a glance that betrayed George's fondness for Olive? Or had George's letters home made it clear that he was more than a little bit in love with his married landlady? Certainly Eliza was jealous of this rival for her first-born son's affections, for there was no doubt that as long as George shared the Chipmans' accommodations he was more under Olive's influence than Eliza's. Eliza may also have been jealous of Olive's appearance, for even as a young woman George's mother had looked forbiddingly grim. Olive was not beautiful by any stretch of the imagination. Her nose was too sharp and her protruding teeth showed even when her mouth was closed. But her complexion was clear, her light brown hair was carefully brushed and her neat clothing revealed a slender figure. More importantly, she was kind-hearted, affectionate and vivacious, always ready to laugh at someone's jokes or chat with friends.

To George's stern and judgmental mother, Olive Chipman was too flighty to be likeable. Worse still, Eliza suspected that Olive's morals might not withstand too close an inspection. When the fair was over, Elon Chipman went back to Buffalo alone. Pleading illness, Olive stayed on in Canada. And so did George.

Whatever Eliza might make of that turn of events, it did not bother Elon Chipman in the least. He had no reason to distrust his wife, who would be among relatives and family friends. Nor did he consider George's decision to remain a little longer in Canada suspicious. He was quite happy to have George continue living with them in Buffalo. Elon must have heard neighbourhood gossip – there are always those ready to interpret any relationship in the worst possible light and try to bring others round to their way of thinking – but he was a sensible man, who loved Olive and their children. Besides, he and George had much in common.

Possibly, Elon was just so close to both George and Olive that he was not fully aware of the depth of George's affection. Neither, for that matter, was Olive. Either George hid the intensity of his feelings, or Olive was simply too busy to notice. She cared for her two young sons and ran the household as usual, spending whatever free time she had with friends or with the Order of Rebekahs, the women's auxiliary of the International Order of Oddfellows (IOOF), a charitable organization created to care for the ill and impoverished. But Olive's sister Lizzie and her mother Ellen knew something about George's emotional state.

Some time after George came to stay with the Chipmans, Olive fell seriously ill. A doctor was sent for, and when he came, he informed the family that the young woman was dying. Either Ellen or Lizzie told George, who began to cry as though his heart would break. Shortly afterwards, he had an attack of vomiting, and was ill for a several days.

Both Olive and George recovered. Despite the young man's intensely inappropriate feelings, he continued to live with the couple. They were both kind to him, although there were times when he felt like an outsider. Whenever Elon and Olive had company, often other members of their family, George would slip out, not returning until the guests had departed. Still, he felt comfortable enough with Olive and Elon.

In the late summer of 1894, news reached Buffalo that George's father, David Sternaman, was dying of stomach cancer. George went home to be with him in his final days and remained in Canada for more than a month.

David died on September 19 at the age of 54. Like many farmers, he had incurred several debts. But he and Eliza were a cautious couple and the insurance on David's life was more than enough to pay all the bills and leave a little extra. George was so impressed with the benefits of life insurance that he told Ambrose K. Goodman, the Cayuga lawyer who probated David's will, that he intended to insure his own life at once. Goodman passed the word along to a Cayuga insurance agent, who drove out to the Sternaman farm. True to his word, George began payments on a policy of his own.

As the late summer days grew shorter, the Sternaman family returned to its regular routine. For George, there was no longer a reason to stay behind. He was unwilling to take on the burden of the farm and so, around the end of September, he returned to Buffalo and the Chipmans' house.

About this time, Elon began to complain of exhaustion when he came home from work. As the weeks passed and he failed to get better, Olive worried silently. But she said nothing, convinced he would recover before long.

"My stomach is burning out of me."

Winter is a changeable season in Buffalo and the entire lower Great Lakes region. One day, the weather is mild, almost balmy. The sun shines, and thoughts of snow and ice are far away. The next, several inches of snow might fall, or icy rain. Knowing this, those who live in the region make the most of the good weather, and somehow muddle through the rest.

Christmas Eve 1894 was much like any other December day. As usual, Olive packed lunches for Elon and George, and the two went off to their separate jobs. At lunch time, Elon stopped to eat with two other carpenters, William Martin and contractor William T. Randall. Randall had a stove going in the attic of the house in which they were working, so the men gathered there, soaking in the heat before returning to their tasks. Elon sat by the stairway and appeared to be enjoying his lunch. He had eaten about three-quarters of a slice of pie when he suddenly he flung it into a corner. "Gad," he joked, "I guess the old woman got cayenne pepper in her pie this time instead of spice." A few minutes later, however, when he rose to return to work, he was no longer laughing. "My stomach is burning out of me," he complained as he went downstairs. By one o'clock, he could no longer bear the pain. Telling Randall that he had never felt so sick in his life, he went home. Elon had been vomiting continuously since lunch, but he was sure it was nothing serious. He even asked Randall whether the crew would be at work the next day. Christmas was a holiday, Randall replied, but the crew would be back to work the day after. "Well, I will be with you again," Elon assured him. On the way home, he stopped at a drug store to get some medicine for the pain.

As the afternoon progressed, Elon's stomach pain became more intense. Olive sent for Dr. Francis Rich, the family physician since early 1889. He examined Elon, noting his symptoms: gastritis, extreme thirst and vomiting. He prescribed some medicine, but it did little to help. As Christmas came and went, Elon continued to suffer terrible pain and a unremitting thirst. The vomiting continued.

When Elon failed to appear for work on Boxing Day, Randall stopped by the Chipman house on his way home. He found Elon in bed, obviously very sick. According to the family, the doctor had diagnosed inflammation of the stomach. By the end of the month, Elon's fingers and legs were numb and his skin was discolored. Rich reviewed the symptoms and Elon's failure to improve, especially after Olive observed that he must have got the wrong medicine from the drug store. Because the illness was outside anything in his experience, Rich decided a second opinion was needed. He suggested Elon be sent to the state hospital, a short distance from the Chipman home in Black Rock.

Olive was horrified. Like many people of her class and education, she believed that hospitals offered little hope of recovery and that Elon's only chance was to remain under her care. In part, she was correct. In the late 19th century, the wealthy usually paid for medical care in their own homes. Most hospitals were charitable institutions where patients went only when there was no other choice. Moreover, because of strict budgets and limited staff, hospital care was not always the best. As a result, there was a widespread feeling among the working classes that a hospital was where one went to die. Knowing this, Olive spurned Dr. Rich's suggestion.

During Elon's illness, George worked each day as usual and handled the few household chores which he and Elon had shared. Olive, worried about her husband, had little time for their boarder, although his presence must have been welcome, if only because of the extra money he brought into the household. And that money was now essential. The few dollars Elon received from the Carpenters' Union as sick pay, as well as some benefits from the IOOF, were hardly enough to pay for rent, food and medicine.

One noticeable change in George's routine over this period was a renewed interest in religion. Olive, whose own faith was simple and unshakable, must have been gratified that some good was coming out of Elon's illness. Despite his mother's example, George had expressed little interest in religion since arriving in Buffalo. Now, with Elon deteriorating every day, he began to attend Baptist church meetings. Some time in January 1895 he was baptized, symbolically washing away his sins and starting afresh.

By January 5th, Elon was so much better that Dr. Rich no longer visited daily. One week later, however, Elon suffered a relapse. This time, there was no recovery. He grew steadily weaker and paralysis set in. Soon after, his mother, Ellen Chipman and his sister, Dora Bonestead, were called to his bedside.

Unable to convince Olive that Elon belonged in a hospital, Dr. Rich tried another tack. On January 19th, he brought a more experienced colleague, Dr. W.L. Parmanter, to the Chipman's residence. Parmanter was 60 and had lived in Buffalo for nearly 30 years, but he had been born in Gananoque, Ontario, and had studied at Queen's University in Kingston before graduating from the Homeopathic College of Medicine in Cleveland in the early 1870s. Like most experienced doctors, Parmanter had reached a point where almost nothing surprised him. There was a possibility that Elon was suffering from syphilis. Although they were men of science, the doctors were reluctant to discuss such a delicate issue with a woman. Besides, Dr. Parmanter was leaning heavily towards a diagnosis of chronic poisoning. Alcohol was certainly a possible cause, but Elon Chipman did not drink. There was, therefore, only one other possibility – metallic poisoning, probably arsenic.

Like Rich, Parmanter urged Olive to send Elon to the hospital, where he would be cared for and his vomit analyzed. Olive refused, pointing out that Elon seemed to be getting a little better, and the doctors backed down.

Doctor Rich was alarmed at Elon's continuing deterioration, but expected no sudden change in his condition. Neither, for that matter, did Dr. Parmanter. To the surprise of both physicians, Elon died in the early hours of January 20, 1895. The death certificate ascribed death to multiple neuritis and paralysis, a description of the symptoms rather than the cause of death. Both doctors knew neuritis was a symptom of either syphilis or poisoning, and as far as they had been able to determine Elon Chipman had not been suffering from the former. Where poison had come from was open to speculation – perhaps Olive's statement that the druggist had made a mistake in preparing Elon's medicine was correct. Or perhaps Elon had accidentally ingested some chemical on the job site. Unwilling to examine the issue more closely, Dr. Rich simply signed the death certificate. Elon's body was embalmed almost immediately.

Dr. Rich may have chosen to shut his eyes to the unusual circumstances of Elon Chipman's death, but the neighbourhood gossips did not. According to rumours, Olive had murdered Elon for insurance money. Moreover, the young widow's reputation was not enhanced by the continued presence of George Sternaman.

"If you marry that woman ..."

The 19th-century women's movement started in Seneca Falls, New York, in 1848. By the 1890s, women had overcome various obstacles to gain access to universities and some professions. Some women found employment as doctors and lawyers, teachers, university professors and secretaries. Most, however, were still in low-paying and menial positions, as factory workers or domestic servants. For the majority, employment outside the home ended with marriage.

Although the need for a woman's income did not necessarily end at the same time, societal pressures on women to care for home and family meant most remained at home until their children were old enough to care for themselves. Mothers who found themselves widowed or abandoned were in a particularly difficult situation: if they went out to work, their children suffered; if they did not, the children might starve. With social services virtually non-existent, women found what solutions they could. Some worked at home, sewing or washing for neighbours; some relied on relatives or friends to care for their children while they went out to work; others took in boarders.

Olive was only a little better off than most young widows. Insurance money had covered Elon's funeral expenses, but what was left over quickly vanished with day–to–day living costs and a loan to Olive's family. Still, she had the emotional support of Elon's family and her own. She also had George.

Simple inertia may have accounted for George's decision to continue boarding with Olive and her children, although some feeling of responsibility was much more likely to have been the cause. Whatever the case, without George's contribution to the household, Olive would have been forced to leave her home.

Nevertheless, Olive paid a price for this small measure of financial security. Few neighbours could resist speculating about the relationship between the virile young carpenter and the attractive widow. Astute observers recognized the depth of George's feelings for Olive, whose own warmth and kindness towards George could easily be interpreted as affection. The mysterious circumstances of Elon's death added a sinister overtone. Inevitably, tongues wagged, and many of the more straight–laced neighbours criticized her living arrangements.

The neighbours were not the only ones who disapproved. In mid–February, Olive and George invited his mother to visit Buffalo. Eliza came and was soon expressing her displeasure. George and Olive were far too familiar for her liking, and she told George so in no uncertain terms. George merely laughed it off, telling his mother there was nothing to worry about.

But Eliza *was* worried, not only about her son's relationship with Olive, but also about the rumours that Elon had been poisoned. She believed the rumours. She also believed Olive was trying to poison her. One day, Olive left the room to prepare tea for Eliza. When she returned, Eliza was weeping, almost hysterically. She refused to explain her behaviour, but after returning to Canada she wrote to George explaining her suspicions.

Over the next several months, Eliza entreated George to find other accommodations. Matters came to a head in the fall of 1895. In September, George and Olive once again attended the Rainham Fair. Olive returned to Buffalo alone, while George remained to visit with his mother. During that time, he told her he was thinking of marrying Olive.

Eliza furiously pointed out that not only was Olive five years older and the mother of two children, but also there were the rumours surrounding Elon's death. Furthermore, as Eliza well knew – since she was the beneficiary – George held one or two life insurance policies. If getting insurance money had been the motive behind Elon's murder, Eliza reasoned, then marriage to Olive was a risky business. "George," she warned, "if you marry that woman, you'll be dead in six months."

"Ollie's all right," George laughed. But Eliza would not be convinced and refused to give her blessing to the union. After George returned to Buffalo, she wrote, pleading with him to break away from Olive, and telling him that, according to his brother Freeman, even in Rainham people suspected Olive of murdering Elon.

In response, George pleaded, that he had "always tried to do the best I could for you and to please you." But she was "asking too much when you want me to give up one that I love." He expressed astonishment at the rumours. "I have never heard anything of the kind over here," and wondered why folks thought "that we were engaged." Reaffirming his desire to marry Olive, he hoped Eliza would not "like anyone to coax you away from one you loved." Then he reassured his Eliza about his filial feelings, while asking her to change her attitude towards Olive:

> Mother I do not want you to die broken hearted. I want
> you to live as long as you can and when your time comes
> I want you to be the same to me and mine as you have
> been to me. Mother I think that you had not ought to
> think so hard of her because you have no proof for what
> you have heard.

Finally, George derided the rumours as "falsehood," which, moreover, were more prevalent in Rainham than in Buffalo. As for Olive's supposed designs on his insurance, if "I had that opinion ... I would not pay another cent to any of my policies."

In the same letter, George told Eliza that once his mind was made up there was nothing that could stop him, and he was determined to marry Olive. On January 21, 1896, a year and a day after Elon Chipman's death, he wrote to Eliza announcing his engagement. She wrote back, pleading with him not to sacrifice his future, and possibly his life, through a foolish move. George ignored her. On February 3, Olive Adell Sevenpifer Chipman became Mrs. George Sternaman. Soon afterwards, George notified his mother that Olive was now the beneficiary of his insurance policies.

The marriage was generally happy. George adored Olive and would do anything to please her. Family and friends remarked on their mutual affection. But there were two problems. First was the bitterness between Eliza and Olive, which preyed on George's mind. One day, while shopping in a grocery store, George encountered Benjamin Morningstar, who tried to interest him in buying some stock in the Chautauqua Savings & Loan Association. George turned him down, explaining that all his extra cash went towards his insurance policies. He went on to say that his mother disapproved of the policies, and that his wife and his mother were on bad terms.

Second was George's own character. He was both jealous and possessive. After Elon's death, Olive displayed his photograph on an easel in the parlor. Whenever George saw it, he flew into a rage, no matter who else was present, insisting that it be covered with a black cloth. He was, in addition, insecure about Olive's love for him and hated to be away from her. On one occasion he remarked that he wished he could be sick for two years so that she would not leave him. And, like a small boy, he had fits of sulking. Olive called them "spells" and put them down to bad temper and worry. Yet George would sit for hours at a time, as if in a trance, neither moving nor responding to any remarks. The fits were frequent enough to cause Olive real concern. Before the marriage, she and her mother visited a doctor to describe them. The doctor had assured them that George was not suffering from epileptic seizures and that there was nothing to worry about. Laughing, he predicted the fits would stop as soon as he married. The doctor may have been right. After the wedding, the spells stopped.

George seemed to be in good health. On April 27, he had been examined by Dr. William Langley, a physician for Metropolitan Life Insurance. In keeping with company rules, Langley had examined George alone while Olive stayed in the back room of the house. With George stripped to his undershirt for the examination, the doctor noted the young man's weight, 148 pounds; height, 5 feet, 8 inches; and girth of chest, 35 inches. Langley examined his lungs and heart, which seemed in good condition. Then he asked several questions about his state of health and family history. George claimed no history of "fits or convulsions" or hereditary disease, although he did mention his father's stomach cancer.

Langley duly pronounced George fit. True, George had complained to Benjamin Morningstar of his occasional stomach trouble, but he attributed the problem to a habit of carrying nails in his mouth while working.

"Peculiar attacks"

Then, on June 2, George suddenly became ill at work after lunch. The symptoms – vomiting, accompanied by a burning sensation in the mouth, throat and stomach – were remarkably similar to those Elon Chipman had experienced. George's foreman blamed it on the drinking water, which frequently went bad during warm weather, and allowed him to leave work an hour early.

At home, Olive worried over his health and the ironic similarities between his mysterious ailment and Elon's final illness. He soon recovered, however, he now seemed moodier than usual. On June 9, George suffered another spell. Olive was remarkably patient, but the sudden return of George's mysterious ailment tried even her forbearance. She snapped, "Merciful God, if Elon could know that I married George, and he had these fits, he would wish him dead a dozen times."

Despite his apparent catatonia, George heard every word. Later, he accused her of not loving him. She reassured him, but warned him that if he continued with such behaviour she might stop. If that happened, George cautioned, he would leave her, although he would always provide money for her support.

Neither George nor Olive could forget the neighbours' suspicions following Elon's death and the accusations Eliza had made. Consequently, on June 10, George wrote an unusual letter. He had "had very peculiar attacks at times during the past 6 mos and of which no one but my wife and a few of her relative know anything of" and wrote the letter "to state that if I should die while in one of them that no person can say that it was by her hands in any way that I died." The attacks came "when I get down-hearted or worrying about anything that does not go to please me." His sole purpose in writing was to "convince all that they may not think that my wife had anything to do with such an uncommon death." He then entrusted the letter to Olive for safekeeping.

For several days, George continued on the job, although leaving early every evening. Then, on Saturday, June 13, about half an hour after lunch, he began vomiting more violently than ever. Olive sent for Dr. Edward L. Frost, an instructor in obstetrics at the Buffalo Medical School for three years and a practising physician for about twice as long. He diagnosed George's ailment as summer complaint, complicated by "gastric catarrh" and did what he could to make him comfortable. Because Olive was concerned about faulty plumbing and had complained to Frost about a bad odour emanating from the "closet", the doctor also notified the Board of Health. The plumbing was inspected, and was ruled out as a source of contamination.

Frost checked George every second day or so, but to his bafflement, George failed to make progress. First, he complained of a backache; then he developed a genital sore. Frost prescribed medication containing a minuscule amount of arsenic, but discontinued the treatment when George failed to respond. By June 20th, George's skin had darkened to a sickly yellow colour, like that of a malaria victim. The genital sore had disappeared, but George's pulse was climbing and he was noticeably weaker. On June 26, Frost called in a colleague, Dr. James R. Whitewell, for a second opinion. Whitewell concurred with both Frost's diagnosis and his treatment. As far as he was concerned, George would eventually get better. With renewed confidence, Frost continued to visit George.

Aside from the family and doctor, there were few visitors to the Sternaman home. One exception was Frank Snyder, a member of the visiting committee of the Carpenter's Union. He made his first call shortly after George fell ill and found him, a little yellowish, walking around the room. Snyder came by weekly bringing the $3.00 sick benefit to which union members were entitled; he was not, however, allowed to see George any more. Olive took the money explaining that George was not allowed to have any visitors.

Meanwhile, George's vomiting increased. On June 30, less than a week after Whitewell had approved Frost's treatment, George developed a sore spot on his throat. Concerned about diphtheria, Frost took a culture and had it analyzed. The result was negative. By July 1, the sore had spread to George's mouth, making eating and drinking so painful that Frost resorted to "rectal alimentation."

Olive began to fear the worst. On July 4 she sent a letter asking Eliza to visit. It was haying time, a hectic period on any farm, and Eliza was reluctant to abandon her work. Nevertheless, she made plans for the journey.

George continued to decline. On July 8, Frost prescribed brandy to stimulate his weakening heart; on the 10th, George complained of a tingling sensation in his fingers and legs. To Frost, this suggested a breakdown of the nervous system. The young doctor reviewed all the symptoms to date and, for the first time, began to suspect poisoning. He again consulted another physician.

Dr. William C. Phelps was a general practitioner who had been the Buffalo police department surgeon in the 1870s, then served as city health commissioner for several years. He had seen many cases of poisoning, and he confirmed Frost's worst fears. George was apparently suffering from arsenic poisoning. Both doctors suggested immediate hospitalization, but George and Olive refused point-blank. Quietly, Frost drew Olive aside and spoke bluntly. "I believe your husband is suffering from arsenical poisoning."

Olive seemed surprised, but made no comment. Frost continued, "You have had, I understand, one husband die under suspicious circumstances, and if another died under similar suspicious circumstances, it would place you in a very unenviable position." Recalling

George's letter absolving her of blame, Olive said simply, "If he dies, I will have an autopsy, and that will clear me." Frost relented.

Two days later, he had a long private talk with George, who agreed to go to the hospital. Olive was furious. "If you go to the hospital, I'll never go and see you," she warned. George capitulated. Frost had lost again.

On July 14, Eliza made the train trip from Haldimand County to Buffalo. It was her first visit to the city since George and Olive married. She was shocked at her son's deterioration. As she later recalled, she found him:

> in a very low condition. He couldn't pick up even a pocket handkerchief in his fingers. His legs were paralysed, he could draw them up, but could not straighten them out. His arms were paralysed but not so bad as his legs. His mouth and lips were very sore, and skin dark.

The old woman asked Olive the nature of her son's ailment. Recalling the genital sore and, undoubtedly all the accusations Eliza had made about her, Olive gave an answer calculated to horrify her God-fearing, church-going mother-in-law. George was, she snapped, suffering from a "loathsome disease." Later, in a more generous mood, she explained that he had fallen ill at work, and that his condition had worsened with the passing weeks. Since the end of June, he had been unable to keep any food in his stomach. Olive refused to discuss any further details. She made no reference whatsoever to Frost's suspicions of poison.

Eliza waited. During the first day of her visit, George vomited immediately after Olive gave him his medicine and a glass of beer. Upset, depressed by his illness, George told his mother that, if he died, he wanted an autopsy. "It would free Ollie and put everything right," he explained.

Eliza agreed, but called at Dr. Frost's office and questioned him closely about George's illness. She asked him outright, "Is there foul play?"

"No," the doctor replied.

Eliza refused to accept the doctor's assurance. Almost as soon as she returned to the house, she insisted that another doctor be called. George and Olive objected, saying Frost was doing all he could. In a huff, Eliza threatened to go back home unless they gave in to her requests. Reluctantly, the couple complied.

On the morning of July 17, Dr. Ward B. Saltsman arrived at the Sternaman household. He had visited once before at the urging of a member of George's church. This time, he found George lying in bed, "unable to move hand or foot." A muslin rag, soaked in water, was in his mouth – the only way he could obtain a little relief from his raging thirst without vomiting. Saltsman immediately advised hospitalization. Just as she had done with Elon, Olive objected. Later, she told Eliza that although George was willing to enter a hospital, he would not go against her wishes.

Saltsman diagnosed atrophy of the liver, a condition which he said he could cure. He prescribed medicine and, after a day or two, George did seem to be getting better. With her son on the road to recovery, Eliza decided to return to Rainham and the farm work that could no longer be kept waiting. But first she asked Dr. Saltsman to send her daily bulletins on George's progress. Concerned about the extra cost, Olive intervened – *she* would write the letters. Eliza seemed satisfied and left for Canada.

The postcards and letters which reached Canada almost every day over the next couple of weeks were encouraging. Under Saltsman's care, George was now able to move around in bed. After a while, he could sit up, pick up a handkerchief and wipe off his face. His appetite also improved. At first, the doctor put him upon matzo. As the days passed, George added buttermilk to his diet, then poached eggs and toast, and, finally, beefsteak and a potato at supper. But the recovery came too late to help the Sternamans out of dire financial straits. George's medicine alone cost nearly $3 each week, leaving little money for rent, food and other expenses. The Sevenpifers tried to help out, and Lizzie shared as much of the nursing with Olive as she could, but they, too, were beginning to feel burdened by George's illness. In early August, Olive told Saltsman that they were behind in the rent and would have to leave. With housing so scarce and with little money to pay for it anyway, they had no choice but to move in with George's mother.

Saltsman was aghast. "It would be next to insanity!" he declared, "He'll collapse." Olive protested that there was nothing else she could do. Very well, Saltsman told her, it was her responsibility.

On August 9th, Olive wrote to Eliza,

> Dear Mother: George has made up his mind to come home Wednesday on the evening train at Cayuga, and I and the children are coming with him, and if my service is needed I will stay and I will take the children to my aunt at Rainham. She will keep them for a while until I come home, and if I am not needed I will come home; but George wants to come, as we are not able to do as we have been, as I cannot take care of him alone and Lizzie

cannot stay. Our income will not keep us anyway, as it takes nearly all for him. There is nothing left for the rest to live on, and my folks have helped me a great deal and they begin to feel as if they would not any longer. So there is nothing left but to have George go to the hospital, and he does not want to go, and I don't want him to, either, if there is any way out of it. Well, mother, George said I should tell you he would rather run his chances and come home than go to the hospital. He asked the doctor to–day, and the doctor said it was quite a big ride from Cayuga home, but as circumstances is as they are, he would not say he should not go. Well, mother, can you meet us and have a rig that the cot can stand in, as he cannot sit up. If it should rain we will be there on Thursday.

Olive had apparently written once before, urging Eliza to return to Buffalo. When the letter went unanswered, she wrote an angry note to Annie Franklin, George's married sister.

Well Mother I hope you will forgive the way I wrote to Annie for I was nearly crazy. Geo was fretting about you not answering that letter I wrote you about our coming over and some times he wished he was dead. Well Mother I spoke as I felt but I hope you will forgive.

Forgiveness, however, was not Eliza Sternaman's strong suit. She believed in hard work, in respectability and religion, in long prayers before meals and regular attendance at church services. Although she had little use for the doctrine of Christian charity, she could not stand by idly and see her eldest son and his family turned onto the street. No matter what she felt for Olive, George was her son and he was in need.

On the day of departure, Ellen Sevenpifer helped her daughter prepare for the trip. She was in Olive's kitchen, packing lunches for the boys, when a knock sounded at the door. Olive went to see who it was and soon Ellen heard voices raised in anger. She found Olive arguing with an insurance agent who had come to collect his premiums.

"It is absurd," the man said, "this woman taking this husband away like this; if he should die to–day he won't get a dollar." In response to Ellen's question, the agent explained Olive was five weeks behind in payments and would not get a dollar.

Olive was nonchalant. She couldn't help it, she said, since she didn't have a cent.

"How much is it?" Ellen asked. "I have got a little money." But she found she had only a dollar in her pocket-book, about two-thirds of what was needed. She gave the money to the agent, along with her address, and told him to call. She would, she promised, keep up the premiums until Olive returned.

It was dark when the wagon reached the Sternaman house in Rainham. Assisted by Peter Hunsinger, the men lifted George, cot and all, out of the wagon, then found the cot would not fit through the door of the house. With Hunsinger holding his feet and one of the Sternaman brothers holding him under the arms, George was carefully placed on a lounge, carried through the door into the parlour, and settled down in the front bedroom. As the rest of the family sat down for an evening supper, a disagreement erupted between Olive and Eliza.

As Olive had hinted in her letter, the Buffalo doctor was concerned about the effect the long journey to Rainham would have on George. Olive wanted a physician's reassurance that no harm had been done, but Eliza had not called in a doctor. After a brief discussion, she agreed to send for one the next day.

Over the past three weeks, George had become more and more petulant, unhappy if Olive was out of his sight for more than a few minutes. She took to sleeping in her clothes, ready to attend to him at a moment's notice. Throughout the day, she took odd moments to cook and clean and care for her sons. In Buffalo, Lizzie's help had been a godsend, but here in Rainham, Olive could count on little help from her mother-in-law. At least she needn't worry about her boys. Walter and Albert were staying with her aunt Olive Walker, who ran the post office in Rainham Centre. Olive settled down for the night, catching whatever sleep she could in a chair in George's room.

Dr. Phillip Park drove over the dusty clay roads from Fisherville the following morning. At the Sternaman farm, he was led to George's room. When Olive and her mother-in-law showed no signs of leaving Park alone with his patient, the doctor asked them to wait outside. Olive and Eliza withdrew, and Park closed the door behind him. For a few minutes, Olive listened at the door, then re-entered the room.

Park conducted a careful examination, mentally noting the symptoms:

> ... desquamation of the cuticle, no elevation of temperature, pulse 120 to the minute, rapid and weak, white patches inside the mouth, also ulcers, marked pigmenta-

tion of the body, also emaciation, marked tenderness on
deep pressure in the legs, and almost complete anaesthesia
over the lower and upper extremities, more over the lower
than upper.

George complained of a tingling sensation in his lower legs. On
examining them, Park found the lower muscles were atrophied, with
a loss of superficial sensation. His diagnosis was multiple neuritis,
caused by either alcohol or poison. But Park "knew that Sternaman
was not a drinking man, and ... entertained the suspicion that his
illness was caused by arsenical poisoning."

Needing to know more about George's illness, Park asked several questions. Because of the illness, George was unable to speak
above a whisper, so Olive answered most of the doctor's queries. If
he had heard the rumours about Elon Chipman's death, rumours
that Eliza maintained were circulating in Rainham Township, he said
nothing. Instead, he left instructions to save George's vomit and
promised to call again the next day. He also asked for a urine sample, which Olive provided in a glass jar. Park took the specimen back
to his office for testing.

Meanwhile, tension mounted between Olive and Eliza. The
older woman made it clear that she still suspected Olive of poisoning
her first husband and of poisoning George as well. So, shortly after
arriving in Rainham, Olive went to George's bedside and reassured
herself that he would agree to a post–mortem. She reminded George
that in the event of his death, Eliza would accuse Olive of killing him,
just as she had accused her of killing Elon. George agreed, Eliza was
called in, and he repeated his request for an autopsy.

The stress of being forced to live with Eliza, along with George's
illness, was proving too much for Olive. Exhausted, she slept in late
on Friday morning. Eliza took the opportunity to serve George a
breakfast of toasted home–made bread and tea. When Olive awoke,
Eliza accused her of being too lazy to look after her husband.

The atmosphere at the farmhouse was thick with tension when
Park arrived a little later. He found George somewhat weaker that
when he had left him. "This case is somewhat peculiar," he told Olive
and Eliza, then asked permission to consult another doctor. Park
suggested two men, Dr. Jacob Baxter of Cayuga, a well–known practitioner and member of parliament, and Dr. T.T.S. Harrison of Selkirk.
Harrison had once been the Sternamans' family doctor, and so the
women agreed to allow him to visit. In the meantime, Dr. Park left
some medicine for George. One was a tonic of quinine and diluted
muriatic acid to restore some of the young man's strength; the other

was an alterative composed of iodide of potassium and compound tincture of cardamom to eliminate the poison from his system.

Except for Olive, George was pretty well left alone in the sick room. It was threshing time and his mother was busy preparing food for the crew that worked on the farm. After dinner, most of the men left the house, ready to return to the fields. But Phillip Hartwick, Peter Hunsinger's brother-in-law and a friend of George, asked one of the Sternaman boys if it would be all right to visit the invalid. Hartwick stayed a few minutes to chat, promising to return another time.

Dr. Park had arranged to consult with Harrison on Saturday August 16 at 10 a.m. Park was there on time, but duties kept the older doctor way until 1 p.m. By then, Park had gone on to other patients. Nevertheless, Dr. Harrison decided to have a look at George. One of the family showed him into the bedroom, where he:

> found the patient in a good, large and light room. His wife was with him … I noticed that his eyes were peculiarly bright and that his face was thin but his countenance was good and hopeful: it was not the countenance of a man that was suffering; it was the countenance of a man that expected to get well. His skin was very dark; about as dark as an Indian's with a little olive tinge in it. They were both at the bed side: she was as close to him as I was and she heard the questions I asked and all the answers he gave and a good part of the answers she gave herself. He had some trouble talking. It was evident that he had some paralysis of the vocal chords.

Nearly 70 years old, Thomas Tipton Steele Harrison was a wily, silver-haired general practitioner, one of a long line of physicians and surgeons. Born in Tring, Hertfordshire, he moved to Ontario with his father in 1837, settling in Selkirk in 1854. At that time, he later recalled, the country was "an unbroken forest, with merely a thin and scattered fringe of settlements on or near the lake."

As a respected member of the community, and an experienced medical man, he was regarded with a certain awe by younger, less prominent residents of the area. There were others, however, such as Toronto journalist Hector Charlesworth, who described Harrison as the Nestor of Canadian medicine, in reference to a Trojan War general noted for giving long-winded but seemingly sage advice, most of which had disastrous consequences. Charlesworth himself was prone to exaggerate, and besides, he did not live in a small rural community. Whatever Harrison said was likely to carry immense weight with Dr. Park.

As it turned out, Harrison had heard of George's symptoms through the local grapevine. Recalling that David Sternaman had died of stomach cancer several months earlier, Harrison guessed that his son might be suffering the same ailment. He changed his mind after examining George. Three other illnesses were also dismissed.

> ... there were several diseases that would have accounted for more or less of the symptoms that I thought over, one of them was syphilis. I asked him if he had ever had the bad disorder. He said not to his knowledge. I described to him some of the symptoms the lesions of syphilis and he said he had never had it, never had anything like that. I saw that there were no scars that I would have expected to find as a result of chancres and buboes in the preliminary and secondary syphilis that must have taken place if the neuritis was the result of it, and I saw none and I excluded syphilis. Another thing was chronic alcoholism that might have caused some of the symptoms: but he had been reared in our neighbourhood; they were known to be a sober family; I knew none of them had been in the habit of drinking and he told me he had lived a regular life in Buffalo: and I excluded alcohol.

Addison's disease might have accounted for George's emaciation, weakness, irritation of the stomach and discoloration but, as far as Harrison was aware, paralysis was not a typical symptom of the disease. Moreover, he reflected:

> The irritability of the stomach in Addison's disease, as far as I know anything about it, is neither so marked nor so uncontrollable as, from the history that I got in this case, it had been. Another thing that struck me, I could not imagine that in a case of Addison's disease the irritability of the stomach and the vomiting would cease so positively and so completely ... I made up my mind that it was a case of arsenical poisoning.

However, George was not Harrison's patient and the old doctor decided to reserve comment for the time being. Instead, he told Olive and George to continue following Dr. Park's advice, and reassured them that he would meet the younger physician at the Sternaman house the following day.

On Sunday August 17, the two doctors conducted yet another

examination, noting that the patient's condition had not changed much. Then they left the sick room to discuss the case outside. As insects droned in the summer heat, the older doctor catalogued the symptoms and concluded that Park's diagnosis was correct – George was suffering from multiple neuritis, probably caused by arsenic poisoning. "We felt certain," Harrison said:

> that no arsenic had been administered to him for several weeks before he left Buffalo. We felt certain that no arsenic had been administered to him, from the history we got, during the whole time he was under the care of the second medical man. We felt certain also from what we saw at that time that no arsenic had been administered to him in Rainham while he was under our charge, and especially from the fact that Dr. Park had examined the urine and found nothing present. We made up our minds, I may say with some hesitation, especially on the part of Dr. Park, to treat the case to the best of our ability and to watch it very carefully for any symptom that would indicate the read–ministration of arsenic ... at my suggestion Dr. Park was to take some of the urine home and examine it every day.

Still, the prognosis was not good, and Harrison warned Olive, "Your husband is a very sick man, and if he gets better it will be only by close attention and good nursing."

"You don't think he will die, doctor?" she asked. "Why the doctor in Buffalo said he was getting better."

Harrison was non–committal, hoping the letter Park had sent to Dr. Saltsman would bring a speedy response. Privately, he asked Park if anyone in the family was discreet enough to watch for a poisoner. Park, whose few visits had made him aware of the emotionally charged atmosphere in the house, could recommend no one. There was nothing to do but wait, and hope that Park's medicines would take effect.

Sunday also brought another visitor. Phillip Hartwick returned to sit with George for a while. When the invalid complained that the heat and his whiskers made his face itchy but he couldn't raise his hands to scratch, Hartwick cheerfully shaved him.

Park continued his daily visits. On Tuesday, August 18, he realized George's diaphragm had become paralyzed, interfering with breathing. Before leaving, he warned Eliza and Olive that George might not survive the night.

The household gathered to watch and wait. Annie Franklin,

George's married sister, was there, along with Mary Hunsinger. Late in the evening, Olive gave George his medicine, remarking to Annie that he was supposed to take it during the day, but had been so much worse that she couldn't give it to him then. By this time, only Mary, Annie and Olive were left in the sick room. The rest of the family was napping in another part of the house. A while later, George vomited over the bedclothes. Annie wiped it up. As Tuesday melted into Wednesday, his breathing became laboured, and, at 5:30, he died.

Peter Hunsinger arrived around 6 a.m. and Phillip Hartwick a short time later. Immediately, the two men set to work washing and dressing the body for burial. As they worked, Peter brought up the subject of the post-mortem. He had heard some talk of it during George's illness, and, wondering how they should proceed if it was to be held, left the room to question the family.

There was some confusion. One of the Sternamans pointed out that George himself had wanted an autopsy. Olive had misgivings, however, saying she wanted to see George at rest. Eliza insisted Olive make the final decision.

Olive confessed her reluctance to Peter – she didn't like the idea of having George cut up. None the less, given George's wishes, she felt she had no choice. Reluctantly, she agreed to an autopsy and Avery and Freeman were dispatched to inform the doctor.

Peter Hunsinger returned to his brother-in-law and the corpse but, as soon as George was washed and dressed, hurried away to Cayuga to meet the milk wagon. Hartwick shaved George one last time. Then, because Eliza felt a man should be in the house and her Avery and Freeman had gone to Fisherville, he sat with George until the doctor arrived.

Through the open door of the bedroom, Hartwick heard sounds of conversation in the kitchen. Eliza was partly deaf and, because most people spoke loudly in her presence, it was possible for him to make out some of the words. At one point, he heard Eliza ask Olive how much insurance George had left. The younger woman replied that there was $770.

Park received the news of George's death from one of the Sternaman brothers before 8 a.m. He immediately sent a message to Dr. Harrison, telling him of George's death and the need to perform an autopsy. Harrison, however, was attending a woman in labour, so he sent the messenger back advising Park to get another doctor. He also warned Park, "Don't let Snider embalm him."

A little after noon, Park sent another message to Harrison, advising him that he was still waiting. Harrison's pregnant patient was still in labour and it seemed she would not deliver for several hours. He calculated that if he drove quickly and wasted no time he could complete the post–mortem and return in time for the delivery. He climbed into his rig and headed for the Sternaman house.

As he hurried along the dusty roads, Harrison mulled over the situation:

> I made up my mind that it would not be doing justice to my patient or safe for me to put my finger upon the cadaver and I told Dr. Park that he would have to do all the work on it and I was merely there suggesting, looking on and making suggestions.

Park agreed and the two physicians moved into George's room.

After stripping the body, Park made an incision in the abdomen and examined the stomach, intestines, kidneys, spleen, suprarenal capsules and liver. He found no indication of either Addison's disease or alcoholism in the kidneys and liver. "Don't put your hand on anything you don't have to," Harrison advised as his younger colleague proceeded. Given the rumours he had already heard and the unusual request George had made, Harrison suspected there might eventually be a second post–mortem. Yet both doctors were still convinced arsenic had been responsible for George's death.

Despite Harrison's warning, the two of them felt it was essential to examine the stomach more closely. Park described the procedure:

> We took two ligatures and tied them around the cardiac, that is the upper end of the stomach where the food goes in, the esophagus, tied them very tight. Then we made two at the other end of the stomach, the outlet, two strong ligatures. Having done that we made an incision between each of these ligatures at either end and removed the stomach from the body and placed it in a clean tin pan and took it to the window and examined it. When we got there I made an incision in the stomach.

Harrison pointed out the thinness of the stomach walls. There were also patches of inflamed tissue and, on close inspection, Park found a fine, moss–like growth throughout the organ. There was also a small quantity of partly–digested food, "semi–fluid, pasty looking stuff, thick and dark colored." Park poured a small portion into a glass vial to be tested for arsenic. Since Harrison was better equipped to conduct the test, he agreed to take the sample home.

Before the doctors' grisly task was complete, undertaker John Snider and his son Abraham arrived with a wagon containing a coffin, embalming fluid and everything else necessary to prepare the body for burial. Olive discussed the arrangements with Snider. After they had settled on a price, Olive enquired whether it included the cost of embalming. "It pays for embalming and all," Snider reassured her. A cabinetmaker by trade, Snider had followed a path taken by many other practitioners of the craft, who had traditionally been called on to manufacture coffins. For some 30 years, the practice of embalming had been spreading throughout Canada and the United States, helped along by aggressive chemical salesmen who supplied cabinetmakers with appropriate supplies and rudimentary instruction. But the line between professional obligations and custom was blurred, especially in the country, and it was neighbours Peter Hunsinger and Phillip Hartwick who had washed and dressed George's body and dressed it once the doctors were through. At the house, only the tasks of embalming, lifting the body into the casket, and placing it the front parlour were left to the undertakers.

While the two Sniders tended to the body, Harrison hurried off to his maternity case and Park called Olive outside for a private conversation. Standing in front of the house, he wondered if George had had any enemies in Buffalo.

"No," she replied. "Why, Doctor, do you ask that question?"

Park explained, "These symptoms might easily be accounted for by poison."

"What kind of poison do you think it might be?"

Ignoring the question, Park asked whether he was the first doctor to suggest poisoning. She said he was.

A steady stream of visitors called to pay their last respects, staying a while to chat quietly with other mourners, to express condolences in conventional phrases and to leave the traditional offerings of food which would help the family cope over the ensuing days. Between visitors and funeral arrangements, Olive and Eliza were apart most of them time. The day after George's death, however, they found themselves alone together, and Eliza used the opportunity to ask some pointed questions about the amount of George's insurance.

She was astounded by Olive's response, and pointed out that there had been much more when she had been beneficiary. Olive explained they had let the premiums lapse during George's illness, and Eliza seemed to accept her explanation. But she was curious as to when Olive would apply for the insurance money.

"Ma has already done so," Olive responded. Eliza's continued suspicion was serious, but with George gone,there was no longer any reason for Olive to be diplomatic. She confronted her mother-in-law. "You still think I poisoned him?"

"Yes, I do, until you prove your innocence," Eliza told her. "I know you killed Chipman."

But if Eliza was hoping the post-mortem would implicate Olive in George's death, she was disappointed. Just as he had promised Park, Harrison examined the contents of George's stomach for traces of arsenic, using the Marsh test. Invented more than 50 years earlier by a British naval surgeon, it was a standard means of detecting arsenic poisoning. Hydrochloric or sulfuric acid and zinc were added to fluid from the body and heated. If arsenic was present, arsine gas was released, burned off, and a black residue – arsenic – collected. Although the test was highly sensitive even under ideal conditions, few general practitioners were sufficiently familiar with chemical procedures to carry it out properly. This was apparently the case with Dr. Harrison, as he later explained:

> I took a little of the contents that I had home and examined it by Marsh's test. But I had not the appliances. If I had had time I could have made them better than I did, but I took a phial, a small bottle with a middling wide mouth and I took a small tube that was drawn to a middling fine point and broken off at the end and passed it through the cork air tight. I put the contents of the stomach in that bottle, put in some chips of zinc and some chemically pure muriatic acid. I corked it up tight so that after the gas was fairly coming off and no danger of an explosion, I lit it expecting that if there was arsenic in the liquid it would unite with the nascent hydrogen to form a gas that will deposit the arsenic on a cold surface above it. I held a cold plate above it and tried but the organic material in it complicated it so that I could not say that the test amounted to anything. Almost immediately it would froth up the tube and put out the flame. I would light it again but I had a patient to see and I put it away. The result was negative and I would not say that it determined anything.

The result did not negate the possibility of poisoning, Harrison argued. He advised Park to list multiple neuritis and paralysis as the causes of death on the burial certificate. This way, the two physicians were covered in case of further investigations, in that they had not ruled out the possibility of poisoning but simply had not gone far enough in their diagnoses. Park, persuaded by the older physician's experience and tenacity, complied.

George was buried in the graveyard of the Rainham Baptist Church. The Reverend John Trickey officiated. Afterwards, Olive stayed only long enough to gather up her few belongings, visit with relatives who still remained in Canada, and comfort her sons. As a homeless widow, there were few people on whom she could depend. But there was one person who would take her in, who would not only help her to overcome her grief, but would also provide affection and care for her two sons. Olive returned to Buffalo to live with Ellen Chipman, Elon's mother.

PART TWO

INQUEST AND EXTRADITION

"I know"

Summer was passing. Goldenrod and wild asters bloomed in the meadows, their burnished yellow and purple providing the last flash of colour before the onslaught of winter. Here and there, in the tree lines between farm fields and the bush lots that dotted the southern Ontario landscape, leaves were turning to scarlet and gold. On the Sternaman farm, Eliza was busy stocking up vegetables in the root cellar. George was gone, but that was no reason for neglecting work.

With George dead, Eliza had little reason to contact Olive; nevertheless, she did write around September 18th. She said she had been expecting some money and was disappointed when it had not yet arrived. Since Olive was coming into a substantial amount of money from George's life insurance, Eliza thought it only fair that she should get $20 or $25. The amount would help compensate her for the expenses she had incurred during George's final illness, as well as repay Avery and Freeman for running errands. In addition, Eliza asked for George's tools, claiming that one of the boys wanted to be a carpenter. In Buffalo, Olive was trying to put back the pieces of her life. Eliza's letter was more than upsetting – it was insulting. Olive showed it to some close friends, and, on their advice, ripped it up and made no reply.

Of necessity, the young widow spent part of her time dealing with insurance agents. One of the first was Jesse Dewe, an agent with Metropolitan Life. Dewe, who had known Olive since October 1895, was riding his bicycle along Dearborn Street when he spotted Olive and her two boys. Noticing she was in mourning, he asked if George was dead. Olive explained that George had died a few days earlier. "Poor fellow, he died a hard death."

They chatted for a few more minutes and before Dewe rode off Olive pleaded with him not to tell anyone about the insurance policy. After receiving the insurance on Elon's life, one of her relatives had borrowed $200 and never repaid it. Olive was convinced if the family knew about the insurance they would get the money from her in no time.

Olive had good reasons to be secretive. No matter what she had told her mother-in-law, she did have quite a bit of insurance on George's life: $200 in the Carpenter's Union, $770 in the John Hancock company and another $1000 in the Metropolitan. However, it seemed she might not get all that was due her. The Carpenter's Union was stalling, claiming there had been foul play. As a consequence, Olive had hired a lawyer to get the money.

The John Hancock Mutual Company was far less difficult. It had quickly paid the policy on George's life. But, despite Jesse Dewe's friendliness, Metropolitan's resident claim inspector, Charles A. Medlicott, had misgivings. Soon after returning to Buffalo, Olive dropped off the papers at Metropolitan's office. A day or two later, Medlicott tried to talk to her at home, but she was out. He finally talked to her one Saturday at the Metropolitan office. He asked about George's medical care, the cause of his death and why Olive had insisted on an autopsy.

Olive was stunned. How could Medlicott have known that?
"I know," he replied. Hesitantly, she explained that she had ordered a post-mortem because of rumours that had circulated the previous year. What rumours, Medlicott asked. Olive was silent. Medlicott pressed her for a few moments about the rumours, then, realizing a woman might not feel comfortable discussing what might be a highly personal matter in an large, open office where almost anyone could eavesdrop, he offered to call her at home the following Monday.

In the meantime, he checked the records of the Buffalo Board of Health and found that Elon Chipman had not died of typhoid fever but of multiple neuritis and paralysis, the same symptoms which appeared on George's death certificate. With a little further investigation, Medlicott also discovered that a total of six physicians had treated George – Frost, Whitewell, Phelps, Saltsman, Park and Harrison – not three, as Olive had indicated.

Charles Medlicott was a deeply suspicious man at the subsequent meeting and one of the first questions he asked was about Elon's death. Why had she mentioned typhoid fever when both husbands had suffered similar illnesses? Olive replied that, as far as she understood the situation, Elon had died of typhoid.

Medlicott might have accepted that answer, persuading himself that Olive was poorly educated and had misunderstood the doctors. But the business of George's autopsy was a serious matter, and Olive was extremely uncooperative. For nearly two hours, Medlicott badgered her, insisting that she tell him what rumours had led her to the conclusion that an autopsy was necessary. Finally, when he convinced her that she would not receive a cent unless she was completely honest, Olive admitted that there were reports that she had done away with her first husband. When Medlicott asked whether "anything else ... was said about you?" Olive reluctantly recounted the details of Eliza's hysterical outburst when she thought her tea had been poisoned. For his part, Medlicott was not satisfied with the results of the interview. As far as he was concerned, the circumstances of George Sternaman's premature death now required careful investigation.

On September 6, the Reverend John Trickey, the Baptist minister who had officiated at George's funeral, called on Eliza. It was not unusual for a minister to visit members of his flock, to comfort them in their sorrows and bolster their spiritual strength. But this was more than a routine call. Trickey told Eliza of a request he had received from the Metropolitan Insurance Company. Its agents needed a certificate of internment from him before they would release payment of George's life insurance to Olive. All the suspicions which Eliza had tried to put behind her flared again. What insurance, she wondered. Olive told her the policies had lapsed. All Trickey could do was reiterate what he had learned from the letter.   Eliza's suspicions were further reinforced a short time later when Charles Robertson, an investigator for the company, called on Eliza and others in Rainham, then visited coroner David Thompson in Cayuga.

Soon afterwards, Eliza hitched up a wagon and rode into Cayuga, where she visited the offices of Colter and Goodman. Ambrose K. Goodman had probated David's will a year or two earlier, but it was not the junior partner Eliza wanted to see. She was more interested in talking to Charles Wesley Colter, the County crown attorney.

Colter was 49, a New Brunswicker by birth who had lived in Haldimand some 30 years. Starting out as a school teacher, then principal of Dunnville High School, he became interested in law, studied diligently, and had been called to the bar in 1879. He listened attentively as Eliza spilled out her grief, her rage and her profound suspicions. She had opposed the marriage and warned George about Olive. Then she described her visit to Buffalo during George's illness, and how Olive alone had nursed the patient. When she was finished, Colter was convinced that Eliza was more than a jealous and possessive mother. He agreed with her that an official inquiry should be held. Colter's instructions alone were enough to convince Thompson that an inquest was necessary. Robertson's suspicions merely added fuel to the fire. He set the hearing date for September 29.

"Deceased came to his death by arsenical poisoning."

Between the time Eliza visited Colter and the inquest on the 29th, rumours floated about Haldimand County. Over backyard fences in town, outside churches and in general stores, the details of the case were discussed, dissected, dismissed. One rumour claimed that Olive had obtained $1000 in insurance on George by having someone else impersonate him. According to reports, the fake was two or three inches taller and of a different complexion. Only imagination limited speculations of this type, and there were plenty of imaginative people in Haldimand. But some preferred to discuss the facts – or what they perceived to be the facts. One such discussion took place at Ivan W. Holmes's general store on the night of the 28th.

Holmes was 26 and a member of a prominent Selkirk family. Some 30 years previously, his grandfather William had built Cottonwood Mansion, a magnificent red-brick building a mile north of town. Ivan's father, Joseph W. Holmes, was active in local politics. Ivan's store, like other general stores throughout rural Canada, was a community gathering place. The atmosphere was laden with the smell of aged cheese, pickles, kerosene, soap and coffee. In the evenings, the air was heavy with smoke as the local fellows gathered amid the nail kegs and cracker barrels for a game of checkers after the day's work was done, perhaps to pass a bottle around (hoping their wives would be none the wiser) and to catch up on the local gossip.

Some time between 7 and 8 the night before the coroner's inquest, Albert Hedden walked into the store on an errand. Several men were around, including proprietor Holmes, John Chevalier, and John Snider. Naturally enough, the dominant topic of conversation was the upcoming inquest. When asked if he planned to attend, Snider responded, "If I go down I will get no pay without being subpoenaed." Snider paused, watching the raised eyebrows and skeptical looks. "They will have to have me there," he stated, "they will subpoena me." He explained that if he swore the body was embalmed that would be the end of the matter. If, however, he swore otherwise – well, that would put a different light on it.

John Chevalier recalled the reaction from the group of men:

> Well, we laughed a little, kind of smiled. We are all neighbors. And I says to him, "Did you embalm him?" Either

Holmes or me, I wouldn't swear positively which one, asked him that, but the question was asked between the three of us.

Snider paused for effect and, just a little pompously, replied, "We always embalm."

The inquest convened at Rainham Township Hall on the 29th. Dr. David Thompson presided as coroner. A member of a prominent family from Indiana, north of Cayuga, Thompson was 32 and had been educated at Upper Canada College and the University of Toronto before finishing his medical studies in Edinburgh and Glasgow. Like his father, Senator David Thompson, the young doctor was a politically active entrepreneur. He had served as reeve of Cayuga for two years, and had funded the construction of several buildings, including the Davis block, a grist mill and the electric light plant.

The first order of business was the swearing in of jurors. For the most part, they were farmers and neighbors of the Sternaman family. Peter Hunsinger was there, as was Phillip Hartwick and William Featherston. Other jurymen included Thomas Fitzgerald, Levi Fehrman, Josiah Sherk, Leander Culver, James Greenbury, Ethan Allen, Stephen Culver, William Kellam, David Daley, Daniel Culver, Isaac Allen and Robert Miller. Elias Overholt served as foreman.

The next task was the exhumation of the body. For several weeks, southern Haldimand County had experienced extremely dry weather, but it was raining as the first shovelsful of clay were pitched out of the grave. On top, the soil was wet but the moisture had not penetrated more than three or four inches. Underneath, the clay was as dry as it had been on the day of George's burial. The rough box was raised to the surface. "It was just as dry as if it had been laid on trestles in a dry cellar," Harrison remarked.

Undertaker John Snider opened it and helped remove the casket from the outer box. He unscrewed the lid of the coffin, as coroner David Thompson, doctors Harrison and Park, and George's brother Freeman looked on. For the benefit of the jury, both Snider and Freeman identified the corpse as that of George Henry Sternaman. Then George's body was carried the short distance to the churchyard shed and placed on an improvised table.

The post–mortem was a more elaborate version of the one conducted by Park and Harrison at the farm house. Remarking how well preserved the body was – the only difference being a slight darkening in colour – the doctors set to work. As George was lifted from the casket, Dr. Harrison noted a slight discoloration on the white muslin lining, corresponding to the places where his shoulders, backbone and buttocks had touched. The doctors stripped the corpse and examined it carefully. Harrison had been attending a maternity case during the night near the lake, and had no instruments with him, so that Park did most of the cutting.

Park noted the sutures from the previous examination were still in place, as he cut open the stitches to expose the internal organs. Harrison was astonished at the condition of the viscera. "It was just as bright and seemed to be just as healthy as it was when we sewed him up. You could see the marks of the inflammation in the intestines." For the first time, the doctors noted yellow patches on the intestines. "Do you think those can be sulphide of arsenic?" Harrison asked Park. Without a test, however, there was no way of knowing, and this time it was not up to the country doctors to perform the test. Instead, they removed a portion of intestine, the spleen, pancreas, kidneys, liver and stomach. To see if the latter still retained its contents, Park held it up. There was no leakage of fluid.

In addition, it was also necessary to examine the brain. Park cut open the skull, and unsuccessfully attempted to lift the entire brain out. As Harrison noted,

> The brain seemed to be about the only organ that was extensively or much decomposed. The brain was in such a fluid state that you could not get it out, but by cutting the duramater and holding the jar under it we could pour the brain into the jar.

All the organs were placed in clean glass jars, "four gem jars, the ordinary sealing, that you put up fruit in; and two jars that screwed down with a tin top," and covered with alcohol. Then, with the jury looking on, Coroner Thompson sealed the jars with tape and sealing wax, before imprinting the wax with his monogrammed ring.

Finally, both doctors were questioned at length as to their treatment of George during his final illness and on what they had found during the course of the original post-mortem. When the inquest adjourned to await Ellis's conclusions, Thompson took the jars containing George's internal organs home to Cayuga, placed them carefully in a wooden box and nailed the lid shut. The next day, he shipped them by train to Professor William Ellis in Toronto.

The newspapers had already caught wind of the story and were eager for news. One reporter spoke to Dr. Park following the inquest, but the physician had little to say.

> We found nothing particular ... at the post–mortem to-
> day I found the organs as we had left them ... The organs
> removed were in a remarkable good state of preservation,
> absolutely no signs of decomposition or putrefaction being
> apparent.

Word of the coroner's inquest had drifted towards Buffalo, and on October 1, a reporter visited Ellen Chipman's house at 165 Annie Place. Ellen was not surprised at the interest of the press and was, in fact, prepared to protect her daughter-in-law. She refused to allow the reporter to interview Olive. "She has nothing to say," she said determinedly. "I have nothing to say. There!"

"Don't you care to answer the rumours of foul play in connection with Mr. Sternaman's death?" asked the reporter.

"We have decided not to talk about it at all," replied Mrs. Chipman. "We have engaged a lawyer and the guilty ones will suffer. We have lots to say, but we do not intend to say it now."

"And who are the guilty ones?" the reporter asked.

Ellen refused, however, to be drawn further into the conversation.

The next day, a reporter from the Toronto *Globe* travelled to Buffalo to investigate the story. Although Olive was always in the company of either her mother or mother-in-law, the reporter was able to speak to her briefly. She expressed shock at the news of the exhumation, although admitted she was not completely surprised. It was, she explained, a conspiracy with Eliza at the bottom of it. George's mother, Olive claimed, had wanted her son to marry a girl from Rainham.

The reporter also spoke to others including one of the Sternaman's Buffalo neighbors, R.W. Kasson. Kasson claimed the whole affair was a malicious plot to injure an innocent woman. He was sure George had taken out the insurance himself and described Olive as an exceptionally devoted wife. But the comments of two carpenters, fellow members of George's union, pointed to the similarity between George and Elon's illness. And Dr. Frost told the reporter that, contrary to one rumour that was circulating, George had not died of diphtheria. Furthermore, he told the reporter, the building's plumbing had been inspected and was deemed no threat to the tenants' health. A little additional investigation by the reporter seemed to overturn the contaminated water theory. In the period between June 3 and 13, the temperature climbed above 83 degrees on a single day, June 5. On all other days, it was between 60 and 75, hardly the high temperatures normally associated with intestinal complaints resulting from bad water.

If the Buffalo newspapers were interested, the local law enforcement agencies were singularly disinterested. Such was not the case in Canada, for, on October 1, John Wilson Murray reached Cayuga and began investigating the curious circumstances surrounding the death of George Sternaman. Murray was already a legendary figure in Ontario, and, in fact, he was also well known in legal circles in the U.S.

Born in Edinburgh, Scotland and brought to the U.S. as a child, Murray's experiences as a detective brought him to the attention of Ontario premier Oliver Mowat around 1875. He seemed just the man Mowat wanted for the Ontario Police Force, and in May Murray was hired at an annual salary of $1500. He spent the remainder of his life investigating crimes throughout Ontario.

Murray was a man who tended to make snap judgements, and, once convinced, he was fully capable of bullying suspects into a confession. Early in his career, his instincts apparently served him well, but as he grew older he relied less and less on the facts of an investigation than on his memories of similar cases. It was almost as if he had begun to believe the newspaper reports which exaggerated his uncanny ability.

When he arrived in Cayuga, one of his first actions was to read over the depositions from the post–mortem and the inquest. By the time he was finished reading and talking to one or two of the officials involved in the case, he was convinced it "deserved careful investigation." He called upon Charles Colter and the two men decided they could do nothing until William Ellis reported his findings.

There was also a little confusion over the legal implications of the case. Both Harrison and Park were convinced that, if arsenic had been administered, it had been done in Buffalo. If so, they wondered, should not the American authorities handle any inquiry? Murray thought not. It was his opinion, given the fact that George had died in Canada, that there was enough evidence to convince U.S. authorities to extradite Olive from Buffalo.

Nearly four weeks passed before the inquest resumed on October 27. Again, the proceedings took place at the Rainham Township Hall. Crown Attorney Colter watched as Dr. Thompson read the letter from Professor Ellis to the jury:

> I have examined the viscera of the late George H.
> Sternaman, and from the contents of the stomach I ob-
> tained eighteen milligrammes of sulphide of arsenic, equal
> to about one-fifth grain white arsenic. I also found arsenic
> in the liver, and traces of arsenic in the brain.

Dr. Park was then called to the stand. He explained that he had
given George iodide of potash to help eliminate any poison in his
system and that arsenite of copper was also administered to stop the
vomiting. But Ellis's conclusions supported his own suspicions –
George Sternaman had died of arsenic poisoning. Dr. Harrison cor-
roborated his testimony.

Dr. Francis Rich of Buffalo also took the stand to describe the illness of Elon Chipman. Eliza Sternaman in her turn described her relationship with George and Olive, including her prophetic warning that
George would be dead within six months if he married the widow.
John Snider and Dr. Frost added their observations to the evidence.

The jury withdrew, deliberating for half an hour before returning. Their verdict was straightforward: George H. Sternaman, the jury
concluded, "came to his death August 19, 1896, by arsenical poisoning,
administered by some party or parties at present unknown to us."

Night had fallen by the time the verdict was rendered. Murray,
Robertson, Thompson and Colter made their way back to Cayuga in
the autumn darkness. Early the next morning, Colter telegraphed the
Buffalo police.

> The adjourned inquest on the body of George H.
> Sternaman, who died at Rainham Center last August,
> under suspicious circumstances, was concluded last night.
> The report of Dr. Ellis of his analysis on the viscera of the
> deceased showed arsenic in the stomach, brain and liver.
> The jury rendered a verdict that deceased came to his
> death by arsenical poisoning administered by some party
> or parties unknown to the jury.

In Buffalo, the chief of police issued a warrant for Olive's arrest
as a fugitive from justice. Two officers, Sergeant O'Neill and Detective
Fiori, were sent to Ellen Chipman's house to take Olive into custody.
When they arrived, Olive showed little surprise. "I was expecting
this." Placidly, she accompanied them to the station house and notified her lawyer, Feldman Duckwitz.

When questioned by reporters, a police spokesman said he did
not believe Olive would return to Canada for trial. Furthermore, he

claimed that the telegram was simply a precautionary measure on the part of the Canadian authorities. For his part, Duckwitz vowed to fight against any bid for extradition. Nevertheless, on the morning of October 28, a few minutes before 11 a.m. Olive was arraigned before Judge King. Dressed in black, she stood before the judge and heard herself committed to jail.

As she was led away, reporters pressed forward, eager to get a statement from the alleged murderess. Duckwitz had already warned her against answering any questions and spoke in her stead.

> This is a serious matter and I do not care to have any statements made at this time. The action of the Canadian officials is not entirely unexpected. While we do not fear the outcome, it is the best that nothing be said by my client at this time.

His advice was wise, because the detailed coverage of the inquest in both Canadian and American newspapers already amounted to trial by media. Typical was a comment from the *Dunnville Chronicle*:

> There is not any doubt but what one arrest will be made before long, and it will require the services of an Osler or a Blackstock to extricate that one from the web of evidence that has been woven around her.

A few days later, Detective John Wilson Murray left for Buffalo, carrying with him the papers required for Olive's extradition.

November 10, 1896

"I am … morally convinced that she poisoned them both."

Much has been made of the friendly co-existence of Canada and the United States, which share the longest undefended border in the world. Although similarities in culture and language have sometimes made for amicable relations, there has always been a certain amount of friction between the two countries. Just beyond living memory was the War of 1812. Around the time Olive was born, the American Civil War was raging and, at one point during the war, relationships between the two countries deteriorated so badly that Canadians travelling to the U.S. were required to produce passports.

By the last decade of the nineteenth century, the two countries were strong trading partners, and the steady flow of people south-ward to jobs in American cities meant that many families had ties in both countries. Still, little provocation was needed to set off a wave of public opinion against the other country. The United States, with its outspoken patriotism was always ready to point out the flaws in the British way of life, including its ponderous class system and hidebound traditions. At the same time, Canadians took enormous pride in being part of an Empire on which the sun never set, pride which would reach its climax in the phantasmagoric celebrations of Queen Victoria's Diamond Jubilee in the summer of 1897. To be part of the British Empire was to be part of the richest, most sophisticated and most technologically advanced empire in history. It went with-out saying that British institutions were best. British law, evolved over centuries, was rooted in traditions that were tried and true, far superior to the democratic notions of the Americans. To many Canadians the notion of rule by the will of the majority in matters of law was anathema: the same mob which would release a person ac-cused of murder on nothing more than popular opinion might just as easily lynch him. Or her. And Olive, as a Canadian–born American resident, wanted by Canadian authorities for a crime which may have been committed in the United States, was caught in the middle of these opposing views of justice.

John Wilson Murray made his living through the administra-tion of British justice, but he was also a man who liked to draw his own conclusions. And he was convinced that Olive Sternaman was guilty. He said as much to reporters after he arrived in Buffalo.

> When the Canadian government decided to investigate the charges against Mrs. Sternaman, accusing her of mur-dering her two husbands, I thought it would end in a fiz-zle. But I am now, after the most thorough investigation, morally convinced that she poisoned them both. There is a great similarity between his writing and hers. It bothered me for some time. My theory concerning the letter ad-dressed 'to whom it may concern,' is that she induced him to write it.

He was equally definite in another interview. "Mrs. Sternaman won't make a confession, but the chain of circumstances is strong enough to convince us that the death was not due to natural diseases or complaints."

Murray's opinion may have carried weight with newspaper readers and probably with his colleagues, but legally it was nothing more than hot air. Olive could not be extradited until the American authorities were convinced a case existed. Furthermore, the death of Elon Chipman was not under investigation, although it would haunt the public, the court officials and Olive for many months to come.

Chipman haunted the case in another way as well. A Victorian sense of delicacy prevented newspaper reporters from dwelling too long on the Chipman–Sternaman *ménage à trois*. In most instances, it was sufficient to mention the living arrangements, the trip to Canada when Elon returned to Buffalo before George and Olive, George's continued presence after Elon's death and his subsequent marriage to Olive. Readers drew their own conclusions and, given the very human proclivity for believing the worst about one's neighbours, most concluded that adultery had been committed. Given the Victorian cult of respectability, especially among the working class, who saw respectability as a means to social advancement, adultery was almost as serious a crime as murder. And, in Olive's case, it seemed the two were inseparable. Although, officially speaking, she was accused of murder, she was also on trial, at least in the public mind, for adultery.

The proceedings opened on November 10, 1896, in a crowded courtroom presided over by U.S. Commissioner J.L. Fairchild. Charles Thomas conducted the case for the Canadian government, while the defense was handled by Duckwitz and Thayer. Olive, wearing a plain black dress and a crepe veil, was escorted into the courtroom. Olive's relatives and friends, as well as several members of the Order of Rebekahs, and other female spectators jammed into the limited space.

Presumably, most of the female spectators were sympathetic. For several decades, whenever a woman went on trial for her life, courtrooms in Britain, France, Canada and the U.S. were crowded with interested females. Men had less free time to sit through a lengthy hearing, but the women who attended were displaying more than idle curiosity. In justice systems where no women sat on juries, presented arguments for the prosecution or defense, or sat in judgement, a woman accused of a capital crime was very much alone. Her isolation deepened when her crime was a blatant violation of the most dearly-held standards of a male-dominated society: that a woman's husband was her lord and master, and that her highest calling was to bear his children and care for his home. A woman accused of uxoricide or infanticide, especially one motivated by an illicit sexual relationship, was a potent threat to the male status quo.

Only other women understood the constricting roles imposed by notions of Victorian respectability and even if they could not condone murder, many could sympathize. By their very presence the female spectators were a strong reminder to the judge, jury and lawyers that there was another point of view.

Charles Thomas began by reading medical evidence, the statement from Dr. Park and Dr. Ellis's report. Often, he stumbled over the multisyllabic medical terms. "I guess Sternaman would have died if he had to pronounce these words," he commented at one point. Amused, Olive smiled.

Thomas continued, but part way through, Feldman Duckwitz interrupted. "Shall I read for you?"

Thomas declined the offer. "No, never mind, it's too interesting to your client to allow you to read it." Again, Olive smiled causing Thomas to comment cryptically, "The more I look at you, the more I think I know you." The first witness was Dr. William Langley, who testified that he had examined George as part of a Metropolitan Life insurance policy application in April. The young man, he stated, was in perfect health. Charles Medlicott was next in the witness box. He explained that the life insurance policies were in order, but that there were difficulties with the evidence Olive had provided following George's demise. Olive, he said, had made contradictory and erroneous statements. For example, she told him that only three doctors had attended George, when, in fact, there had been six: Frost, Saltsman, Phelps and Whitewell in Buffalo; Harrison and Park in Canada.

William Ralph Leity, another insurance agent, took the stand and reiterated his encounters with Olive. A third insurance agent, Frederick Dodsworth, followed. He was questioned at length by Thomas, whose interrogation was obviously designed to show that Olive had deliberately lied or misrepresented facts in order to benefit from the policies.

Wallace Thayer objected to Thomas's approach, contending that it was ridiculous to suppose Olive would have killed either husband. The amount of the policies, he argued, was hardly enough to compensate her for the loss of the household's main source of income. It was a weak argument: the Metropolitan policy alone was more than George could have earned in a year. Taken altogether, the policies totalled more than three years' income.

Detective Murray was the last witness called before lunch. After taking the stand at 1 p.m. he verified that he was the provincial detective appointed in the case and that he had gathered all the medical evidence submitted.

Dr. Frost was scheduled to appear immediately after lunch. Some mix-up occurred, however, and the proceedings were delayed until his arrival around 3 p.m. He testified for half an hour regarding his treatment of George, including how he had urged the young man to go to the hospital and how Olive had objected. The testimony of Dr. Phelps, which wrapped up the day's session, more or less confirmed what Frost had said.

November 11, 1896

"This may be the handwriting on the wall for you."

The hearing continued the following afternoon, beginning at 2 p.m. Olive was the first witness called. Calmly, she took her seat and related the story of her life a voice so low that Commissioner Fairchild had to ask her to speak up.

> I was born in Canada, near where the parents of Sternaman live. I came to Buffalo with my parents when 12 years old, and am now 29 years of age. Shortly after coming here I went to work for a Mr. Simpson of Bouck avenue, and worked with him for three years doing general housework. Then I met my first husband Ezra E. Chipman. He was a carpenter, and I believe he came to this city from Canada. Our courtship lasted while I was working for Mr. Simpson. I married him and we went to live at Hampshire and Fourteenth streets. I married him on Feb. 3, 1886, and we lived at the same place until he died, which was on Jan. 20, 1895. Two children were born. One is now 9 and the other 7 years old.
>
> I first met Sternaman when my husband came home one night and told me the next morning Sternaman would call and arrange to stay at our house for a few weeks, until a job nearby, on which he was employed, was finished. Sternaman came and after the job was finished he did not say anything about leaving. My husband and I talked it over and decided that he could stay if he wished. He remained with us steadily until his father was taken sick. Then he went to Canada, remained there a month or more, returned to Buffalo and came to our home again.
>
> My husband and Sternaman often worked together, and I

did up both their lunches. We were all friendly and I
never saw anything in the conduct of Sternaman that led
me to believe that he loved me, that is while my first husband was alive. I noticed nothing suspicious in his manner, and he and my husband seemed the best of friends.

To Fairchild's right, Assistant Attorney W.F. Mackey watched
every move, every expression on Olive's face, while Charles Thomas
scribbled notes as quickly as he could. Also scribbling were a pack of
reporters. The trial was of great interest and the scribes were eager to
capture all the drama for their readers. One point they stressed was
Olive's demeanour. She was, one reporter hypothesized, "either an
innocent woman or has the hardihood and fortitude of a Stoic." For
many readers, Olive's composure was the most telling bit of evidence. If she could remain so calm when facing the massed forces of
justice, was it not logical to suppose she had the *sang-froid* needed to
commit murder?

Most of the time, Olive's eyes were cast demurely downward. If
a question was directed at her, she looked up, gazed steadily into the
eyes of her interrogator, and answered straightforwardly.

When she finished making her statement, Thayer asked, "Were
you ever accused of murdering your husband excepting through the
letters and statements of Mrs. Sternaman?"

"No, not until then."

"You know that you are accused now?" Thomas interjected.

Thayer turned his opponent's statement to his own advantage.
"And from the same source?"

Olive indicated that she understood both men. "It was Mrs.
Sternaman who told the insurance company and they riled up the
Canadian Government," she said as a ripple of excitement spread
through the court. For many of the spectators, the relationship between the two women, George's mother and George's wife, was an
important part of the proceedings. The personal battle between two
rivals for the affection of one man, between the aging and often cantankerous Eliza and the young, attractive Olive, was one played out
on domestic stages all over the country. Any woman (and likely
many men) who had been forced to put up with demands and disapproval from a mother or mother-in-law, responded instinctively
to Olive's plight.

Wallace Thayer began the proceedings by introducing a letter
from Eliza Sternaman in which she strongly objected to the marriage
of George and Olive. In it, she told of rumours floating about
Rainham Center, rumours which accused Olive of killing her first

husband, and demanded that George end the liaison. It was clear, Thayer contended, that Eliza entertained a lively dislike for Olive.

Thayer also read George's reply, and asked Olive to identify the handwriting. She confirmed it was that of her late husband.

"This may be the handwriting on the wall for you," quipped Charles Thomas.

Thayer turned on him, and the two sparred verbally until Commissioner Fairchild reproved them.

Olive described George's illness, explaining that she always went for his medicine when he could no longer do so, and that she usually administered it to him personally, except for once or twice when her sister did it. She also explained how things stood between herself and her mother-in-law. "She treated me harshly. She complained to Dr. Park that I wasn't caring for George properly." Other details emerged: George's petulance, his agreement to a post-mortem as a means of clearing all suspicions surrounding Olive. The postmortem had been carried out, just as George had wished, Olive added, but the doctors had not told her the results. She also recalled the conversation with Eliza in which the older woman accused her of poisoning George.

The morning session lasted until 2 p.m. After a brief recess for lunch, Charles Thomas took up the cross-examination. Olive answered all his questions calmly, although many of them ruffled Wallace Thayer's feathers. Several times, he objected to the line of questions and to Thomas's manner, and a few heated arguments erupted between the two lawyers. Olive was the only witness called before the court adjourned at 4 p.m.

November 12, 1896

"I will leave that for you to discover."

She was back on the stand the following morning, November 12, fielding questions from Thomas.

"Do you think that Sternaman poisoned your first husband?"

"No, not until it is proved."

Then what, the prosecutor wondered, had caused his death.

Olive was growing angry. "I don't know. I will leave that to you to discover. I would be as glad as any to find out!"

Thomas turned to the circumstances of George's death.   " D o you think that he poisoned himself?"

"I am beginning to think so."

"When did you begin to think so?"

"When I got back from Canada after the funeral and saw the doctor's papers about arsenic poisoning."

Thomas was not the only one to question Olive at length. Assistant Attorney Mackey also probed the circumstances surrounding George's illness.

"Did you ever hear Dr. Frost telling you that if Sternaman received no more poison he would get well?

Olive admitted she had.

"Why did you keep this fact from the knowledge of Drs. Saltsman and Sternaman's mother? For fear of scandal and suspicion?"

"Yes. I knew that if his mother learned of it she would create trouble."

When Olive's testimony concluded, her sister was called to the stand. Most of Lizzie's testimony focused on the relationship between her sister and George, and she had not quite finished when the court adjourned for the day.

When the fifth day of the extradition hearing fell on Friday, November 13, the crowd of spectators had thinned out somewhat. As the session got under way, Lizzie was shunted aside in order to give Dr. Ward B. Saltsman an opportunity to testify with minimum disruption of his schedule.

Dr. Saltsman described the pitiful condition in which he found George, ascribing it to arsenical poisoning. How it was administered, though, Saltsman could not say. "During the period I visited Sternaman I do not think poison was administered. If it had been the original symptoms would have returned after I succeed in stopping the course of the disease."

Thomas probed further. "During the period you attended him did you ever suspect that poison had been administered?"

"No; it could not have been given without a marked return of the symptoms of his disease."

"Did Sternaman improve under your treatment?"

"Yes. He recovered the use of his limbs and could move about the bed. He was unable to move a muscle when I first saw him."

He admitted to Thayer that the couple was unusually affectionate, and that George meekly submitted to anything Olive suggested. He also reiterated the conversation he had with her regarding the move to Canada and how he ultimately washed his hands of any responsibility if she chose to undertake the journey.

Then Thomas interrupted. "Is atrophy of the liver inevitably followed by paralysis?"

"It is."

"Now, assuming that the body of a person who has died from this had been buried six weeks and had not been embalmed, was exhumed at the expiration of that time, and upon the content found in the stomach being submitted to chemical analysis, arsenic was found, what would your opinion be regarding the discovery of the arsenic?"

"I should certainly say that it had been administered but a short time previous to the man's death."

Thayer could barely hide his surprise. He jumped to his feet, peppering Saltsman with questions in an attempt to prove that the arsenic was introduced in the embalming process.

Thomas interrupted, pointing out that evidence showed that George had not been embalmed. Murray had obtained the documents to prove as much before leaving Canada. Once more, the attorneys were off on a mudslinging match.

When the lawyers were through with medical testimony, Lizzie Sevenpifer returned to the witness box to answer more questions. She was followed by her mother, Ellen and Eliza Chipman. Most of their testimony centred on the relationship between the couple.

Elon's mother, who was ailing, was shaky when she entered the witness box immediately after lunch. Thomas began by asking her to describe events when she was called to her son's deathbed. Required to relive a grief that was still fresh, the woman began to weep. Other women in the court burst into tears as well, although Olive maintained a stoic fortitude. Gallantly, Thomas refrained from asking further questions.

But Eliza Chipman's ordeal was not yet over. Thayer questioned her about her husband, and she continued to weep as she explained they were separated. Chipman was also called to the stand, and the bulk of his testimony dealt with the relationship between Elon and Olive. As he described the marriage that had endured for more than a decade, Olive began to cry.

Before the afternoon was over, Thomas called Dr. Saltsman back to the stand. "You swore that under your treatment Sternaman recovered in a remarkable manner and was able to retain extraordinary quantities of food upon his stomach, something which he was unable to do when you first saw him."

"Yes I did."

"Could this remarkable improvement in this specific case have been due to a suspension of the administration of arsenic?"

"It could have been due to that, most certainly."

This exchange was considered one of the most telling bits of evidence presented that day. Thayer, apparently feeling at something of a disadvantage, requested an adjournment. He wanted to visit Canada to examine the testimony of the experts himself. Commissioner Fairchild granted his request and the case adjourned.

November 17, 1896
"All the evidence in this case is circumstantial."

The extradition hearing resumed on Tuesday, November 17. Again, the poorly-lighted courtroom was crowded with women, who murmured sympathetically when Olive appeared. They had little sympathy for Thomas, however, and, in fact, there were some contemptuous whispers whenever he questioned a female witness too closely.

All eyes were on Olive. When she entered the courtroom, her father greeted her. Christopher Sevenpifer looked "brighter and more hopeful" than he had on earlier occasions, but Olive, if anything, was more serious. They shook hands, then Olive took her seat beside her lawyer.

Thayer opened the proceedings by asking that a certified copy of the testimony taken by Coroner David Thompson be admitted as evidence. Thomas objected and, as he looked up the statute on which his objection was based, Thayer turned to Judge Fairchild and asked if it would be possible to get better ventilation in the room. The heat was stifling, and several of the women had already been forced to leave or risk fainting in the heat.

Thomas made his argument. The papers Thayer wanted to present could not be used since, he claimed, they had not been properly authenticated. Therefore, they could not be employed to contradict earlier papers that had been validated by the Canadian government. The original papers, Thomas argued, had to take precedence over Thayer's documents.

Fairchild overruled the objection. Olive beamed – it was important to her that the new testimony be admitted – while Thomas glowered. Throughout the hearing, not one of his objections had been sustained. Short of a definite statement, Fairchild was making it clear that he intended to give the Thayer every possible opportunity to block the surrender of an American resident to Canadian authorities.

Having gained his point, Thayer proceeded to read the testimony into the record, beginning with Eliza's account of George's illness. Olive wept bitterly, wiping her face with a black-bordered

handkerchief, and breaking down completely when the description
of George's death was read.

The next affidavit came from an equivocal John Snider.

> I think that I did not embalm the body. It was in good
> condition, and I did not think it necessary. I simply punc-
> tured his intestines in order to let the gases escape. I
> would not say positively that I did not embalm the body.

But Thomas had a statement in which Snider swore that he *had* embalmed the body. It seemed Snider was not certain one way or another.

The next deposition came from Charlotte Hunsberger, Eliza
Sternaman's cousin, who swore that Snider told her that he was uncertain whether he had embalmed the body. Thomas had had
enough. He was on his feet crying that Hunsberger's testimony was
worthless since she was a relative of Eliza. The courtroom erupted in
a buzz of speculation.

When peace was restored, Dr. F.P. Vandenburg of Buffalo was
called to the stand. A practising analytical and consulting chemist, he
concurred with Park's and Harrison's conclusion that George had
died of arsenic poisoning. He explained that Canadian doctors
would have used the Marsh test only if they were looking for arsenic. Vandenburg also pointed out that the amount found in
George's stomach had no bearing on the cause of death because
only arsenic which had been dissolved and made its way to various
part of the body would be lethal. Then he addressed the embalming
issue, explaining,

> In the event of the body having been embalmed by inject-
> ing arsenical fluid in the stomach, the condition of the soil
> containing moisture and numerous alkaline deposits
> would have a tendency to draw the poisonous fluid to
> other parts of the body after six weeks of burial.

The final evidence centred on insurance policies. Benjamin
Morningstar stressed that it was George, not Olive, who had wanted
the policy. However, when Thomas questioned Morningstar about
George's physical appearance and mannerisms, the Chautauqua
Savings and Loan agent was unable to answer.

Thayer viewed Morningstar as a friendly witness. Such was not
the case with Charles R. Roberts. Although Roberts claimed he had
first suspected poisoning after talking to Eliza Sternaman, Thayer ac-

cused him of purposely looking for irregularities, of drumming up a case against Olive in order to save the insurance company money. Roberts vehemently denied these allegations, swearing he was an absolutely disinterested party. When questioned about the evidence he had rendered at the coroner's inquest, Roberts said he had attended because he had been asked by Canadian authorities.

That statement may have drawn skeptical comments from the spectators. In the late 1890s, insurance companies were under fire from many quarters. Frequently viewed as corrupt, money–making enterprises, they were blamed for convincing the working poor to spend what little spare money they had on policies which, for one reason or another, were never paid. And there were even more sinister accusations. Some people believed that the insurance companies' policy of encouraging working people to insure their children encouraged neglect and abuse. If a poor family could make money from the death of a child, critics argued, what was to stop them from arranging an "accident" or simply failing to provide the necessities of life?

Thayer wanted Roberts' testimony kept out of the record, and this sparked yet another clash between the two lawyers. Throughout Thayer's examination, Thomas had interrupted repeatedly. At one point, Thomas accused Thayer of insulting a witness. "Will not the court protect the witness?" he demanded. When Thomas criticized Thayer's method of handling the case, Thayer became furious. "Will not the Court protect me from insult?" As Commissioner Fairchild tried to intervene, his voice was drowned out by Thayer and Thomas's arguments.

The questioning continued. Thayer tried to force Roberts's admittance he had gone to Canada in hopes of persuading Eliza to bring her suspicions regarding George's death to the appropriate authorities. "Decidedly not," he protested. "I went there only for the purposes mentioned."

Thayer was skeptical. "Mr. Roberts, I ask you to name a single case you have proceeded to investigate without a feeling of doubt as to the cause of death."

"I cannot reveal such information. It would be a breach of confidence." He appealed to the court, and Commissioner Fairchild upheld him.

"And did you not persuade the authorities to exhume the body of George Sternaman?" Thayer asked.

"I had nothing to do with the exhumation."

The day's proceedings ended with Thomas re–reading John Snider's deposition. Detective Murray was needed back in Toronto, so that the case was adjourned until the following Tuesday.

In the interval, Olive's mother Ellen took the train to Canada. In the Selkirk area, she spoke to many people, hoping to find someone with the evidence needed to clear her daughter. But there was no new information, and the extradition hearing proceeded without any dramatic surprises.

The summing up was scheduled to begin at 10 a.m. on November 24. Somehow, the information was not passed along to Deputy Marshall Kane and Olive was not in the courtroom. She had to be brought from the jail, and only arrived at 10:40 a.m. As soon as she entered the courtroom, Thayer began to speak. As far as he was concerned, "the prosecution has not made out a case. There is not in the whole of the testimony one fact that leads to the justification of her extradition." He argued that the facts did not show that any crime had been committed. Moreover, he stated, after reviewing the *Federal Reporter*'s synopses of murder trials, he could find nothing which would justify Olive's extradition.

He quoted several legal precedents, reiterating the concept of probable cause.

> The question here is whether any legal grounds have been shown; any proof establishing the actual commitment of a crime, not the suspicions of an old crone. And again I repeat, have they shown the slightest bit of evidence, even circumstantial, which would justify her extradition? They have not made out a prima facie case. All the evidence in this case is circumstantial.

Again, he emphasized the affection between George and Olive and the fact that George was worth more to her alive and working than dead. Furthermore, Thayer concluded, it was his suspicion that George himself was the culprit – that he had poisoned Elon in order to marry Olive. Surely his attitude toward Elon's picture supported this conclusion, as did his jealousy and his desire to have Olive with him all the time.

Throughout, Olive sat quietly in the courtroom, looking as pleasant and unruffled as she had through most of the hearing.

The court broke for lunch, after which Thayer wrapped up his summation. Around 3:20 p.m., it was Thomas's turn. He was brief and concise, citing legal authorities and technical evidence. Among his chief arguments was his contradiction of his opponent's statement that the failure of the Marsh test proved that George had been embalmed. He re-read Dr. Phelps's statement attesting that the finding of the Marsh test were inconclusive, since few physicians could carry it out competently. Finally, he raised a question that at least some of the onlookers had probably wondered themselves:

> Why is it that this woman wants to remain here under the weight of condemnation and continual accusation, injuring herself and her children, when she could go to Canada and be tried by a fair tribunal, and if, as she claims, she is innocent, be for all time hereafter freed from such a burden?

With that, Commissioner Fairchild was left to review the evidence and to reach his decision.

December 4, 1896

"I ... will issue a warrant of commitment."

On December 4, 1896, Fairchild reconvened the extradition hearing. Once more, the room was packed with people, including the usual crowd of women spectators and Olive's two sons, Albert and Walter. When Olive was escorted into the room at 10:15 she looked calm and placid, completely unruffled, as though she were a spectator rather than the accused. Tension built as the spectators and court officials waited for the arrival of Thayer, who had been inexplicably delayed.

Finally, about half an hour later, Thayer arrived and the proceedings got underway. Commissioner Fairchild spoke, while Olive's boys played and laughed quietly. "After a very careful examination and hearing of a great amount of testimony in the case, and the laws and reports and decisions in extradition proceedings, I deem the evidence herein sufficient –"

Olive's face brightened and she rose from her chair. She smiled, her cheeks flushed with pleasure. A murmur arose from the female spectators, because, like Olive, they had heard "here insufficient."

Fairchild continued:

> ... to sustain the charges under the provisions of the treaty between Great Britain and the United States, and I will therefore certify the same, together with a copy of the testimony taken before me, to the secretary of state of the United States, and will issue a warrant of commitment in pursuance to section 5170 of the laws of the United States.

The women now realized their error. Olive's smile vanished, but she betrayed no other sign of her disappointment.

As soon as Fairchild had finished, Thayer was on his feet, vowing to appeal. Fairchild agreed. Olive was certainly entitled to an appeal and he entertain motion the next morning. After an affectionate farewell to her family, Olive was escorted back to jail by Deputy Marshall Kane. Meanwhile, Detective Murray prepared to make an application through the British Legation for the extradition papers. He had 60 days in which to make the arrangements.

"I do not believe that I will ever go to Canada."

Four decades earlier, Charles Dickens had attacked the slowness of the British judicial system in his novel *Bleak House*. While there was little likelihood of Olive's case dragging on into the next generation, proceedings certainly were not moving fast enough for her. Thayer made his appeal, assisted by Frank C. Ferguson while Assistant Attorney Mackey and Thomas appeared for the prosecution. Meanwhile, Olive prepared to spend Christmas in jail. It was impossible for her not to think back to the last two Christmases. In 1894, Elon was ill and whatever joy the celebration brought the Chipman household had been mitigated by his condition. A year later, she was a widow, but already contemplating a second marriage. Now it was Christmas once more, and she had not only been widowed again, but was also separated from her beloved boys, imprisoned on suspicion of murder.

There was hope, of course, but whatever hope she had entertained must have been allayed by a newspaper report which the prison matron, Mrs. Halliday, read to her. The article revealed that Judge Coxe had upheld Commissioner Fairchild's decision – Olive would be extradited.

Coxe reviewed Fairchild's decision at a district court in Utica, New York, in mid-December. Olive's lawyers objected to the extradition order on three counts. First, they also quibbled about the method in which the complaint had been prepared. Secondly, they questioned whether the complaint presented by Murray gave him jurisdiction to issue a warrant resulting in the arrest of a Buffalo resident. Finally, they asked, did the evidence warrant extradition? Coxe dismissed the latter issue in no time. As far as he was concerned, Fairchild had made the right decision. Although the evidence was circumstantial, it was sufficient to warrant Olive's extradition. As for the jurisdictional question, he reserved judgement to give Thomas and Mackey time to cite authorities.

On December 24, the ruling came down. Coxe conceded that "the complaint shows evidences of having been hastily drawn, that it is inartistic from the point of view of the accomplished technical pleader and that it might be more ample and exact." Nevertheless, it was sufficient, and time was of the essence if there was the least possibility that the suspect might flee from justice.

As far as jurisdiction was concerned, Coxe pointed out that Olive had been amply informed of her rights and the crime with which she was charged. Although he hinted that it would be possible to dismiss the charges on a technicality, it would be of no benefit to the accused since it would be a simple matter to issue a new warrant based on the evidence submitted at the extradition hearing. Dismissal would only delay the proceedings further and cause additional hardship for Olive. In consequence, Coxe dismissed the appeal.

Before Olive received formal confirmation of the decision, she was interviewed by a reporter from the *Buffalo Evening News*. His first impression, when he saw her sitting with Mrs. Halliday, was that she looked quite well for someone who had spent eight weeks in custody. When she caught sight of him, Olive rose, nodded politely, and moved forward. She was, he thought, remarkably calm. "Well, you are the first newspaper man I have consented to talk with this morning," laughed Olive. "It was the advice of my attorney, Mr. Thayer, that I have been trying to follow." Possibly Thayer saw a chance to capitalize on Christmas spirit. Surely few scenes could have been more poignant than a young mother separated from her fatherless children during a season that emphasized family reunions and Christian charity.

Q: You have been notified of Judge Coxe's decision, I suppose?

A: No. I have received no official notification either from the United States District Attorney or Mr. Thayer. The first I knew of it was when Mrs. Halliday read it to me from the newspaper this morning.

Q: You don't feel particularly apprehensive as to the result in Canada?

A: No. I do not. I feel quite confident that I will be acquitted if I be ever tried. But, I do not believe that I ever will go to Canada. I cannot account for this feeling, but something tells me that my attorneys will eventually find a loop hole through which I will crawl out of this disagreeable affair. I never poisoned either of my husbands and that will be proved so clearly that no one will ever entertain a suspicion against me.

Q: In the event of your acquittal in Canada, what do you purpose to do?

A: I shall certainly bring actions against the chief instigators of this conspiracy. It was George's mother, the old Mrs. Sternaman ... that instigated this affair. I do not doubt that she was aroused by the insurance agents. Now that I have mentioned insurance, I want to publicly state that I never was a party to George's getting insured. It was of his own free will and I had nothing whatever to do with it. The way he came to be insured was this: I, and my children, were insured in the Metropolitan and the agent, when he came to collect the premiums, would get into conversation with my husband, and he at last prevailed upon George to get insured.

Q: You do not feel very friendly toward your mother-in-law, do you?

A: I almost despise her. I cannot understand how a mother could ever do such a thing as she has. She professed to love dearly her son George, and said she did everything in his interest. But she listened too much to the suspicions whispered into her ears by the insurance agents. How could anyone like a woman who has done to me what she has?

For one of the few times since her arrest, Olive's face betrayed her anger.

Q: Then you think the entire affair was done through motives of jealousy and hatred?

A: Yes I do.

Q: Do your children visit you often?

A: Yes. That is about the only comfort I derived out of this situation. Of course I could wish a better place in which to spend my Christmas, but I have to submit to the inevitable. My children will not come to see me Christmas. I do not wish it, anyhow.

Asked about the treatment she was receiving in jail, she described it as:

the very best. Mrs. Halliday always treats me with propriety and decorum. My food is of the best, and I am satisfied. I will however, never go to a Canadian jail if I can

possibly help it. Their jails are dark and gloomy, I understand. My friends could not see me, and I would be iso-
lated from everybody. But I hope never to go there. I am
not afraid to stand my trial, however, because I know I
will be acquitted.

What most impressed the reporter was Olive's calm and her
simple pleasantness, as though they were having a social visit. She
even made a small attempt at humour. As he was leaving, the reporter asked the matron's name and Olive quipped, "You will not
forget mine very easily."

A short time later, Thayer notified Olive of Judge Coxe's decision. He
also told her of his plans to appeal, plans he shared with a reporter
for the *Buffalo News* on the morning of December 26.

If the Circuit Court of Appeals sustains the decision of
Judge Coxe, I intend to appeal her case to the United
States Supreme Court. This is as far as we can go and we
must abide by whatever decision is rendered by that court.
I do not want the woman to be tried in Haldimand
county, because I know that she will not get a fair trial. I
was through that section a short time ago, and was surprised at the deep-rooted prejudice there is against her.
Everyone in her community is satisfied that she is guilty,
and it would be impossible to get an unbiased jury. I am
perfectly satisfied that the woman is innocent. Public sentiment is aroused to a high pitch in Haldimand county. The
people there reason it out by the process of elimination.

Apparently, locals felt that no one else had the motive, means
or opportunity to murder George but Olive. Because of this, Thayer
wanted a change of venue.

What we are trying to have done is to have her tried at
Toronto or some other large Canadian city. Two weeks ago
I wrote to the Attorney-General of Canada, asking him to
transfer the seat of the trial from Haldimand county to
Toronto. I have received no reply from him yet. Mr.
Sternaman is not afraid to stand trial for this alleged crime,
but I will not have her tried before a jury tainted with
prejudice.

It would be a long time before Thayer would have to worry about a biased jury, for the appeals dragged on. On the afternoon of March 18, Thayer obtained an order from Justice Lambert, empowering Andrew T. Thompson of Cayuga to take the testimony of key witnesses, specifically Doctors Harrison and Park, William Ellis and Eliza Sternaman. For Thompson, a lawyer and brother of coroner David Thompson, it was probably the last bit of professional business to be wrapped up before he sailed to England to take part in Queen Victoria's Diamond Jubilee celebrations. He was to begin his work in Toronto on April 3, and Thayer was convinced that the testimony of these five individuals would prove Olive's innocence beyond a shadow of a doubt. Meanwhile, Thayer was preparing his case for presentation in New York City. Just as he had at the Buffalo hearing, Thayer based his argument on his belief that the case was weak. He insisted that a *prima facie* case had not been made – too much of the evidence was circumstantial – and therefore no extradition could be ordered. Again and again, he would tell judges, colleagues and the press that Olive was not guilty of the crime.

The appeal was argued in New York City on May 4. Judges Wallace, Lacombe and Shipman listened to the evidence presented by Thomas and District Attorney Mackey, along with Thayer's refutations. Olive remained in prison in Buffalo, where she learned that the tribunal had upheld Judge Fairchild's ruling.

She refused, however, to give up hope, pinning her future on Thayer's energetic support. The Buffalo attorney now carried his case to the highest court in the land, the United States Supreme Court in Washington. Although he added a new twist – the contention that if any poison had been given it had been administered in the United States and so Olive should be prosecuted in American courts – he failed once more. The *Federal Reporter* summed up the decision of July 10, 1897, succinctly: "One accused of poisoning resulting in death in Canada, may be extradited, though it appears that the poison, if administered at all, was given in this country."

On July 28, 1897, the State Department issued a warrant ordering Olive's surrender to Canadian officials. Although a last-minute attempt to stop the process came a month or so later, there was nothing that could be done. Before the summer was out, Detective Murray arrived to escort Olive back to Haldimand County.

PART THREE

TRIAL FOR MURDER

"Absolute self-possession ..."

*T*he route Olive travelled to Cayuga was the same she had covered with George little more than a year earlier. Once more, she
changed trains at Canfield Junction, then steamed towards the
Haldimand County seat in Cayuga.

Cayuga had a population of little more than 1000. It was a
pretty town on the east bank of the Grand River. It boasted a new
town hall, as well as a red brick post office "considered the hand-
somest and most durable public building in the county," which told
of recent prosperity. The court-house, records office and jail on the
north side of town commanded an unparalleled view of the mean-
dering waterway, for they were built atop the only hill in an otherwise flat countryside.

A handsome stone and brick structure in the Classic Revival
style, the Haldimand County Court-house had been built nearly half
a century earlier. The imposing central block featured Ionic pilasters
and a massive dome or cupola housing several windows. To the
north was the jailer's house, completed in 1877, a red and yellow
brick Italian villa with a large front verandah and twin chimneys.
Behind the court-house, enclosed by a high stone wall, was the jail.
Built along with the court-house, it was a solid-looking two-storey
structure of grey brick, with a flat roof and low wide windows.

Despite its attractive appearance, the jail-house fell short of
standards set by the province. In January 1897, Haldimand County
Sheriff A.A. Davis called the county council's attention to the "precarious condition of the water supply to the jail." Dr. Baxter, who saw to
the medical needs of the inmates, had also written a letter complaining about the water supply, but by late summer, a visiting committee still found problems with the water in the jail's kitchen.

Olive reached the jail-house grounds through an opening on
the north side of the stone wall. Immediately on the left was the governor's brick house, with the kitchen door opening into the jail yard.
The yard itself, still green in the late summer sunshine, was smooth
and grassy, bearing no evidence of the drama it had witnessed, or the

bodies of convicted felons which lay buried beneath. Olive entered the jail-house through a low door and was led up a winding set of iron stairs to a landing, where a wooden partition screened all sight of the women's quarters from curious eyes. Then, there was a second set of stairs. Reaching the top, Olive found herself facing a blank wall. To the left was the cell in which she would await trial or, more correctly, cells, for there were two. The larger one contained two windows with curved stone archways that offered a view of the river. The smaller one had a single window, which faced onto the whitewashed wall of the prison yard. Furnishings were minimal – a wooden table painted yellow and two matching yellow chairs were in the larger cell. A cot and a wash-stand occupied the smaller.

The jailer, John Alfred Murphy, was an unusual character considering his occupation. Born in Caledonia in 1859, he was only eight years older than Olive. A former school-teacher, he had spent several years in Lucan, now famous as the home of the Black Donnellys. Although he had taken a post in Cayuga at the time of the notorious massacre of the Donnelly family, Murphy probably knew several of the characters in the drama. School-teachers normally knew most residents of a small rural community and, furthermore, Murphy and the Donnellys shared a common Irish heritage.

John Murphy became jailer around 1885, succeeding his father, Peter. An intelligent and curious man, John was fascinated with the court proceedings carried on so close to his home, and he took up the study of law. By the time Olive was placed in his charge, he had also acquired a wife, Susan Higgins of Walpole Township. Together, they had three children.

Convicted felons were expected to earn their keep during their sojourn in the county jail. Men sentenced to hard labour were often put to work improving Cayuga's streets and sidewalks. Women, as the weaker sex, were exempt from such burdensome work, but were still given various domestic tasks, including the laundering of prisoners' clothes and bed linen. Olive found that needlework and reading religious tracts were not enough to fill her time, so she helped Susan Murphy with sewing and mending. The two women, born in neighbouring townships, raised in the country, and close to the same age, struck up a tenuous friendship.

The preliminary hearing opened at Cayuga on September 2, 1897, despite Wallace Thayer's belief that the case could not be fairly tried in Haldimand County. He, of course, could not act on Olive's behalf. Instead, she was represented by William Manley German of

Welland, QC. Born in eastern Ontario's Prince Edward County in 1851, German studied law in Belleville after graduating from Victoria College, Cobourg. Upon admittance to the bar in 1882, he set up a practice in Welland. A handsome and genial man, he had a knack for getting his own way without offending too many people. In fact, his admirers said his "dominant manner" instilled confidence. In 1884, he was elected Deputy–Reeve for Welland by acclamation. Seven years later he was elected to the Ontario legislature, but "was unseated". Nevertheless, he ran again in 1894 and this time he re-tained his seat. An aggressive and ambitious character, German's eloquence served him well both in politics and in the courtroom. By the time he agreed to defend Olive, he had built himself a beautiful mansion on Division Street, one of Welland's finest residential areas.

County Crown Attorney Charles Wesley Colter, who had been involved in the case from the beginning, represented the Crown at the preliminary hearing. Presiding over the courtroom was Mr. Justice Adam A. Davis. An emigrant from Eniskillen, Ireland, Davis was 69, a doctor by training who had been Haldimand county sher-iff for 20 years. Genial and courteous, "a real Irish gentleman," he had recently retired as commanding officer of the Haldimand militia.

The evidence presented at the preliminary hearing was already familiar to most newspaper readers and, indeed, to almost anyone who lived in Haldimand County, Buffalo and parts in between. What excited most interest was the appearance of the defendant. Olive ap-peared on the first day, still dressed completely in black although the requisite year of mourning had passed. She also wore a black hat, with a black veil pulled down over her face. According to news-paper reports, "At times her face took on a sad look, but as a rule she looked very pleasant." Olive's appearance and behaviour inspired much speculation. According to one newspaper description, she

> did not appear to be much more concerned than the rest
> of the community. She sat throughout the day beside her
> counsel, most of the time with a listless air of being some-
> what bored by the whole business, though now and again
> she would look up sharply and fix her steel–grey eyes in-
> tently on the witness as though to read into his very heart
> and brain, or again she would lean forward to whisper
> into her counsel's ear some instruction or information
> upon a point brought out by the testimony. She was qui-
> etly dressed in a neat, black cashmere gown, plainly but
> fashionably made, the throat concealed by a high collar of
> the same material, unrelieved by any edging of white;

around the waist a plain black band, fastened with a dull
jet buckle and holding a gold watch, the only piece of
adornment or jewelry visible, save the plain band of gold
on the third finger of the left hand. Her neatly-brushed
brown hair was surmounted by a broad-brimmed black
straw hat, trimmed with black ribbon and osprey feathers,
and her face partly shaded by a light black net. Absolute
self-possession was the characteristic of her whole demeanour, and, whatever the outcome may be, one cannot
but admire the courage with which she is facing the terrible ordeal of the twelve months, an ordeal which will cul-
minate   two   or   three   months   hence   in   the
anxiously-awaited verdict of the Assize Court jury.

But where did that self-possession originate? A woman of
Olive's class was not expected to manifest such incredible self-con-
trol and certainly not over the period of months in which she had
been under public scrutiny. For many, her apparent lack of interest
in the proceedings and her stoic *sang-froid* were the most damning
evidence against her. It suggested she was perfectly capable of committing a husband to a horrible, painful death – not once, but twice.

Yet there were displays of emotion, as the *Spectator* revealed on
September 11. It was a particularly hot and humid late summer day
and, with the courtroom packed with observers, the temperature became unbearable.

The coolest person in the sweltering crowd, both mentally
and physically, during the first two hours of the morning's
session apparently was the prisoner herself. With mar-
velous self-possession she sat through the tedious hours
never once showing signs of fatigue, and giving little indication of special concern in the testimony being offered.

Then, a few moments before adjournment, and without any warning,

She gave a little start and shuddering, burst into tears, at
the same time burying her face in the black-bordered
handkerchief which she had carried in her hands throughout the morning. The fit of weeping was unaccountable
just at that moment as no special point of interest or importance, nothing particularly harrowing or pathetic, was
being elicited. Neither did it last long. Five minutes later

she dried her eyes again and sat motionless as before, the only remaining indication of the passing wave of feeling being the reddening of the lids and moistened lash.

Observers could draw their own conclusions. Was Olive reacting to the pangs of conscience? Or were her sudden and inappropriate outbursts indicative of an unbalanced mind?

But not all her outbursts were inappropriate. As the opposing lawyers summed up their arguments, William German waxed eloquent in his description of Olive's separation from her children. For her part, Olive wept silently. Surely a woman with such strong maternal instincts could not be a murderer. Still, a show of emotion was not enough to convince the law of her innocence. Mr. Justice Davis ruled that there was sufficient evidence for Olive to stand trial at the fall assizes.

The crowd watched Olive receive the sentence. "All eyes turned to the graceful, sombrely–draped figure as the Magistrate announced his decision, but she was evidently prepared for it, and showed no embarrassment or distress." John Murphy then escorted her back to the jail house to await the next chapter in her dramatic ordeal.

Just before the trial, a reporter from the *Hamilton Evening Times* slipped into the jail and, with Murphy's and High Constable John Farrell's permission, and Olive's cooperation, conducted an interview.

The jail is situated just in the rear of the Court-house, and although old–fashioned, is a model institution, Every nook and corner of the old pile is as sweet and clean and white-looking as a newly–erected mansion. On the ground floor are the cells for male prisoners and the jailer's office. A winding iron stairway runs to the upper flat, and it is here that Mrs. Olive Adele Sternaman is confined. Her cell, or rather chamber, is the first door on the landing to the right, and is about fifteen feet by ten.

When her cell door was thrown open Mrs. Sternaman came forward with a smile and heartily shook the proffered hand of her visitors. Mrs. Sternaman is just thirty years of age, and although the constant confinement for more than a year has told on her a trifle, she is young looking yet, and although not decidedly handsome, is

pretty. She is a blonde, [in fact, her hair was light brown]
with large, dreamy eyes, prominent cheek–bones and nose,
large mouth, and a narrow chin. She is always smiling and
her present embarrassing position does not seem to trouble her."

Q: Well, it is nearly time for your trial. Are you
     glad it is at hand?
A: Indeed I am. I never was so thankful for any-
     thing in my life. I want to go to that court and
     have my name cleared. I am confident of suc-
     cess, and am sure I will be acquitted.

Olive stopped to introduce Lizzie, who was spending a few
hours with her in her cell. The reporter remarked on the resemblance between the two women, noting later that Lizzie was "a decided brunette." Then he asked Olive how she spent her time.

Oh, Mr. Murphy treats me well, and Mrs. Murphy is an
angel. I have my three afternoons out on the pretty lawn
there, and altogether I manage to get along fairly well. You
see I do a lot of fancy work, and this is what I am at just
now.

She hurried over to a table and returned with a *jardinière* made
of tissue paper and decorated with "life–like chrysanthemums." Once
the reporter had admired it, he asked why Olive had fought so hard
to avoid extradition.

I was anxious to come only my friends prevented me, and
advised me to stay and fight the proceedings. You see I
was nine months in jail in Buffalo, and they did not treat
me half as well as they do here. I was glad when I got here
on Aug. 7th, and I am still better pleased now when I
know my trial is so near. Of course I dislike the ordeal of
facing the crowds of people, but I'll do it, and be acquitted.

Olive's comparison between her treatment in American and
Canadian jails was intriguing. The previous December, in an interview with a Buffalo reporter, she had expressed a desire to stay in
the United States where, she said, jail conditions were better. Perhaps
experience had changed her mind; perhaps she was trying to elicit
support from Canadian newspapers, motivated either by her own

instinct for survival or by advice from William German. Then again, Olive may not have made the comment at all. Newspaper reporters often embellished their stories for dramatic or political effect, or to increase sales, and this journalist might have been making a less-than-subtle hint about the superiority of Canadian legal and penal institutions. In any event, the interview ended with Olive saying goodbye "with a hearty laugh and some jocular remark."

Indictment

Throughout Ontario, in Buffalo and elsewhere in Canada and the United States, newspapers transported their readers to the Cayuga courtroom. Olive Sternaman was the topic of conversation in parlours and clubs and on the street. Those who knew the facts – at least the facts as presented in the newspapers – drew their own conclusions. Regardless of their decisions, the courtroom drama still had to be played out. And, in this instance, the county court of rural Haldimand would be the stage for one of the giants of the criminal justice system, Britton Bath Osler.

"Brick" Osler, as his family and friends called him, was 58 and at the peak of his career as a criminal lawyer. The third son of an Anglican minister, he was born in Simcoe County and educated at the Barrie Grammar School, where he first showed the business acumen and ambition that would make him a fine lawyer. He followed his older brother, Featherstone, into a legal career after graduating from the University of Toronto in 1862. At first, he practised law in Dundas, at the head of Lake Ontario, afterwards moving to Hamilton. From May 1874 to December 1882, he served as Crown Attorney for Wentworth County; two years after his appointment, he was made a QC. He resigned in 1884 to move to Toronto, where he became a partner in the firm of McCarthy, Osler, Hoskin & Creelman.

Osler was one of the team of lawyers prosecuting for the crown at Louis Riel's trial in 1885. His reputation was further enhanced when he secured a conviction in the Birchall trial, in which an English con man was accused of murdering a compatriot in a swamp near Woodstock, Ontario. He flirted with politics from time to time, running unsuccessfully as a Liberal candidate for Welland in the federal election of 1882, and making speeches on several occasions – including one in Haldimand County in June 1896. There were also rumours that he had turned down an offer to serve as Minister of Justice under Prime Minister Charles Tupper.

In the courtroom, he was eloquent, cogent, logical and conscientious in his presentation of the facts. One writer for *The Canadian Magazine* described his address to the jury in the Birchall trial:

> His powerful voice, rich and magnetic, rang through the court-room ... His short and effective sentences, unornamented and unpolished, but simple, fluent, crushing and terrible, swept everything in one overwhelming and engulfing torrent before them. There was no seeking for effect, no attempt to display a finished style, no refinement of speech, and no careful discrimination in the use of words and phrases.

In short, Osler eschewed literary references, convoluted phrases and complicated words, and frequently made grammatical errors, in order to present evidence clearly and concisely. Instinctively, he knew that although legal and literary pyrotechnics might impress his colleagues, they were wasted on juries. By speaking to businessmen, artisans and farmers in their own language, Osler immediately set up a rapport that could only strengthen his case.

For all Osler's appeals to the average man, his closest ties were to other officers of the court. As Liberals, both he and German had much in common. And Osler's relationship with the presiding judge, John Douglas Armour, went back many years. Although the two men had opposing political views – Armour was a Conservative – they had much in common. Armour, born in Peterborough County in 1830, was also the son of a clergyman who studied at King's College (later the University of Toronto). Widely read and very shrewd, Armour had a well-developed sense of humour, even in the courtroom.

Although Armour appreciated courtroom repartee, he had a deserved reputation as the sternest judge in late 19th-century Ontario. He had little patience for involved technical arguments and took perverse pleasure in "tossing aside technicality and pinning everyone down to the facts which facilitated the course of justice." Consequently, he made enemies, most of whom used every opportunity to have his decisions reversed.

The first order of business was the indictment. A grand jury, consisting of Jacob Albright, John Booker, John Bouk, James A. Burwash, William Dobbin, Thomas Gracey, John Neweitt, William H. Hull, Robert Jamieson, Peter Kinsman, R.F. Lattermore, James Pitt and Alex Mitchell was empanelled; Mitchell was elected as foreman.

After receiving instructions from Armour, the grand jury spent a few hours listening to witnesses. Then they withdrew to discuss what they had heard. Around 6 p.m., the grand jury returned a true bill of murder and Olive was indicted.

Preliminaries – November 17, 1897

"Hearken to the charges."

Selection of the trial jury began on the morning of November 17. Osler asked six men to stand down and German challenged one, but the final selection did not take as much time and effort as had been anticipated. Without exception, the jurors were all from Haldimand County, and most were farmers; all townships except Rainham were represented. Six of the jurymen, David J. Forest, James Bragg, Robert Kelly, Edward Hyland, John N. Irwin, and John H. Lewis, came from Walpole, the township immediately west of Rainham, and one, Jacob Sitter, from South Cayuga, immediately to the east. Two, William Myers and Philip Houser were from Moulton; John Mino of North Cayuga, Henry Jackson of Oneida and Alfred James of Seneca, made up the remainder of the panel.

No matter how much time Olive had spent in American court-rooms, nothing could have prepared her for the Canadian trial. In a small county court, ten miles from her birthplace, her life hung in the balance. Theoretically, she was to be tried by a jury of her peers, but in practice this was impossible. Women still did not serve on Canadian juries, although a few had managed to enter the legal pro-fession. True, the men of the jury came from farming communities, just as Olive had, and like her most had little more than a rudimen-tary education. Some even shared a similar ethnic background. But, in a society where the roles of men and women were clearly defined, where women collected in one part of a room and men in another at social gatherings, there was a great, unbridgeable chasm between the sexes.

As a member of the "weaker sex," Olive was an enigma to the men of the jury. As a widow who had lived with a younger man prior to their marriage, she was regarded as immoral. As a woman accused of killing her husband – to whom, in law and tradition, she owed complete obedience, respect and devotion – she was suspected of one of the most despicable crimes. Any juryman who had ever fought with his wife, who had seen a flash of anger and pure hatred, however brief, in her eyes could not look at Olive Sternaman with-out discomfort and the thought "there, but for the grace of God go I."

Any man of perception quickly realized the fate of George Sternaman might have been his own. And, in fact, whoever had murdered George, a brother farmer, cousin to innumerable Hoover descendants and neighbour, had struck a blow at the entire tightly-knit rural community. If Olive was the guilty one, no matter what compunctions might exist about capital punishment for women, it was the jury's duty to see that she was duly convicted, if only to prevent other young men from falling prey to women who had been led to murder by the twin corruptions of city life and the United States.

Mr. Justice Armour addressed the men regarding their duties. He explained that a jury's duty did not extend to a choice of the case they could hear. If there was enough evidence to put the accused on trial, it was required to render a true bill. Furthermore, he said, in this instance the work would be fairly light, for there was only one charge, that of murder.

Then Armour proceeded to define murder as, "the unlawful killing of any person, providing the person who committed the deed was in his right mind, reason, memory and understanding." He went on to the specific details of murder by poisoning. It was the jury's task to determine if death had resulted from poisoning, and whether malice was expressed through the purchase and preparation of the poison. It was not necessary, he explained, to prove the exact substance or quantity given, or to prove that such a quantity was found in the body of the deceased. What was necessary was to prove the guilt of the accused, the motive of the crime, the means of purchasing or obtaining, and the opportunity of administering the substance. Furthermore, it was not even necessary to prove that the poison was administered by the accused, if there was sufficient evidence that the accused had prepared the poison and had a motive. It was entirely likely the poison could be administered by an innocent third party.

Finally, Armour honed in on the specifics of the Sternaman case. It was not necessary to examine the testimony of every witness, he explained, if, after examining a few, it seemed there was enough evidence to place the accused on trial. He finished with the hope that the jurors would act promptly so that the trial could proceed. The trial, he hinted, should be finished before the end of the week.

Selection, instruction and other matters took most of the day. By 6 o'clock, the crowds of spectators had thinned out considerably. Judge Armour ordered Sheriff Farrell to place the prisoner in the dock. Escorted by Murphy, Olive climbed down two flights of winding stairs and passed through a narrow doorway into the courtroom.

She was wearing a black cloak, tossed hastily around her shoulders, as if anticipating her freedom. She also wore a black straw hat. As always, she seemed composed, although a careful observer saw her glance straying from face to face, never resting long, as though searching for some clue of what was about to happen.

Farrell escorted her to the prisoner's dock. Nervously, she entered and sat down. Meanwhile, lawyers were addressing the jury on another case. Olive waited, and the pause seemed to give her time to recover her composure. By the time Justice Armour asked her to stand, she was as impassive as ever.

"Hearken to the charges," he commanded in the ancient language of the British courts. The clerk read the documents accusing her of the wilful murder of her husband, George Sternaman, and asked for her plea.

Firmly, in a voice that could be clearly heard from one end of the courtroom to the other, Olive replied. "Not guilty."

The plea was entered and Armour called for the trial to begin at 9 a.m. the following morning.

The Crown's Case – November 18, 1897

"All skilled and crafty crimes are done in the dark."

Two minor matters on the docket postponed Olive's case until 10:30 when Judge Armour ordered Olive to be brought in. Her sister Lizzie accompanied her from the jail and, as always, Olive seemed oblivious to the drama of the situation. In fact, she appeared to be in an extraordinarily good mood, laughing from time to time at humorous remarks made by female acquaintances who sat behind her.

Around 11 o'clock, B.B. Osler began his address to the jury. Demonstrating his characteristic conciseness and logic, Osler reiterated the facts of the case: how George had died under suspicious circumstances and why Olive now stood charged with his murder. It was the jury's duty, he explained, to judge whether or not she was responsible for her husband's death.

He elaborated on the process. The jury must arrive at the fact of the exact person causing death, and then how far the accused is connected with the administration of poison. But, he warned, the Crown would not attempt to prove the actual administration of poison by the accused because no one had claimed to see such action. Circumventing one of the obvious defense tactics, he continued:

You will have to deal with circumstantial evidence entirely, because the Crown has none other to submit. All
skilled and crafty crimes are done in the dark, after a long
preparation of all details, which leave only circumstantial
evidence possible. Some persons object to this class of evidence, but it has to be considered that without it none of
the crafty crimes committed could be brought home to the
accused.

Osler pointed to the motive – $1900 in life insurance, but said
the Crown would not submit evidence of quarrelling between Olive
and George because the deceased had great confidence and affection
for his wife. The implication, of course, was to make the betrayal of
George's trust all the more heinous. He also referred briefly to the
death of Elon Chipman and summarized critical elements of the
Crown's evidence, beginning with the letter written in early June
asking for an autopsy. Osler claimed it had been written at Olive's
suggestion and had been deliberately constructed to counter any of
Eliza's suspicions.

Osler also stated he would not attempt to prove that Olive had
procured poison; instead, he would show that it was possible for
anyone to do so in Buffalo and escape detection. He summed up
with a short chronology of the events leading up to the trial: the
marriage in February, the arrangement of the insurance policies in
May, George's curious letter of June, his death in August, and the
contradictory and misleading statements Olive made when claiming
the insurance.

The summary, delivered in his characteristically clear style, was
deliberately designed to help jurors follow the Crown's case as it unfolded. Repetition was the key: like later-day propagandists and
public relations experts, Osler understood the tenet that if you repeat
something often enough people are likely to believe it. By outlining
the case in clear, cogent language, Osler was planting a seed he
hoped would grow as each of the 35 Crown witnesses presented
their evidence. Not all testimony would be as readily understood as
Osler's presentation, but that, too, was part of the strategy. Osler
clearly understood the weight normally given to the testimony of
expert witnesses, especially doctors. No matter what their feelings toward the medical profession as a whole, the men who made up rural
juries usually had great respect for anyone with a good education.
Doctors certainly fit into that category, so that by parading no less
than 10 physicians – plus two forensics experts – before the jury,
Osler hoped to overwhelm them with irrefutable evidence that

George had died of arsenic poisoning. The same tactic would be applied to other aspects of the case, through testimony from a handful
of insurance men and from those who had observed the Sternamans
during the final days of George's life.

Borrowing a tactic that good teachers have used through the
ages, Osler started with the familiar. Eliza Sternaman was part of the
Haldimand farming community; she was the first to suspect her son
had been murdered and the first to notify authorities, and so it was
fitting for Eliza Jane Stermanan to be the first on the stand. She appeared worried and very nervous as the oath was administered, perhaps because the noise of the crowd made it difficult to hear with
her ear trumpet. She testified that George had always enjoyed good
health and that she had visited Buffalo three weeks after Elon
Chipman's death. She also recited her objections to the match: Osler
avoided probing into her reasons. Although the crowd was visibly
disappointed, it was a wise move. Eliza's strong dislike of Olive could
have generated more sympathy for the accused.

Eliza recounted the symptoms of his illness, his return to her
house in Rainham, and the care he had received there. Eliza recalled
that the day after George's death she asked Olive about his insurance and had been told it amounted to $770.

After dwelling on the relationship between Eliza and the young
couple, and Eliza's visits to Buffalo, Osler also produced the letter
George had written in June. He asked Eliza to identify it and she
confirmed the handwriting as her son's. Osler returned to George's
illness and asked if Olive had ever revealed the nature of it. "She
told me at the first the doctors said it was a loathsome disease," Eliza
replied. Later, Eliza went on, Olive explained that the doctors had
treated George for that ailment for two weeks, then changed their
diagnosis.

After probing, unsuccessfully, for suspicious remarks Olive
might have made to her, Osler asked about the statements made by
the Buffalo doctors. Eliza repeated them, especially those made by
Dr. Saltsman, who had claimed that he knew what was wrong with
George, and could help him if he was not too far gone. Saltsman,
however, could not state the exact cause of the illness.

At 12:30, W.M. German began his cross-examination. Arrogant
where Osler was confident, he was far less concerned about dealing
tactfully with the aged witness. He went over most of the same
ground as Osler without turning up new revelations. He did provoke
some amused smiles and perhaps a few embarrassed blushes when
he questioned Eliza on the name of George's illness. "You stated that
the prisoner said that the doctor had told her his disease was a

loathsome disease," the barrister said, and asked Eliza the name of it. She hesitated, and when German asked again whether Olive had mentioned the name of the ailment, Eliza made it clear that she had little use for medical jargon. "She gave it to me in the words that the doctor told her to use, to keep people blind from knowing what was wrong. I can't remember that." German suggested syphilis, then gon-orrhoea, but all Eliza could offer was that "There was two words ... they seemed to be in Latin or something."

German changed his tack to concentrate on one inconsistency, regarding the post–mortem. Was the witness aware, he wondered, "that the prisoner caused the post–mortem examination to be held in consequence of the suspicion you had as to the cause of death?" "I ain't aware of that," Eliza replied, but she did confirm her evidence before Magistrate Parker in the Cayuga court-house. When German asked if she had sworn that Olive had ordered the post–mortem be-cause of her suspicions, Eliza denied it. "How could she have a post mortem when I didn't accuse her until after the post mortem?"

But German had evidence to the contrary. He read the deposi-tion Eliza had made to the magistrate, stating that Olive had asked for the post–mortem because she, Eliza, had suspected foul play. A confusing series of questions and answers followed, in which it be-came clear that Eliza had misunderstood the lawyer's questions at some point. Finally, in exasperation she confessed, "My head isn't clear like it used to be. That was a misunderstanding of mine."

When his opponent had finished, Osler asked a few more questions, again returning to the name of George's disease in hopes that Eliza might provide some clues. Their exchange made it clear that Eliza had no grasp of medical terminology and would be little help in that area. In fact, she seemed singularly ignorant of all as-pects of George's health except his final illness. When Osler turned to the "spells" George was alleged to have had, and the rumours that had circulated about them, Eliza denied George had suffered from any such spells at all. Approaching the topic was a calculated risk on Osler's part: if Eliza had made a good impression, her word would probably be accepted by the jury. If not – or if any of the jurors had heard rumours of George's spells from other residents of Rainham – the rest of her testimony might not be given credence. However, it was worth the risk. Eliza might be an ageing, cantankerous, un-schooled woman, suspicious of doctors and confused by legal pro-ceedings, but she was also a bereaved mother and part of the farming community to which most of the jurors belonged. A signifi-cant portion of her testimony would be accepted as fact, and German's cavalier treatment of the old woman would offset any negative impression created by her querulousness. Osler had made a good beginning.

Medical Testimony

As soon as Eliza stepped down from the witness stand, Judge Armour ordered a half-hour adjournment for lunch. When proceedings resumed shortly before 2 o'clock, the first of the medical witnesses took the stand.

Shortly before 2 o'clock, Dr. Park took the stand and recounted the details of George's treatment at length. He recalled what he knew of George's treatment in Buffalo, and listed medicines he had prescribed: morphia to allow George to rest at night and some "cathartic pills" for constipation. But it was not until Osler asked a direct question that Park discussed the cause of George's many symptoms.

Q: What did you treat him for?
A: I treated him for arsenical poisoning.
Q: That was your diagnosis?
A: That was my diagnosis, multiple neuritis due to arsenical poisoning.

After explaining the symptoms which had led to this conclusion, Park took the courtroom through the details of the post-mortem, and how he and Harrison had checked for signs of Addison's disease and syphilis. When neither appeared the older physician had administered the Marsh test.

In hopes of catching Park off guard, German began his cross-examination with the delicate issue of venereal disease.

Q: I suppose that syphilis, spoken of to a woman at any rate, would be considered as a loathsome disease. You would not be surprised at a woman describing that as a loathsome disease?
A: No.
Q: As a matter of fact it is?
A: Yes, it is considered so, a loathsome disease.
Q: And you would not be surprised at a doctor, telling Mrs. Sternaman, from your diagnosis of the case, that he had the appearance of syphilis?

In Buffalo, there had been suggestions that George was suffering from syphilis. Presumably, German was fishing for an admission that Park might have made a similar diagnosis. He was also trying to persuade the jury that, when one of the doctors had suggested syphilis, Olive had misrepresented George's ailment out of delicacy, rather than a deliberate attempt to conceal the truth. However, he was beating about the bush too much for Park's liking. "Just put your question so as to make it plain to me," the doctor demanded.

Unruffled, the Welland lawyer continued. "You would not be surprised at a doctor telling Mrs. Sternaman that her husband's disease had the appearance of syphilis?" Park conceded that this might happen.

"You had syphilis in your mind as a probable cause of the illness?"

Finally, the doctor rose to German's bait. "I did when I first saw him."

That admission was precisely what German needed to launch his campaign against the medical experts with a line of questioning designed to suggest that George might not have been poisoned at all. Counting on the likelihood that the experience of a young country doctor like Park would be limited, German proceeded to question his familiarity with arsenic and, by extension, his ability to make a competent diagnosis of George's ailment. "Have you had much experience with arsenic or arsenical poisoning?"

A: Never before in my life.
Q: I suppose [German's tone was sarcastic] you had seen what is termed white arsenic before?
A: I don't know whether I ever did or not. White arsenic is not used in medicine as such.
Q: So you could not say now whether or not you had seen white arsenic?
A: I couldn't say. I might have seen it in my college days.

Convinced that he now had the physician off balance and that he had introduced a shadow of doubt about the doctor's ability, German moved to the crux of his defense. "I presume you never had any experience with Addison's disease."

The sarcasm was too much for Park, especially since German's presumption was wrong. "I have seen cases of Addison's disease," he said. "At least I made a diagnosis in one case and saw cases in Edinburgh. It is more common in Edinburgh that in this country." If the mention of the Scottish capital not once, but twice, was deliberate, Park was sending a clear message to the jury that he had studied at one of the best centres of medical education in the world.

German continued with his questioning, establishing that Addison's disease was most common among people between 20 and 40. "Is it not a disease which is peculiar to the labouring class of people rather than people of leisure," he asked. The lawyer's purpose was now transparent to Park, who decided to be as specific as possible.

> "About that I never had much experience. My experience is not extensive enough. I would think it would be probable. It may occur though in others, in tubercular history, where there is consumption it is more apt to occur."

Slowly, German built up an argument that George Sternaman might have suffered from Addison's disease. As the doctor responded, the jurors and court-room spectators learned that Addison's might be caused by an injury to the back, typical, it was implied, of the type a carpenter such as George might suffer. The symptoms, emaciation, vomiting, anemia, discoloration of the skin, extremely bright eyes and rapid pulse sounded all too familiar.

As to the effect on the supra-renal cavities, Park had already testified that he had specifically examined George's kidneys for Addison's disease without success. Now, in response to German's question, he admitted, "You may have Addison's disease without those being affected."

"So that as a matter of fact all of the symptoms which you saw in George Sternaman when you examined him might be developed from Addison's disease?" German crowed.

Park deflated his triumphant mood with two words. "No sir."

"Will you tell me one that could not be?"

"I would not expect to find multiple neuritis in Addison's disease."

For several minutes more, German peppered the doctor with questions about the comparative symptoms of Addison's disease and arsenic poisoning, turning at length to tests for the presence of the poison. Although Park agreed that analyzing urine was one method of detection, he favoured a prior examination of the patient's vomit. He also stressed that negative results were not necessarily conclusive. "He might be taking small quantities and with our facilities we might not be able to find it."

German felt it important to point out to the jury that, in fact, Park had found no trace of arsenic.

"How many times did you examine the urine?"

"Two or three times I would think."

"Then you examined the urine nearly every day that Sternaman was under your charge."

"No, I cannot say nearly every day. I only had the deceased six days under my care and I examined the urine I think two or three times. The urine was handed to me; I don't know whether it was his or whose it was."

German then asked for an account of the events following George's death. Park noted that, at his request, John Snider had not touched the body. And that response led to German's second line of defense: an attempt to prove that the arsenic found at the second post-mortem had been injected by the undertaker."If embalming fluid had been injected in George Sternaman's body after death, after you hade made your post mortem examination, would you or [would you] not expect to find arsenic disseminated through the parts of the body?"

Park said he would expect to find it. Furthermore, he stated, the embalming fluid might account for the excellent condition of George's body upon exhumation.

After a few more questions, German brought up the topic of Addison's disease again, reminding the jurors of the similarities between the two ailments. Then he questioned Park about Olive's behaviour.

"Did Mrs. Sternaman at any time exhibit any desire to keep anything hid from you at all as to George's symptoms?"

"I cannot say that she did excepting in giving the history he gave a certain version of the affair, of one part of the symptoms and she gave another version. That is the only thing. On other points she was quite free."

German's attempt to discredit Park was only partly successful. While he had managed to introduce the notion that George might have suffered from Addison's disease, he had not persuaded anyone that the young doctor was incompetent. Furthermore, his tentative attempt to shore up Olive's credibility was swept aside when Osler returned to Olive's rendition of the facts in his re-direct. "Did you have any talk with the prisoner as to arsenic?" he asked. The only time the subject was discussed, Park said, was when George died. At that time, "She said I was the first and only doctor that ever mentioned poison." For anyone familiar with newspaper accounts of the case, the statement was an emphatic reminder that Olive had not always told the truth.

Osler had planned to call Dr. Harrison as his next witness. However, as he explained to the court, "I have to go a little out of order to call a foreign witness." He saw no reason to irritate American witnesses by causing them to miss their trains home. Dr. Edward L. Frost was the next witness.

For the benefit of the jurors, he recounted his treatment of George including the administration of medication containing minute traces of arsenic. "The amount that he took altogether would not exceed one-thirtieth of a grain of the arsenite of copper," Frost explained. When George, after ten days, failed to respond, Frost called in Dr. James Whitewell. Whitewell concurred with Frost's diagnosis, but by June 30th George had developed a spot on his throat. It spread to his mouth by the following day, making eating and drinking so difficult that Frost had ordered "rectal alimentation." By the July 10, George was failing; moreover, he was now experiencing marked numbness in his fingers. On the 12th, Frost called on Dr. W.C. Phelps, who had considerable experience with poisoning cases. "At that time I had a suspicion that possibly my patient had had arsenic."

Phelps advised putting George in a hospital, where a doctor would be available at all times. After 45 minutes of coaxing, George agreed. Olive insisted that if he went to the hospital, she would never visit him. At that point, Frost drew her aside and revealed his suspicions that George had been poisoned. And later, when he was discharged, he warned Olive that if anyone heard about the possibility of poisoning, it would be from her, not from him

Osler then questioned Frost about his knowledge of George's life insurance policies. Because Olive had come to see him after her husband's death, Frost knew a little.

Q: What did she say?
A: She asked me to fill out the certificate.
Q: And did you do so?
A: I did.
Q: In what Company or Association?
A: It was in the Metropolitan.
Q: Do you know for how much?
A: I have since learned that it was for $1,000.
Q: Did you know how much it was at the time?
A: I was misinformed regarding it at that time.
Q: How were you misinformed?
A: She told me it was for a burial benefit.
Q: A funeral benefit.
A: Yes. I think she stated that it was $200 and that had he carried it for some term of years it would have been for

the full amount of $1000.

Olive did not mention any other insurance policies. On the certificate, Frost listed the cause of death as unknown.

As he had with Dr. Park, Osler asked what, in Frost's opinion, had caused George Sternaman's death.

> Take the symptoms as you found them from the 13th June, with the history of the case, and presume that we find arsenic as a result of an examination, in the stomach, liver, brain. What in your opinion was the cause of death and the cause of this illness?

Frost chose his words carefully. "Eliminating all contact of arsenical solutions in any way with the body after death, and showing the abdominal organs to be healthy, then I should say that he died from arsenical poisoning."

Again, Osler had produced an expert witness who believed George had died from arsenic poisoning, and who, moreover, had testified that Olive had lied to him. German's cross-examination, which continued to focus on the similarity of symptoms between arsenic poisoning and Addison's disease, failed to elicit any admission that the cause of death was other than arsenic poisoning.

"I have seen druggists sell poison."

To reinforce Frost's testimony, Osler called Dr. William Phelps next. The jurors and spectators listened to yet another account of George's medical care. Phelps revealed he had considerable experience with poison, including the use of arsenic as a medical treatment. He explained that in the embalming process, arsenic was usually disseminated throughout the body. He knew nothing of John Snider's embalming methods; nonetheless, he was convinced that George Sternaman was suffering from arsenic poisoning when he called on him in Buffalo.

In his cross-examination, German returned to the question of the specific treatment. "Did you know at that time that Dr. Frost had administered doses of arsenic?"

"Yes, he told me that he had given him very small doses of the sulphate of copper. It is about what we would give children. It is a very common remedy with children."

"What is the smallest dose of arsenic that will cause death?"

"That varies with the individual. Some people can stand more than others. I can only tell you what the books say. I have never killed anybody with arsenic that I know of. The books say from one to two grains."

German contradicted him. "Two to four isn't it?"

"Two grains will kill. A grain and a half has killed."

German moved on to Phelps's connection with Metropolitan Life. The doctor, by his own admission, examined applicants for insurance policies. And, as German pointed out, Metropolitan Life was holding back payment of George's policy. German did not ask Phelps to speculate on the reasons, nor did he ask if Phelps had discussed George's case with the insurance company. Instead of elaborating on the conflict of interest inherent in Frost's position, German chose to dwell on the availability of arsenic in Buffalo. According to Phelps, druggists were required to record the name and address of anyone who purchased poison. This was customarily done, he stated, and he assumed that it was the law.

"Does not the law require them to take down the name and residence of the person receiving the poison," German asked, "together with the kind and quantity of the poison and the name and residence of some person known to the dealer as a witness?"

"I did not know the witness part," Phelps replied. I have seen druggists sell poison lots of times and I have never known them to ask for a witness." When German suggested this might be the case when the customer was known to the druggist, Phelps conceded that it was possible. Still, the overall effect of his testimony suggested that anyone could purchase poison in Buffalo, regardless of the law. No great leap of logic was needed to conclude that Olive might have purchased poison undetected. German's tactic had backfired.

To allow two American insurance men to catch their train, Osler briefly interrupted the procession of medical witnesses. Dr. Harrison was next. With a captive audience, Harrison chose to enumerate every little act that had occurred from the time Park asked him to provide a second opinion on George's condition. He was thorough, painstaking and spoke without interruption for nearly half an hour. Harrison recalled how Olive had answered most of his questions because George was unable to speak. He also testified that his preliminary diagnosis was that George was suffering from one of four ailments: cancer of the stomach, syphilis, Addison's disease or arsenical poisoning. After discussing the case with Park, he settled on poisoning.

Harrison saw George only once more before his death, and was somewhat surprised at the evident deterioration. He provoked some smiles from the spectators when he recounted his advice to Park prior to the post-mortem: "Don't put your hand on anything you don't have to; there will be most certainly another post mortem and I don't wish to give any of these lawyers a chance to say we might have contaminated any of the organs." He also revealed that the Marsh test, performed during the post-mortem, had failed to produce conclusive results. Nevertheless, when Charles Coulter, who was now handling the questions for Osler, asked what he believed was the cause of death, Harrison was unequivocal. "I came to the conclusion that death was caused by arsenic."

Throughout the day's proceedings, Olive had remained stoically silent. But the old doctor's contribution took its toll. Whether it was stress, or the knowledge that Harrison's standing in the community gave much more weight to his testimony than the previous doctors, Olive could stand the pressure no longer. Through Harrison's long, detailed responses she sat with one hand up to her face, silently weeping.

If German could get a prominent local doctor like Harrison to admit he might be wrong, all previous medical testimony would come into question. At first, Olive's lawyer had some success. "I suppose you would not like to say but what you might be mistaken?" he asked.

A: Oh yes.
Q: Doctors are fallible?
A: Often are mistaken.
Q: And you might be mistaken.
A: Yes.

Under German's interrogation, Harrison revealed that he had cared for both George's father and his maternal grandfather and that David's final illness bore some resemblance to George's. German reviewed Harrison's reasons for diagnosing arsenic poisoning and the possibility that embalming might account for the arsenic in George's exhumed body. Harrison even admitted that he might not have detected the marks of an embalming needle. But he made clear to the defense counsel and to the court his conviction that George had died of arsenic poisoning. He responded definitively and at great length to most questions, revelling in his dual roles as medical expert and a respected community leader.

Frustrated by the doctor's seeming obduracy, German attacked his ethics. "Though a test had been made of the urine and no arsenic had been found and you had the contents of the stomach home to find arsenic, believing that a man was being murdered, you went so cavalierly about it that you did not care whether you found it or not?"

The old doctor became defensive. "Well, I did not know whether it was particularly my duty to find it."

Q: It was your duty to protect human life was it not?
A: I felt that it was a very serious charge to make and except that we had more evidence than we had I didn't feel like making it. Our evidence was what we saw in the patient—
Q: Don't go off so long. You say that with the evidence you had at that time you did not feel like making a charge?
A: No, I did not.
Q: You had a suspicion of arsenic?
A: I felt as certain as I could be that it was arsenic.
Q: You had a suspicion that if arsenic had been administered it had been administered by this prisoner for the purpose of murdering her husband?
A: I couldn't say about that. I couldn't say who gave it to him.
Q: You cannot say now?
A: I cannot.
Q: It might have been given by anybody?
A: I couldn't say anything about that."

Since German would not accept the veracity of his statements, Harrison would not commit to anything.

Q: Is that what you wish the jury to understand, that it might have been given by anybody else than Mrs. Sternaman?
A: I wish the jury to understand that I am saying only what I know about the case. That as to who gave the poison, I don't know anything about that.

After a few more questions, German concluded with the matter of embalming. In a transparent attempt to persuade the jurors that any arsenic found in the body had been introduced by the under-taker, he asked, "If embalming fluid was injected into the body after death, it would account for the well preserved condition of the body that you found when he was exhumed?"

"Yes," Harrison said. "If there was enough of it injected and it spread over the whole parts."

Judge Armour asked the final question. "If it were injected into the body would it spread to the brain?"

"I don't think so," Harrison told him, "unless injected into the circulation, and there was no mark."

Every doctor had come to the same conclusion: George had died of arsenic poisoning. German's suggestions that George might have suffered from Addison's disease and any arsenic found had been introduced through embalming were unconvincing. All he had done was to establish the fact that poison was easily obtainable in Buffalo, and that fact could do Olive more harm than good. But the Crown had several more witnesses, and German had plenty of opportunity to recover lost ground.

The Embalming Issue

The insurance agents who preceded Dr. Harrison provided brief but telling information. First was Ralph Liedy, the Buffalo agent of the John Hancock Mutual Life Insurance Company. He identified two policies carried on George's life, one for $500, the other for $270, and verified the signatures on the policies as George's and Olive's. He added that the premiums were paid weekly; he collected them himself, usually from Olive. Frederick Dodsworthy, Buffalo superintendent for John Hancock, followed to corroborate Liedy's testimony.

Mary Hunsinger, her husband Peter and Philip Hardwick followed Dr. Harrison. Their testimony was of little importance except to paint a vivid picture of George's final days, Olive's feelings about the post–mortem, her attentiveness as a nurse and the conflict between Olive and Eliza about the insurance policies. By the time they had answered the lawyers' questions, night had fallen. The feeble lamplight in the courtroom did little to dispel the heavy shadows that fell over the witnesses and the spectators.

Undertaker John Snider was the last important witness called. The moment he was sworn in, German rose. Recognizing that Abraham, Snider's son and business partner, would avoid contradicting his father, he said, "I want the son out while this witness is being examined." Osler readily agreed, and after verifying that John Snider would be the last witness of the evening, dismissed Abraham and the other witnesses. Only Abraham and a few spectators departed. Most remained, well aware that Snider's testimony was crucial to the proceedings. If George had not been embalmed, then nothing but the administration of poison would account for the presence of arsenic in his body.

Osler led Snider through the preparation of George's body for burial. "It is suggested that you embalmed the body, what do you say to that?"

"We did not," the undertaker replied.

"Did you puncture or open the body in any way?"

"No sir, we did not."

"Did you do anything with the body except put it in the coffin?"

"No."

Osler's questioning was brief, lasting only two or three minutes at most. German, however, was not prepared to let the witness off so easily, not when his entire case rested on proving arsenic had been introduced in the embalming process. He began slowly, with routine questions, establishing that Snider lived in Selkirk, had been in business 22 years, and understood the process of embalming. Or so Snider claimed. A little probing by German showed his understanding to be rudimentary.

Q: The embalming fluid is composed largely as you understand it of arsenic?

A: We don't know anything about the composition, that is the formula of the composition. We know nothing of that. We buy that.

Q: What is the preservative element in it?

A: We don't know that.

Q: You have been embalming for 22 years?

A: No.

Q: How long?

A: At the outside ten years and very little in the ten years, from the simple fact that our trade is, you might say, purely a country trade and the majority of people are prejudiced against embalming.

When a second attempt to get Snider to admit he knew arsenic was used in embalming fluid failed, German took a slightly different approach.

Q: During the summer months it is your custom to use the embalming fluid?

A: No sir.

Q: Not your custom.

A: No, it is not.

Q: Did you embalm any of the dead bodies in the summer of

'96?

A: I think so, yes.

Q: How many?

A: Well, not very many, perhaps two or three.

Q: Not more than that?

A: I wouldn't speak positive.

Q: You remember being sworn here before Andrew T. Thompson, the Commissioner, at his law office here in Cayuga?

A: I remember it, yes.

Q: Do you remember him asking you a question like this: "And all of the embalming fluid you use contains arsenic?'

A: No sir.

Q: You don't remember him asking you that?

A: No.

Q: Do you say he did not ask you that.

A: I wouldn't say that.

Q: And that you answered, "We think so." Did you answer that in that way?

A: Not to my recollection.

Q: Will you say you did not.

A: I think it would be safe in saying so from the fact that we have no knowledge of what it contains.

Q: "Did you also have this question asked you: "The preservative agency in embalming fluid, as you suppose, is arsenic?" Do you remember that question?

A: No.

Q: Will you say it was not asked you.

A: It might have been asked me, yes.

Q: And your answer was, "Yes, sir."

Now the undertaker had no doubt. "No, it was not."

"This evidence was taken down in shorthand," German told him. "Are you prepared to deny that those were the questions asked you and the answers you gave."

Snider dodged the question "I won't deny the asking."

Q: Will you deny the answering?

A: I will deny the answering so far as to have any knowledge as to the formula of the composition.

Q: I am not asking you about the formula of the composition. Of course you will say that, but I am asking you about the answer you gave to this question when you were asked the question as to the preservative agency in embalming fluid; did you not say it was arsenic?

Snider was falling into the defense attorney's trap.

A: Arsenic is one of them. We read that.
Q: And it is one of them in the fluid you use?
A: We don't know that.
Q: You read it?
A: No, we don't read it.

Seemingly exasperated, German worked on the contradiction. "Well, where do you read that arsenic is a preservative in embalming fluid?"

"We read it in the journal that is issued for the undertakers." He explained that two companies supplied the embalming fluid, the Globe Casket Company of London, Ontario, and Simmons & Evel of Hamilton. When George died, Snider had both kinds in stock. Under German's questioning, he recounted how, with his son Abraham, he had gone to the Sternaman house to prepare George for burial. "We took the case, that is the coffin, the outside shell, and we took the instruments and I think a couple of bottles of the fluid."

Q: And you took your needle that you inject the fluid with?
A: Yes.
Q: And why didn't you tell us that?
A: I told you the instruments. Do you want me to enumerate them.

"He said the instruments," Judge Armour chided German.
"That includes the needle," Snider interjected.
German continued, questioning Snider about his actions at the Sternaman house. Knowing undertakers sometimes wiped the faces of the deceased with cloths soaked in embalming fluid, German asked whether it had been done. Snider denied it.

Q: Then you did not take your embalming needle into the house with you?
A: No.
Q: You are sure about that?
A: Yes, we are sure about that.
Q: And when did you become sure of that?

Olive Sevenpifer Chipman Sternaman.
No photograph of Olive as a young woman survives, but this sketch was widely published in Canadian newspapers during the trial.

George Sternaman
*Probably taken on his wedding day, this photo gives no inkling of
the tradegy that was about to unfold.*
Harry Sweet

Canfield Junction
To reach Cayuga, Olive and George had to switch trains at Canfield Junction.
Sam Gowling

Cayuga Station
George's last stop before reaching his mother's house.
Haldimand County Museum

Eliza and David Sternaman
When David died, George was greatly impressed with the
benefits of life insurance.
Harry Sweet.

Dr. Thomas Tipton Steele Harrison
*Highly regarded locally, Harrison was president of the Canadian Medical
Association in 1894.*
North Erie Shore Historical Society

Eliza Sternaman
Eliza's suspicions led to an investigation of the circumstances
surrounding her son's death.
Harry Sweet.

John Wilson Murray

Dr. William Ellis
*"The Provincial Analyst" provided conclusive forensic evidence that arsenic was
present in George Sternaman's body.*
University of Toronto.

Wallace Thayer
Convinced of Olive's innocence, the Buffalo lawyer continued to fight for her
release after her extradition to Canada.
Buffalo Historical Society.

Erie County Buildings
Olive spent the Christmas following George's death in the Erie County Jail.
Buffalo Historical Society.

Haldimand County Courthouse ca. 1870
Justice was administered and executions carried out in the confines
of the county buildings.
Harry Sweet

Haldimand County Courthouse ca. 1910
Olive awaited the outcome of her trial in the adjoining jail.
Haldimand County Museum.

Britton Bath Osler
Member of a brilliant family, "Brick" Osler was one of the best lawyers of the day.
Archives of Ontario.

William Manley German
A politically ambitious Welland lawyer, German may have taken the
Sternaman case to raise his profile prior to an election.
Welland Historical Museum

Olive in later life.
Olive lived in obscurity after the publicity surrounding the murder trial abated.

German's ironic tone was not lost on the undertaker. "Well, to the best of our recollection."

Q: Never mind "our", speak for yourself.
A: Well to the best of my recollection.
Q: Who do you mean when you say our recollection?
A: Well the two of us.
Q: You and your son?
A: Yes.
Q: You have been discussing this matter between you and arrived at a similar conclusion.
A: Oh no.

A minute or two later, German rephrased the question. "You have talked that over together have you?" Snider replied, "Well no doubt we have, yes."

Watching the proceedings, Brick Osler must have shaken his head in despair. Snider's lack of credibility was obvious to all, and the situation was about to get worse. When Snider denied puncturing George's intestines to allow gases to escape German read the sworn statement he had made to Andrew Thompson.

> Then we took the casket into the room and put him in it and my son turned to me and asked if I was going to embalm him, and I said no, I didn't think it was necessary for he seems to be in good shape; I think all we will do will be to puncture the intestines and let the gas escape; we punctured the intestines; I don't think we put any embalming fluid in but will not swear to it.

"Did you swear so before the Coroner?" German demanded.

"I did." Then, a second later, "I did not." And, after a question or two from German, Snider denied all recollection of ever having made the statement.

The probing continued, with Snider becoming hopelessly entangled in a web of conflicting statements, denials and lapses of memory. In the end, the undertaker swore that no embalming had taken place, because no charge had been entered for it in his account book. When court adjourned at 7:30 that evening, many spectators gave Snider's testimony little credence.

The hash Snider made of his recollections, however, brought Olive hope. While German questioned the undertaker, she watched him closely. As he grew more and more muddled, her eyes brightened and for the first time since the beginning of trial, she smiled. When the court adjourned, she seemed positively pleased with the turn of events.

The Crown's Case Continues
– Thursday, November 18, 1897
"Digging up the first husband"

Long before court resumed at 9 a.m., crowds poured into the courthouse. Nineteen–year–old son Abraham Snider was the first witness Osler called. Initially, he was somewhat more consistent than his father. He swore that George's body had not been embalmed, nor had the intestines been punctured. Had there been any embalming, he said, the charges would have been listed in their account book, and they were not. But, when William German conducted his cross–examination, Abraham became confused and uncertain. At first he stated that he and his father had brought a pint bottle of embalming fluid into the Sternaman house. Then he conceded that they might have had more than one bottle. When reminded him of the statement he had previously sworn to, Abraham hedged, saying he could not be "real positive" that there had been only one bottle. He denied that he and his father had discussed the details of the case at any length.

German led Abraham over the details of the work he performed that day, establishing the fact that John Snider had done most of the work. German then returned to the matter of the embalming fluid, eliciting Abraham's testimony that the embalming fluid was normally carried in a pint bottle in the front rig. This was virtually the same information Abraham had given to the magistrate, as German demonstrated when he read the young man's sworn statement. The lawyer asked, "So that if there were two large bottles in the wagon you know nothing of it?"

A: I would know it if they were there."
Q: So if your father thinks there were two large bottles, either he or you would be mistaken as to that?"
A: As to being two large bottles?"
Q: Yes.
A: I would know if they were there. Of course I am not really sure whether there was two or not.

Satisfied, German asked Abraham about other embalming work carried out during the summer of 1897. Young Snider could recall two bodies, that of Mrs. Gideon Swartz and a Mrs. Anderson from Walpole Township. Other than that, he said, he would have to consult the book in which his father recorded all the charges. As far as he was concerned, if the work had not been charged for it had not been done.

George's brothers, Freeman and Avery, were next on the stand. Both testified that Olive had always given George his medicine, except once, when Eliza gave him some tea and toast. Neither suspected foul play. In fact, both exhibited a decided lack of interest in their brother's fate. In Avery, perhaps, this was understandable. During the months of George's illness, he was courting a local girl, Barbara Hoover, and, as it turned out, married her a few days after Olive's arrest in Buffalo.

Avery testified that he had heard about plans for the post-mortem, not from his mother but from one of the men who laid out George's body. According to her, Avery said, George had requested the examination during his final illness. Moreover, he had not heard anything about the doctor's findings, although he had heard from local residents that there was some suspicion of poisoning, and according to rumours, Dr. Harrison had confirmed the presence of poison. Once George was dead, however, Avery claimed the family harboured no suspicions until Roberts, the Metropolitan Life representative, visited Mrs. Sternaman.

"And if Mr. Roberts hadn't come there to interfere, George Sternaman never would have been taken up?" German asked.

"I don't think so," Avery replied.

The stream of witnesses continued. Mrs. William Featherstone said she had seen Olive serve George egg–nog at the Sternaman home. "Well, she called it egg–nog. It was white, very white. I couldn't see any symptoms of egg in it."

Together, Mrs. Featherstone and the Sternaman brothers had painted a picture of an extremely attentive wife. This image was further reinforced by the testimony of James Stewart, a Goderich resident employed on the Grand Trunk Railway. He had been on duty when Olive and George left Black Rock. Although unable to swear positively that Olive was the woman he had seen on the train, he did remember her care of the invalid:

> The lady that was with him was all attention to him; she
> was giving him something to drink, or something, most of
> the time, and I remember that the express messenger got

some ice for her. He seemed to be very thirsty or something and I remember the express messenger getting
some ice for her.

Alfred Cox, the brakeman from the GTR, followed. He had seen
George and a woman who strongly resembled Olive on the train
from Canfield Junction to Cayuga. Frank Snider, a Buffalo carpenter,
and Magistrate A.A. Davis were next, followed by Dr. Park.
    The Fisherville doctor had been recalled to explain the absence
of Annie Franklin, George's sister. She had been present at his death
but was unable to travel, having given birth two weeks earlier. Park
felt it unwise for her to ride a buggy over ten or eleven miles of
rough road to the court-house. Once that fact had been established,
Park was again asked to provide details of George's medicine. Under
cross-examination, he also went over what he knew about the couple's insurance arrangements. As far as George had told him of a
$1000 insurance policy with Metropolitan Life. Following his death,
Olive, "said they didn't count that anything as they hadn't kept the
premiums paid up ... She said he was insured for $750."
    Most of the second day was taken up with the testimony of
various insurance agents. Jesse Dewe of Buffalo, the agent for John
Hancock, told of his encounter with Olive on Dearborn Street when
she asked him to say nothing about the $1000 policy. Under cross-
examination, Dewe explained that he had met George through
Olive. Mrs. Chipman, as she was then, had taken out a policy on her
own life, and Dewe usually collected the weekly premiums of 10
cents himself. Asked to explain how George had come to take out a
policy, Dewe described his initial reluctance. German attempted to
represent Dewe as a typically pushy and unethical agent. Instead of
discrediting Dewe, the result was to depict Olive as a woman who
had taken out insurance she could barely afford, scrimping and sav-
ing to pay the premiums. But to what purpose? Dewe's evidence
considerably damaged Olive's case, although German pushed the
flippant agent to reveal that George had been aware of the policy.
"He signed the application himself?" German asked.
    "Why certainly," Dewe replied. "We couldn't insure him if he
didn't. Can't insure dead people."
    U.S. Commissioner Fairchild then took the stand. Osler had him
identify the letter from George exonerating Olive of all blame in his
death, and the transcript of Olive's testimony at the extradition hearing. Then Dr. Ward Saltsman gave his testimony. After reiterating his
treatment of George, he told how he had heard of his death in
Rainham, and how it had been no surprise. He also revealed that,

while caring for George, he had had no suspicion of arsenic poisoning; moreover, that he thought Addison's disease was a highly unlikely diagnosis. Saltsman contended that George was suffering from atrophy of the liver. However, there was some dispute in medical circles whether the disease existed at all, and this was apparently Saltsman's first encounter with it.

For the next several minutes, Saltsman described George's symptoms and the various possible diagnoses. Finally, German asked, "From what you saw of George Sternaman, assuming that a test had been made on a post mortem examination of the contents of the stomach with Marsh's test and no arsenic found, would you sat that George Sternaman had died from arsenical poisoning?"

"I certainly would not."

Saltsman's statement contradicted all previous medical testimony. Armour found this a little difficult to accept. "Supposing the arsenical poisoning had taken place before you took care of the patient at all," the judge asked, " would it be found in the contents of the stomach?" Saltsman, citing one expert, replied negatively.

German then asked if a large dose, or perhaps two doses, administered to George before Saltsman's examination, might account for his subsequent death. Saltsman thought not, but responded affirmatively when German asked, "If he died from an administration of arsenic it must have been administered after he left your hands. In response to a long, hypothetical question from Osler, Saltsman went on to explain that only if arsenic had been administered 48 to 72 hours before death would traces later appear in the stomach.

Buffalo doctor, George W. Sales was then called. Under examination by Charles Colter, he told the court that it was relatively simple to get arsenic in the Queen City. A pharmacist himself, he explained that pharmacists who sold poisons were supposed to be record the sale in a special book, along with the date and the hour of the transaction, the name and address of the purchaser, the type and quantity of poison and the purpose for which it was required. The purchaser was not required to prove his identity, "... although the druggist generally exercises some precautions in regard to selling to strangers." When German's turn to question Sales arrived, he asked whether a witness was required when poison was sold. Sales said it was not.

Q: Sure?
A: I am very sure.
Q: What makes you so sure?
A: The simple reason that I am a graduated pharmacist and I

have sold pounds of it, sold a great deal.

Q: And you are not aware that it is necessary not only to
     have the kind and quantity of the poison but the name
     and residence of some person known to the dealer as a
     witness to the transaction, except upon a written order or
     prescription of a practising physician, you are not aware
     that that is the law?

A: I am not.

German elaborated, explaining that he had taken his information directly from the American Criminal Code. Sales denied any
knowledge of the requirements. He also said that Olive had never, to
his knowledge, purchased any arsenic from him.

Charles Medlicott, resident claim inspector for Metropolitan Life
reported his troubles in meeting with Olive and the discrepancies in
her statements regarding the insurance policies, the cause of
George's death and the cause of Elon Chipman's death. When he
was finished, the statement made by Charles Roberts was read into
the record by Osler's brother Featherston, who was assisting the
prosecution. Then Dr. Rich took the stand to describe what he had
witnessed during his treatment of Elon Chipman.

As one newspaper reported sardonically, German objected to
"digging up the first husband."

> I object to this evidence being taken, because no arsenic
> was discovered. Chipman died and was buried. He had
> peculiar symptoms which might have been symptoms of
> arsenic or anything else. What I say is there is no evidence
> of arsenic as the cause of the death of Chipman and there
> will be no evidence, and that being the case I submit it
> cannot be gone into here.

The objection sparked a dispute between German and Armour,
with the judge arguing that there was ample legal precedent for discussing the circumstances of Elon's death.

> What do you say if there is evidence of symptoms of ar-
> senical poisoning? Supposing they establish symptoms of
> arsenical poisoning – evidence from which a jury might
> infer that arsenical poisoning was the cause of death, is
> there any difference between the symptoms and the poi-
> son itself being found?

"There is a difference," German insisted, "that the symptoms might be the symptoms of any other disease."

Armour suggested that it might be up to the jury to determine whether the symptoms were those of another disease. German countered that to do so would be supposition at best, but Armour disagreed. "The evidence would have to amount to such evidence as the jury could reasonably infer from it that he died of arsenical poisoning. I think I will have to receive the evidence, Mr. German." Osler was allowed to proceed with his line of questioning.

Throughout the day, Osler had been straightforward in his questioning, drawing out facts and leaving most of the speculation to his opponent. Whether he had planned it deliberately, or the order in which the witnesses appeared was dictated simply by circumstances beyond his control, the return to medical evidence worked in his favour. If the spectators and jurymen had not been convinced before, the repetitive vocabulary of the medical men was enough to convince them now. Like the other doctors who had attended George, Dr. Rich described the same symptoms: multiple neuritis, vomiting, gastritis, intense thirst, numbness and paralysis. On the one hand, he admitted, the symptoms might have indicated syphilis or arsenic poisoning, but Rich had not considered poisoning at the time. On the other hand, Dr. Parmenter, who followed him to the stand, said poisoning might have been the cause.

The morning ended when carpenters William Martin and William T. Randall, workmates of Elon's, each took the stand and re-created the day he fell ill at work. Again, the parallels with George's case were remarkable. An hour-long recess followed. When the afternoon's proceedings began at 1:30, Osler immediately introduced Olive's testimony given on November 11, 1896 before Commissioner Fairchild. It required nearly five hours to read her testimony into the record.

Until a revised criminal code came into effect in 1892, accused murders were not allowed to take the stand in their own defense in Canadian courts. There was no legal impediment to Olive taking the stand at this point. Why neither Osler nor German called her as a witness is not known. The reason may have been simple as habit or the innate conservativeness of most lawyers. On the other hand, Osler might have considered the sight of an attractive, bereaved mother too likely to win sympathy from the jury, especially if she broke down while he was questioning her. For his part, German may have felt he was acting in his client's best interest by not calling her as a defense witness. Previous testimony and the Buffalo deposition clearly showed that Olive might say anything when questioned and sometimes in a facetious or flippant manner. Given Osler's skill and Armour's reputation for sternness, German apparently decided against the risk. Thus, the only instance in which Olive's version of the events was heard in the courtroom was when the evidence was read into the record.

Although the newspapers had carried extensive accounts of the statement, many of George's friends and relatives heard his widow's account of his mental condition, his fits, his profound jealousy and her suspicion that he may have attempted suicide for the first time in court. For some, it was riveting entertainment. For others, her statements were suspect. And for a few, there was utter disbelief. Many people still subscribed to the notion of "bad blood", and any hint that George had been not quite normal was a serious blow to the reputation of his extended family and the community as a whole. Psychiatry was in its infancy: if George had been mentally disturbed, most of his neighbours would have concluded the condition had been inherited and might crop up somewhere else among his numerous relatives. In a close–knit community like Haldimand County, believing Olive's testimony about George's mental state was tantamount to believing one's own family, friends and neighbours might also be unbalanced. It was simply too much for many to accept.

Once the statement was read, Osler introduced other items of evidence, chiefly documents from the various insurance companies. After Annie Franklin's deposition was recorded, Dr. Harrison was recalled. He stated unequivocally that, no matter what Saltsman said, George had not been suffering from atrophy of the liver. Most of his brief testimony centred on embalming. He had found no incision which would have suggested arterial embalming. He had heard, however, that some embalmers injected fluid through the nostrils, mouth, or rectum, but:

> In this case no embalming fluid could go any distance by the mouth or nostril by the esophagus because it was tied just where it passes the diaphragm, consequently a very few ounces would have filled it, two or three at the most. Then by the rectum it would take a very large amount of embalming fluid to do any good whatever. It seems to be it would take pretty nearly half a gallon to fill the large intestines, the colon, and if that had been done certain that embalming fluid must have been in when we opened him. If it was not it must have either percolated through into the abdomen or poured out by the rectum ... There was

certainly no pouring out of anything. I should say there
was no embalming.

Anxious to ensure the jurors understood correctly, Osler
rephrased Harrison's statement as a question. "You would say as a
result of your examination of the body that there was no embalming?"

"I could not think there would be."

Perhaps it was the lateness of the hour, or perhaps German was
simply unprepared for Harrison's evidence. At any rate, he had no
questions for the elderly doctor. The county coroner, David
Thompson, was then called. He described what he had witnessed
when George's body was exhumed at the second post-mortem, then
answered a few questions regarding statements John Snider had
made during the examination. The Selkirk undertaker was then recalled to the stand. Despite some minor objection from Brick Osler,
German asked Snider whether he knew John Chevalier and Ivan
Holmes of Selkirk. Snider said he did.

Q: Do you remember seeing those two gentlemen in Mr.
Holmes store the night before the inquest before the
Coroner?

A: No, I don't.

Q: Do you remember having a conversation with John
Chevalier that night?

A: No.

Q: Will you swear you did or did not?

A: I won't say that I did or did not. I don't remember.

Q: Did you say to John Chevalier that night, in speaking
about the inquest that it all depended upon your evidence, that if you said he was embalmed, meaning
Sternaman, that would end it and if you said you did not
embalm him that would knock them out. Did you say
that?

A: To Chevalier?

Q: Yes.

A: No.

Q: Did Chevalier on that night ask you if you did embalm
him and you in reply said, "We always do." ?

A: No sir.

With a wave of his hand, German dismissed the witness. Snider
either could not or would not provide him with solid testimony that

George had been embalmed. Without that evidence, German would be hard pressed to explain the presence of arsenic in George's body. The court adjourned for the day moments later. As Olive was returned to her cell and the spectators shuffled out of the court-house, it must have been apparent to many that Osler still had the upper hand.

The Crown's Case Continues – November 19, 1897

"Sufficient indications of arsenic ... to produce death"

Word had spread that Friday would likely be the final day of the trial. Long before 9 o'clock, crowds gathered outside the court-house. As soon as the doors were opened, the spectators packed the building. The majority were women who sat, tense and watchful, as the final act of the legal drama unfolded.

A few moments before Mr. Justice Armour entered, Olive arrived. She looked strained, her eyes betraying a restless night. Like the women who watched her, she was anxious for the trial to be over.

Brick Osler began by calling Edith Curzon, Assistant Provincial Analyst. She was about Olive's age and something of a curiosity. All the other women who testified were living out traditional female roles, as wives and mothers. Curzon not only had a university degree, she had studied science and was as comfortable in the laboratory as in the kitchen. She had examined the samples sent from the second post-mortem.

> I went to Dr. Ellis' house and got the key of the room in which he keeps such material locked. I then took to him the jar which was mentioned that I should take, took it back to him to identify, and he having identified it and given it to me, I took it back to the room and locked it and left it until next morning.

The jar, she explained, contained the spleen and intestine, which she tested for arsenic. Osler asked about the results.

Q: And what did you find?
A: I found arsenic.
Q: In any quantity?
A: 168 milligrammes to 100 grammes. That is about .168 per cent.

Osler then asked her to estimate the total amount of arsenic that might be found in the spleen and intestine, based on the amount she had found in the sample. Because she could not recall the total weight of the organs, Curzon was unable to do so. Osler said, "Give us an idea as between a trace and a quantity."

Curzon was emphatic. "Oh, there was a quantity; a large quantity."

German's brief but patronizing cross-examination consisted mostly of forcing the young woman to prove her familiarity with measurements and mathematical calculations; she was unshaken. Her superior, Dr. William Ellis, followed.

Born in Derbyshire, England, William Hodgson Ellis was 50. A quiet, kindly man who wrote poetry and fished in his spare time, he was a graduate of the University of Toronto, head of the Faculty of Applied Science and Engineering there, and a university senator. For those who followed newspaper reports of sensational crimes, his name was a familiar one. As Provincial Analyst, he was frequently called upon to provide forensic data at trials.

Ellis made his way to the stand, carrying a wooden box under one arm. Inside, in glass jars, were samples of George's vital organs. When Ellis removed the bottles from the jar, Olive paled visibly and held a handkerchief to her eyes. Ellis testified that he had received four bottles from David Thompson and tested them for arsenic. The results were positive. "I understand that it is not the arsenic you find in the contents of the stomach which is fatal but that which has been absorbed?" Osler queried.

Ellis agreed. "That which is absorbed. That which is in the stomach acts to a certain extent by the local irritation on the coats of the stomach, but the absorbed arsenic is what is the most fatal."

"Then did you find sufficient indications of arsenic in this body to produce death?"

"Yes."

German's cross-examination was lengthy, his questions designed to establish whether arsenic might have been administered before George's death and, if so, how it would act in the body. Ellis explained that arsenic could be eliminated from a man's system in 12 to 14 days. German presented a hypothesis:

> Assuming that no arsenic was administered to a man for four or five weeks and at the end of four or five weeks no arsenic was found in the urine by a test of the urine, would you not naturally suppose that all the arsenic which had been administered prior to the four or five

weeks had been eliminated from the system?

"Yes," Ellis said. "I don't think it is absolutely certain, but that is what one would expect."

After some discussion about the symptoms of arsenic poisoning, German returned to the matter of embalming. Although other preservatives were used in embalming fluid, arsenic was in most and in large quantities. Before Ellis stepped down, Osler posed a few additional questions. "Do you use Marsh's test?"

"Yes."

"Take some of the stomach organic matter and so on, and take Marsh's test as you heard Dr. Harrison describe it."

Ellis stressed that he had not heard Dr. Harrison's description at the trial, although he had heard it at the preliminary hearing.

"Well that is the same way," Osler told him.

"Dr. Harrison said that the contents frothed so that it was impossible to perform the test. I would not use an organic liquid without attempting to get rid of the organic matter, for that test."

"Would you think it likely to be successful in the way Dr. Harrison tried it?"

"I should think that it would be very apt to fail in exactly that way, owing to the frothing, no result occurring."

Following Osler's lead, German also had some questions about the Marsh test. When a dispute arose over exactly what Harrison had said, Judge Armour had part of his testimony read aloud. Ellis concluded that "you could form no opinion at all as to whether arsenic was present or not."

Realizing that Harrison's failure to find arsenic in the Marsh test was itself inconclusive, German tried another tack. "What would you say of the probability of an ignorant person giving doses of arsenic to a healthy man and keeping him in that chronic state of arsenical poisoning for two months or more so that the doctors could not absolutely determine whether there was arsenic or not?"

At this point, Armour was confused. "Determine by what?" he asked.

"By the diagnosis of the case, not by test but by diagnosing the case as they saw it," German explained.

"It has often been done," Ellis stated.

German was skeptical. "By persons absolutely unskilled in the use of arsenic or medical knowledge?"

"Unskilled in ordinary medical knowledge."

The defense attorney remained dubious. "Is not arsenic when administered even by professional men, a very difficult drug to administer in proper quantities?"

"It produces poisonous effects, you mean?"

"Yes. It does produce poisonous effects?"

It produces poisonous effects if given in too large doses," Ellis explained, but it produces a toleration if given in small quantities, so that the patient will bear larger quantities without showing the usual effects of arsenic."

"But if an unskilled person was administering arsenic to an ordinarily healthy man, during the time of the attendance on this man of a doctor, is it likely that this unskilled person could so skillfully administer that arsenic as to deceive the practiced eye of an intelligent physician?" German's line of questioning was obviously designed to eliminate Olive as a suspect.

"I should think that they would suspect that the man was getting arsenic or some other irritant poison," Ellis conceded, but German wanted something more solid from the witness. "Would they not more than suspect it, would they not feel it to be an absolute certainty?"

"I couldn't answer that."

At this point, one of the jurors raised a question. "If there was arsenic injected into the intestines in the embalming fluid, would it be more likely to be found in the inside or outside of the liver?"

"If it were injected into the intestines?" Ellis asked

"Yes. You said in your evidence that you found more arsenic, comparatively, in the inside than the outside of the liver."

Ellis admitted he had.

"If it was injected into the body in the embalming fluid, where would you expect to find the most, in the liver?"

"You say if it were injected into the intestines?" Ellis repeated

"Well, into the abdomen, or into the body;" the juror suggested, "not into an artery."

Ellis reflected, then stated simply. "I should expect to find it more on the outside."

After a brief re-examination of David Thompson, who identified the seals on the sample jar Ellis had produce, Osler rested the crown's case.

In his opening address to the jury, Osler had announced his goals: to prove that George had died of arsenic poisoning, that the insurance policies provided Olive with motive and that she could easily obtain arsenic in Buffalo. As he had warned, much of the evidence was circumstantial. But the sheer volume of medical testimony – much of it presented in similar terms and reaching similar conclusions – was convincing. In all likelihood, George had died of arsenic poisoning, not Addison's disease or any other ailment. The slight possibility that the arsenic in George's body had been introduced through embalming was effectively eliminated by Snider's garbled version of events. Insurance policies that would provide more than most members of the jury would earn in three years certainly provided motive. It was clearly possible to obtain poison with relative ease in Buffalo. As George's only nurse during much of his illness, Olive had the opportunity to administer poison; moreover, the discrepancies in her statements to various witnesses, her reluctance to send George to a hospital, and her unsubstantiated suggestion that George was mentally unstable all told against her. Osler had presented a strong, comprehensive case which German would find difficult to destroy.

Up to this point, German had had little success in undermining the Crown's witnesses. His stubbornness in clinging to one line of questioning, no matter how fruitless, was one of his major weaknesses. The other was a lack of foresight: more than once, his questions had elicited responses that were damaging to his client. German's witnesses would have to produce strong evidence of Olive's innocence to put the defense on solid ground.

The Case for the Defence
– Friday, November 19, 1897

"A loving husband and wife "

As it turned out, German's defense was brief and extremely weak. He called only eleven witnesses, and the first four were family members who would be expected to take Olive's side. From Eliza Chipman, Elon's mother, he elicited testimony that Olive and Elon had lived happily together, that Olive was a good wife

"Extravagant at all and eager for money?"

"Not at all," Mrs. Chipman said. " I never heard a complaint, that wasn't satisfied."

Osler objected. "Do not lead her," he admonished his opponent.

German ignored him. "Did you ever hear her and her husband say anything about life insurance?"

"I did. I often tried to induce her to permit my son to be insured and she always objected. I don't think my son would have had the small insurance he had, only for me. Shortly before his death, that same fall, the last time he visited me I spoke to him concerning it and he said that he had taken out a small one."

"That is not evidence," Osler protested.

"You spoke to him about it?" German asked the witness.

"I did. I think only for that he would not have had what he had."

"What was his condition of health at that time when you saw him last?"

"Well, I thought he wasn't looking very well, but he was working very hard."

"Did you mention anything to him about it?" German asked.

"I said to him that I thought he looked as if he was working too hard."

Again, Osler objected. "That is not evidence. We cannot go into these conversations." And finally, Armour stirred himself enough to utter one word: "No."

German turned to Elon's death, arousing Osler's ire with questions about the cause. According to Eliza Chipman, it was "Inflammation of the stomach, and Dr. Sage pronounced it typhoid fever."

"She does not know that," Osler protested.

"Did you hear him pronounce it?" German asked.

"No," Eliza admitted.

"She should not tell us that," Armour chided.

German was apologetic. "I thought that she had heard him, my lord."

Dora Bonestead, Elon's sister was next. She described the symptoms of his final illness. Ellen Sevenpifer, Olive's mother, followed. She reported how the insurance agent had called just as Olive and George were leaving for Canada, how Olive had let the premiums lapse and how she had taken over the payments herself. She also recounted what she remembered of George's illness.

Olive's sister Lizzie recalled being with her when she paid Snider for George's funeral. "He handed her the receipt and she asked him if that included everything and he says yes, and he named over embalming and all the funeral expenses."

In cross-examination, Osler centred on the relationship between Olive and George as Lizzie had described it in her testimony in Buffalo. "You said this, as I have it: 'And when the wife treated him kindly', that is referring to the dead man, 'he would do almost anything she asked'?" Lizzie confirmed the statement along with others indicating that George would obey Olive in most things and "would be led by her ... more than most couples."

"He was singularly under her influence apparently," Osler remarked, then abruptly switched to the matter of embalming. Lizzie conceded that she could not recall the exact words of the conversation.

"What you would remember was that everything was included?" Osler asked.

She agreed. "Everything was included."

German rose to ask a few more questions. "You say in answer to my learned friend that he was under her influence, that is that she could get him to do what she wanted?"

"I don't know that she could get him to do everything she wanted," Lizzie explained, "but I know he was always kind and if she asked him to do anything he always did it."

"He was a particularly loving husband?"

"He was."

"And how was she to him?"

"The same."

"And when you speak of influence, was there any influence the other way?"

"Well, it was always the same on both sides."

Once more, in case anyone in the court-room had missed the point, German inquired, "They lived together as a loving husband and wife?"

"Yes."

Albert Hedden, John Chevalier and Ivan W. Holmes took the stand next. All three recalled John Snider coming into Holmes's store prior to the post-mortem, and how the undertaker had boasted about the importance of his testimony. Chevalier wasn't sure who posed the question, but when someone asked if he had embalmed the body, Snider replied, "We always embalm."

The next witness was Wallace Thayer, Olive's American defense attorney. The first thing he did was detail the laws of the United States regarding the sale of poison, as German attempted to prove the difficulty Olive would have had in getting arsenic. When Osler examined him, though, German's strategy failed. "And the druggists all obey the law?"

A: I don't know anything about that.

Q: Does that apply to sales of such poisons as Rough on Rats and Paris Green, arsenical compounds, commercial arsenic?

A: I am unable to say that. If sold by druggists and if they are poisonings it does.

Q: But you go into a hardware store or grocery and buy Rough on Rats or Paris Green, you don't know as to that?

A: I know well enough that no such record is kept of sales in stores other than drug stores. I don't know whether drug stores keep such records or not.

Armour interjected. "Paris Green is sold in hardware stores?"

"I know it is sold in other than drug stores," Thayer admitted.

"And Rough on Rats," Osler added.

When Thayer stepped down German brought in the medical experts. Dr. McFadden, a toxicologist from Buffalo, argued that George had died from something other than arsenic poisoning. He had, he explained, treated him for a liver complaint before his marriage to Olive, and the symptoms were the same.

Dr. William Kerr, a Cayuga doctor, ventured an opinion that Addison's disease was responsible. Under Osler's cross–examination, however, he admitted he had never treated a case of Addison's disease in eight years of practice. Furthermore, Osler forced him to admit that the symptoms of Addison's and arsenic poisoning were similar.

Kerr was the last witness for the defense. The witnesses German had called had done little to weaken the Crown's case. His attempt to suggest disease, rather than poison, as a factor in George's death had failed utterly. Still German had one last chance. More than one trial had been decided on the basis of an emotional summation, rather than on the evidence presented. When Kerr stepped down, around 11 o'clock, German began his summing up.

The Summations

"She was murdering for insurance."

After a few introductory remarks, German referred to newspaper coverage of the case.

> It is almost impossible for a human being, having read the reports given in newspapers of cases of this kind not to form some sort of opinion as to the guilt or innocence of the prisoner; not knowing of course that they will be on a jury and that the duty will be incumbent upon them to say whether or not the prisoner is actually innocent or guilty on the evidence. But I am sure, gentlemen … that whatever any of you may have read, whatever any of you may have heard, you will not for one moment allow that to bias or influence your mind in arriving at a decision."

Referring to the Crown's duty to prove guilt beyond a reasonable doubt, German said, "The first difficulty, it seems to me, that we have to get over in this case is, where did the arsenic come from? And who administered it? Assuming that arsenic was there." There was, he concluded, "Not a tittle of evidence from beginning to end that this prisoner ever had any arsenic in her possession; that she ever bought any arsenic from any place." He reviewed the availability of arsenic in Buffalo.

> Now, that is a factor. You have got to find certainly that she had arsenic before you can find that she administered arsenic to George Sternaman or to any person else .... Not a tittle of evidence from the beginning to the end that she had arsenic or that she could have administered it.

Turning to the medical evidence, he pointed out that multiple neuritis, which had appeared on both husbands' death certificates, was not a disease, but rather the result of any one of a number of diseases. "Can you, because some doctor happened to say in Buffalo that Chipman had multiple neuritis, and some other doctor in Canada said that Sternaman had multiple neuritis, say that both or either of those men were poisoned with arsenic or poisoned with anything?"

As for motive, German contended that no motive had been proven. He pointed out that since Olive and Elon had lived happily together, that Elon was a good provider and father of two children, it hardly seemed feasible that Olive would poison him. The argument that insurance money had been the inspiration for the crime was dismissed.

> What does it say for a woman as a criminal if she has the idea of insurance in her mind, if she is getting her husband insured for the purpose of murdering him and getting the money,. isn't it quite reasonable to suppose that she would get all out of her crime that there was in it? Would it not be absolutely inconsistent with the theory of guilt if we find a woman getting her husband insured and killing him without making all out of it she could?

German seemed to forget that his client was on trial for the murder of her second husband, not her first. He then spent several minutes discussing the circumstances of Elon's death in an attempt to undermine the Crown's argument. When he finally turned to the events leading to George's death, he began with George's feelings for Olive.

> Sternaman is strangely infatuated ... so tremendously fond of this woman that he has these spells, as they are called, arising out of that. A great degree of jealousy. Why, gentlemen, if you were looking for a motive as to the cause of Chipman's death and considering the peculiarities of Sternaman and the excessive and overpowering desire that he had to marry Mrs. Sternaman, would it not be just as reasonable, if not more reasonable, to say that he administered a dose of poison to Chipman to get him out of the way in order to marry the widow?

He pointed out that when this suggestion had been made to Olive, her response was "I don't think so." As far as German was concerned, this response was strongly suggestive. "An innocent woman herself, she could not bring her mind to believe in guilt in others."

Point by point, German examined the Crown's arguments. Whenever Olive's actions seemed suspicious, he presented a plausible explanation.

> Suspicion, as I said, there might be. When a person dies and some one is arrested by a detective for that murder, you may rest absolutely certain that there will be suspicious circumstances. They would not go into Court if there were not suspicious circumstances. But if you were to convict on suspicious, you would have to convict every prisoner that was every arrested in a case worked up by a detective.

One of German's strongest arguments concerned the attitudes of Drs. Harrison and Park following the post–mortem. The Welland lawyer had already dismissed the senior physician as, "A nice old gentleman in his way; one of the old school," who had been mistaken about George's condition from his very first encounter with the young man. Now German asked the jury to put themselves in the place of the doctors who treated George.

> One thing that strikes me as very peculiar is the conduct of some of these doctors who believed in arsenical poisoning. When a man believes a thing, particularly if it is murder, he would not try to cover it up. I will venture to say

none of you gentlemen would try to cover up a murder; if you believed that a woman was deliberately, foully murdering her husband with arsenic, that you would try to cover it up, particularly if you were a doctor. It strikes me as peculiar, in the light of Dr. Park's sworn statements as to his opinions, that he would make these answers as to the cause of death: 'Was death the result of deceased own's hand or act?' Answer, 'No.' 'Are there any other particulars relating to the sickness or habits of deceased with which you think the Company should be made acquainted? If so, please specify.' Is murder a particular of which the Company should have been made acquainted?

Does it not strike you, gentlemen, that if Dr. Park believed murder was being done then he would say to the Company, 'There is one particular that I think you ought to know of in justice to you and in justice to society, I believe this man died of arsenical poisoning.' 'None that I know of,' is his answer. "Was death caused directly or indirectly by the use of intoxicating, drink, opium, or other drug?' Arsenic is a drug. If his death was caused by arsenic, there was only one answer that he could give to that question. What is the answer he does give? 'No.'

German had really warmed to his subject. "In the light of those answers, what do you think really affected Dr. Park's mind?" he asked the jury.

How could he consistently as a doctor of medicine, living in this community, bound to see that the law is observed, feeling, if he did feel, that there was arsenic poisoning, how could he answer those questions in that way? ... There is only one place for Dr. Park, he either did not believe that Sternaman was poisoned by arsenic or he was deliberately lying to the insurance Companies. I would not like to say the latter. There are the two horns of the dilemma. Which of them is the most reasonable in view of the evidence? Is Dr. Park a man who would deliberately deceive an Insurance Company, by which they could be swindled out of $1000? Or is it not the case that at the time he did not believe it was arsenical poisoning?

After discussing the various doctors' opinions a little further,

German turned to the events immediately following George's death. The Crown, he reminded the jury, suspected that George had vomited on his deathbed because Olive had given him a dose of arsenic that night. Furthermore, German argued, it had been implied that Olive "knew so much about arsenic that she could give it in doses to carry this man along for weeks and months, so skillfully as to deceive the practiced eye of the physician." If she understood arsenic so well, German asked, why would she allow the post-mortem? And it *was* Olive herself who had ordered the post-mortem, because, as Eliza Sternaman and her sons had testified, the final decision had been left to her.

Could the presence of arsenic be accounted for by embalming German wondered. He turned to the testimony given by the undertaker.

> Snider says here, 'I did not embalm.' You heard his evidence; perhaps many of you know him. I never had the pleasure of meeting him before; I don't know what reliance can be placed upon his testimony and perhaps you do not but as far as that is concerned we take his evidence as we find it given here in Court, and can you say that he impressed you as being very certain as to the exact state of affairs?

Embalming was a logical explanation for the presence of poison, he argued, dismissing the Crown's contention that Olive was "such a fiend of hell that she could pour into that stomach six or seven grains of arsenic on that night before he died." It was unreasonable, he suggested, even if Olive had murdered George. Playing devil's advocate, he continued. "She was murdering for insurance. She could have let her husband die that night, as he would have died, without administering any more poison." The doctors had testified that if George had been poisoned in the United States, no traces of arsenic would likely have remained in his body by the time of death. Administering yet another dosage would have made detection inescapable. If Olive were a murderess, it made no sense, German concluded. "Would she shove her hand into the fire to burn it off? Would she put her head under the axe? Would she tie the rope around her own neck to hang herself with?"

In summing up, German appealed to the emotions of the jury.

> I ask you find that the circumstances are quite consistent with her innocence. That she did not murder the first man.

That she did not murder the second man. And by your verdict declare her not guilty and allow her to go from this room to her young boys in Buffalo, who await her return, rather than to send her to this cell where she will not leave until she walks out to the time of the hangman's tread.

Consider the position, gentlemen, in all its bearings. It is better to err on the side of mercy than to err on the side of strict justice. If you have a reasonable doubt in your mind I ask you in the name of high heaven to give that doubt in favor of the prisoner and say we cannot find on that evidence sufficient to hang this woman, to tear her from her friends and consign her to a felon's grave.

German's argument had taken two and a half hours, during which he had used every oratorical trick at his command. Some of the points he raised were valid. Although evidence had shown that almost anyone could obtain poison in Buffalo, there was no proof that Olive had ever had arsenic in her possession. Her relationship with Elon had been a happy one, and neither his mother nor his sister suspected Olive of any wrongdoing. With no evidence of an illicit affair, it was hard to accept that Olive had murdered Elon in order to marry George. As for financial gain, German pointed out that Elon earned more than George, and was far more valuable to Olive alive than dead. German's appeal to listeners' emotions also carried weight with some. But oratory did not make up for solid evidence and German's last ditch appeal was almost inevitably doomed.

After a 30-minute recess for lunch, it was Osler's turn to try to persuade the jury of the Crown's point of view. His approach, was quiet and logical, unlike his antagonist's emotional and dramatic presentation; his language was simple, direct and easily comprehensible. His summation was also about half as long as German's.

He began, as German had, in defining the jury's task.

We are here to consider things without sympathy, without mercy. For if sympathy and mercy were to influence your judgement I might as well appeal for sympathy for men in the position that the deceased was in if there is a presumption of guilt. Mercy to men in such a case; mercy to the community in danger of such crimes being repeated.

Carefully, he reiterated the evidence, stressing the fact that for

four weeks prior to his death George had been unable to feed himself, "so that all that entered his mouth, medicine, meat or poison,
came from his wife's hand." He conceded that George's symptoms
might be attributed to other diseases. Nevertheless, he maintained,
there were definite signs of arsenical poisoning.

> Was there embalming? No witness says that there was.
> Abraham Snider, the young man, whose evidence is not
> impeached, swears that there was not. Dr. Harrison, whose
> evidence has not been impeached, swears that there was
> no appearance whatever of embalming, and gives you the
> reasons why he concludes there was not embalming. Can
> you reject these witnesses?

The prisoner, he said, was resting her hopes for acquittal on gossip,
"the idle talk, half remembered talk of John Snider."

As for insurance, Osler reminded the jury that the total amount
payable was $1970. Furthermore, the Metropolitan policy – a policy
George felt was unaffordable – went into effect just six or seven
weeks before his illness began. According to one witness, Olive had
wanted more insurance.

> She was not going to be left in the lurch ... Now you see
> there was the temptation before her of large money to re-
> ceive all in one sum, probably as much as her husband
> would earn in four years. The temptation of large money
> was there. Did it enter into her mind?

As for George's condition, he pointed out that there were two
days – between the time Olive announced their plans to move to
Canada and Dr. Park's arrival at the Sternaman house –when George
was not seen by any physician. According to Saltsman, the patient
was on the road to recovery, able to sit up, to walk with a stick, to
eat steak and eggs. But when Park visited him, George was paralyzed. Osler presented a chilling possibility. "Was she letting him
progress towards health when it suited her and letting him progress
towards death when it pleased her? It is for you to conclude."

Turning to the descriptions of Olive's tender nursing, Osler
contrasted it with her silence on the matter of poison.

> What shall we say of the tender and affectionate wife ...
> who is told by the doctor that there is poison, that if he
> gets no more he will get well? ... What should we say of

an honest woman who does not tell that to Saltsman, who
does not tell that to Park, who does not tell that to
Harrison, who does not tell it to the man's mother? ...
What honest woman, anxious for her husband's health,
the husband whom she is said to love, whom she has
sworn to cherish, getting information from the doctor as to
what was the matter, would say, 'Let the doctors find it out
for themselves?' Does that mean guilt or does it mean innocence?

Osler urged the jury to review the circumstances of George's
illness, keeping in mind that "the person who proposes to commit a
crime proposes always to have every circumstance which would indicate innocence surrounding it." He dismissed the bad relations between Olive and Eliza Sternaman:

There is often a natural, instinctive aversion between two
women in those situations, both deeply engaging the affections of the one man as a son and husband, and it takes
very little to make bad blood between the mother–in–law
and the daughter–in–law.

He also pointed out that Olive was not on trial for the death of
her first husband. "Ordinarily we have no right to suggest one crime
when another is being tried, but there are some exceptions to that
rule of law and his Lordship has ruled that this is one of them." He
described the similarities between Elon's sickness and death and
George's. "Two men in the same house; under the charge of the
same woman'; commences alike; die alike; the last man is exhumed
and arsenic is found, and all symptoms are consistent in both cases
with arsenical poisoning. There was insurance in the other case as
well."

He could not accept German's suggestion that George had been
responsible for the poisoning. There was simply no evidence, Osler
contended.

Sternaman did not put up the lunch ... Sternaman got no
benefit from his death. No evidence of any love passages
between them or any improper conduct. They seemed to
have waited the year before they married. No suggestion
of any sexual impropriety either way.

After reviewing why Addison's disease was not likely to have

caused George's death, Osler turned to the duty of a doctor who suspects poison, ensuring that the ethical questions German had raised
would do little harm to the Crown's case.

> He has no opportunity of getting that knowledge which
> we have; the knowledge that a post-mortem gives. All he
> can say to a relative is, 'There are indications of poisoning;
> send him to the hospital; change his surroundings; change
> his attendant.' To charge an attendant without more evi-
> dence than symptoms of arsenic in the lifetime, is to
> charge a person who may be entirely innocent of attempt-
> ing to murder. It is not for Dr. Park, suspecting; it is not for
> Dr. Frost, suspecting; to tell the conclusion that you ought
> to come to here now after hearing all the evidence and
> after the body has been exhumed. All a proper and pru-
> dent doctor can say, having regard both to his reputation
> and to his cash ... is, " I suspect poison here; see to it that
> he is moved to the hospital.

It was mid–afternoon and, perhaps sensing the jury's fatigue,
Osler quickly summed up.

> It is a very, very grave responsibility that is cast upon you;
> the highest responsibility that can be placed upon any
> man; the responsibility of the life of a fellow–being. That
> responsibility is on you to–day. You have got to accept it.
> You cannot shirk it. The easy word is to let her go free. It is
> the pleasant thing to do now. But do such verdicts against
> evidence help a community? The moment jurors shirk re-
> sponsibility and allow their emotions to govern their
> judgement, that moment the people and their laws and
> the safety of the lives of the community are in peril. You
> must stand to your duty no matter what the consequences
> are. You are the community, fixing the standard of morals;
> fixing the safety of life. Do justice by her. Give her the
> benefit of every lawful, every reasonable doubt; but re-
> member at the same time the solemn duty that you are
> sworn to perform, and that you must perform if the con-
> clusion in your individual minds is that there has been
> guilt in connection with the death of this man, guilt of the
> prisoner.

Every argument made for Olive's innocence was refuted in

Osler's detailed review of the case. Motive, means and opportunity were all present, he contended. Osler even twisted Olive's affectionate treatment of George into something sinister. His *coup de grâce* – an appeal to each and every member of the jury to put justice above sentiment – was the perfect counterattack after German's emotionalism. With Osler's reminder of their moral obligations ringing in their ears, the members of the jury awaited instructions from Justice Armour.

Justice Armour Charges the Jury

"We must each do our duty ... and let the consequences take care of themselves."

Much of what Osler said was echoed in the opening words of Judge Armour's charge. He explained his responsibility and the jury's:

> Your responsibility is to find on the facts, to ascertain upon the evidence, upon such of it as you believe to be credible, ascertain what the truth is and a true verdict give according to that truth. That it may have consequences is nothing to you. That the law imposes consequences upon such a finding as you may make is no responsibility of yours. It is no responsibility of mine. We must each do our duty in our own sphere and let the consequences take care of themselves.

Next he explained the two key requirements to find Olive guilty: that George had died by poison and that Olive had administered it. Then he reviewed specific bits of testimony. John Snider's evidence took up several minutes, in which Armour pointed out that, although the undertaker had reputedly said "We always embalm," the truth was otherwise. He went over the medical testimony, particularly the fact that both Frost and Phelps believed George had suffered from arsenical poisoning, and that both had treated George on a daily basis. Armour stressed Olive's refusal to send George to the hospital, and especially her reaction when she first learned that poison was suspected.

> Is she alarmed? Does she say anything to the doctor, "How in the world could he get arsenic?" Does she say anything of that kind? Does she exhibit any alarm about it? She

suggests suicide. But was there anything in the circumstances to show any intention to commit suicide? At this
time, you must remember that this man for some length of
time was in his bed, unable to help himself at all and she
was the person who was helping him. How was she to see
that he would get no more arsenic? It is a very important
point indeed for your consideration.

Armour continued with this point a little further, quoting
Olive's statement to Dr. Park, "You are the first and only doctor that
ever mentioned poison to me." Her excuse, the judge pointed out,
was that Frost did not want her to tell.

But was that any reason for her not telling? If her husband
was being poisoned by arsenic, was that any reason why
she should not tell the doctor who was coming in to take
his place what the symptoms were? ... An excuse she
gave, read to you yesterday, a very flippant remark she
made, 'It was for the doctor to find out.'... What did that
indicate? Is that what a woman anxious for her husband's
health would answer? Is that what she would do? Is that
the way she would conduct herself?

Diverging to the medical evidence for a time, Armour eventually returned to the crucial questions: "... did the deceased die from
arsenical poisoning or not? If he did die of arsenical poisoning, then
the next question is, who is responsible for that? Who administered
the arsenic to him?" A little later, he added yet another question. "If
arsenic was administered, was it administered by design or by accident or was there suicide?" Then, once more, he recounted the details of Elon Chipman's illness dismissing the possibility that George
was implicated in the murder of Olive's first husband.

If Sternaman had known of it, if Sternaman had done it,
he would have known what he did it with. He would have
known the kind of poison he used and when he was getting the same sort of poison himself he would have
known of it. If Sternaman knew that the prisoner had
done it, would he have been likely to have married the
prisoner? Would he have been likely to run the same risk
that Chipman ran?

For a man who had been involved with the legal system for many

years, these questions showed Armour singularly lacked an understanding of human nature. Time and time again, throughout history,
men and women had helped lovers dispose of an unwelcome
spouse only to step into the spouse's shoes. George Sternaman, an
unsophisticated farm boy with little apparent experience with
women, might easily have fallen into similar circumstances.

As Armour continued, it was impossible for anyone to doubt
his belief in Olive's guilt. When he talked of the lunches reputedly
containing poisoned food, he said,

> She it was that put it up. She herself said that no one else
> but she did it. No one else is suggested as having done it.
> It is clear then that if arsenic was in ... the lunch that her
> husband partook of it was she the must have placed it
> there.

He reminded the jury that it was not necessary to prove how Olive
had obtained arsenic.

> If the arsenic is found in the deceased's person; if the
> symptoms are of arsenical poisoning; and she is the only
> person who could have administered it, then the fact that
> she had it, that she procured it at any place, is immaterial.

He went on, repeating the questions that the jury had to answer in order to reach a verdict, He then summed up.

> It may be said that it is an extraordinary thing that a wife
> should poison her husband, and a motive is spoken of.
> Wives do poison their husbands. Husbands do poison
> their wives. We do not know the motive. Sometimes the
> husband gets tired of his wife. Sometime the wife gets tired
> of her husband. We cannot tell what are these hidden
> springs of human action which are figments of the brain
> alone. We cannot tell what the motive existing in any
> man's mind is. We can only tell by the results, by the lan-
> guage made use of and by the conduct of the party. Now
> referring again, the strongest evidence, as it strikes me – I
> do not know how it may strike you, is the fact that this
> woman–

Here he interrupted himself to discuss the suicide theory again.

> Do the circumstances indicate that Sternaman was intend-
> ing to commit suicide when he ate that lunch on the 13th
> of June which brought him to this end? ... If a man com-
> mits suicide he generally does it by one impetuous, rash
> act. He may cut his throat; he may hang or drown himself;
> he may take poison; but he takes enough or intends to
> take enough to deprive him of life. We do not find a man
> taking poison and continuing to take it from time to time
> to put an end to himself.

Picking up the thread he had dropped momentarily, he told the jury,
as far as he was concerned, the strongest piece of evidence against
Olive was her silence on the doctors' suspicions of poisoning and, in
particular, her statement to Dr. Park that he was the first doctor to
mention it. "Now, gentlemen," Armour concluded:

> your duty is to say upon the evidence, uninfluenced by
> sympathy in any way whatever – if this wife designed to
> kill her husband, if she is guilty of this crime, she deserves
> no sympathy; if she is innocent she does not require
> any–it is for your to determine upon the evidence, without
> fear, favor or affection, just as the evidence strikes you,
> whether the prisoner at the bar be guilty or not guilty.

Suddenly Olive called out. "Judge, may I add one word to the
jury?"

Armour refused. "Your counsel has addressed the jury. I cannot." With a warning glance from German, Olive lapsed into silence.

The Verdict

"Is that all the justice there is in this place?"

It was 4:35 p.m. The jury, 12 solid citizens from Haldimand County,
retired to deliberate the fate of Olive Sternaman. During the next
four hours, the spectators sat quietly, waiting for some sign of what
was taking place in the jury room. Around twenty minutes to nine, a
message came that the jurors wanted instructions. The men filed
back into the courtroom, guarded by the constables in their bright
red badges. Olive was sent for and, pale but still looking calm, she
took her place in the dock.

Judge Armour took his seat. "You wanted to make some en-
quiry from me, I believe?"

The jury foreman rose. "Your Lordship," he asked, "what power have we as to any recommendation to mercy?"

"Oh, You can recommend to mercy if you think fit," Armour replied.

The court was heavily shadowed, lighted only by the feeble glow of a few smoking lamps. Mr. Justice Armour sat in the full glare of one lamp, its flickering light illuminating his bulldog face surrounded by white hair and bushy side-whiskers. Olive was half-hidden in the gloom as the jury foreman walked from the box and handed the verdict to the judge. The silence deepened as the clerk accepted the paper from the judge's hand.

"Gentlemen of the jury," he cried, "hearken to your verdict as the court records it, a verdict of guilty, so say you all."

Some women in the gallery hid their faces in their hands and moaned. Others strained to watch the final act of the drama unfold. "Olive Adele Sternaman, stand up," Armour commanded. "What have you to say why the sentence of the court should not be pronounced upon you for the murder of which you have been found guilty?"

Pale, but still controlled, Olive rose. "I am not guilty – in the eyes of God." Her voice was clear, her eyes lifted to face the judge and the others in the court. "I will have a new trial and be acquitted."

Armour was stern. "You have had a very full trial. You have been defended very ably by an able counsel–"

"Yes Judge, but–"

> – and a very intelligent jury has given your case a very patient hearing, and a very deliberate consideration, and have come to the conclusion that you are guilty – a conclusion in which I entirely concur. It only remains for me to pass the sentence which the law pronounces upon you for the offence of which you have been found guilty: and that is, that you be taken hence to the place whence you came, and that you be thence taken on Thursday, the twentieth of January next, to the place of execution, and that you be there hanged by the neck until you are dead." Armour's voice quavered. "And may the Lord have mercy on your soul.

A female spectator fainted. Another cried out in agony. Olive protested, "Oh, judge, is that all the justice there is in this place?" as she sank to the bench.

Armour ignored her, turning instead to the jury. "Your recommendation, gentlemen of the jury, I will forward to the Executive Government in order that they may take action upon it."

Moments later, John Murphy and Chief Constable Farrell led Olive back to her cell. Olive's mother, Eliza Chipman, Dora Bonestead, Lizzie Sevenpifer and Murphy's wife Susan were waiting. When Olive entered the jail house, she was greeted by a flood of tears from her relatives and friends. Susan Murphy was so distraught that she had to be carried across the yard to her own house.

As for Olive, her first reaction was to sit heavily on a rough bench, as though stunned. The silence was broken only by the sobbing of the other women. Nor were the women the only ones affected. Both Murphy and Farrell were in tears.

"Oh, this is terrible," she said at last. "My God, but it cannot be." Choking with emotion, she was unable to continue for a few seconds, but her eyes remained dry.

> Can't I have a new trial? The judge was so severe. Had it not been for him it would have been so. Justice! Everybody told me that would be the justice I would receive in this country. I was told to expect none. I did, but I did not get it. He was cruel, and only for him it would have been different. Surely I am not to be hanged. Oh, this is terrible; my God, it is terrible!

She buried her face in her hands.

Olive's outburst was too much for Eliza Chipman, who left the second-storey cell and went down the winding staircase, calling for the judge and demanding a new trial for an innocent woman. She was exhausted, close to hysteria, and someone had to take her in hand. Meanwhile, in the jail cell, Olive fell to the floor and wept bitterly.

PART FOUR

IN THE SHADOW OF THE GALLOWS

"The thought of hanging a woman is repulsive, but ... the woman was very like a fiend ..."

There were mixed reactions from the public and the press when the news of Olive's conviction was released. The *Toronto Star* published a brief editorial under the heading "Canadian Justice":

> Mrs. Sternaman says she will have a new trial. She should remember that she isn't in San Francisco or any other United States city, where the law operates for the benefit and pleasure of the condemned rather than for the protection of society and the punishment of the guilty.

Elsewhere, the newspaper predicted:

> Mrs. Sternaman will not hang. We do not hang women in Canada; it has gone out of fashion. In its wise mercy, the Government of the Dominion will probably commute the sentence to life imprisonment. But no more just judgment was ever given by a jury, nor was ever judgment so warmly approved as must be the judgment which finds Mrs. Sternaman guilty of poisoning her husband. In his organs was found arsenic sufficient to kill three men, and as he was unable to lift a hand, the simple question is, How did that poison get into his body?

In yet another article, the *Star* continued:

> The thought of hanging a woman is repulsive, but in the case which Mr. Mills [federal minister of justice] will have to review it has been proven that the woman was very like a fiend, that she coolly and deliberately poisoned two husbands for the sake of small sums of insurance, sat by their bedsides, ministering to them patiently, and, with loving words on her lips, administering to them the deadly drug which was sapping their lives. She smiled,

and kissed them, as she tortured them to death ...

This vivid image of evil incarnate was one which a large segment of the public accepted as truth, and one which cried out for
the sternest justice. Olive was guilty not only of murder, but also of
hypocrisy, Victorian Canadians reasoned. She had acted out woman's most important role, that of tender loving wife, while systematically poisoning not one, but two husbands. It was an act of domestic
treachery as threatening to society as betrayal of one's country, and
she deserved the ultimate penalty.

Yet the Canadian public could be merciful under the right circumstances. One of the results of Olive's conviction was a flurry of
newspaper articles reviewing the trials of other Canadian murder-
esses. Among the most poignant was that of Elizabeth Workman of
Sarnia, a kind-hearted, devout woman who had killed her brutally
abusive husband. Despite the jury's recommendation for mercy, a
delay in execution, and several petitions, Workman went to the gallows in May 1873. Public horror at her fate was such that every
woman convicted of murder over the next 25 years had her sentence
commuted by the federal government. The closest Canadian parallel
to Olive's case was that of Eusebie Boulet, who had been convicted
of poisoning her husband in 1884. Her sentence was commuted to
life imprisonment.

Given the precedents, many were justifiably convinced that
Olive Sternaman would not go to the gallows. And this conviction
was further strengthened by the jury's actions. The 12 men had rendered their verdict on the night of Friday, November 19, with a recommendation for mercy. By Sunday, it was apparent that the jurors
had serious misgivings. That day, eight of them met again to discuss
the case and signed a petition asking for commutation of Olive's
sentence. Several later stated publicly they would not have convicted her if had they known in advance that she would receive the
death sentence. Early the next month, they formalized their hand-
written petition with an affidavit stating that all 12 had recom-
mended mercy, and:

> That the jury were under a serious misapprehension in re-
> spect to the powers of the trial judge, in thinking that he
> could give effect to the recommendation aforesaid and ...
> that our recommendation would have prevented the
> judge from imposing the supreme penalty of the law.

The affidavit concluded, "We would certainly have disagreed upon our verdict but for the misapprehension aforesaid."

Elsewhere, others too were clamouring for commutation. One of Olive's most outspoken champions was the Reverend James Gordon Foote, her spiritual mentor. Born in Varan, Huron County, Foote was a few weeks short of his 50th birthday. When Olive went on trial, he was just winding up his term as Methodist minister in Cayuga, where he had supervised the building of a new parsonage. Normally, he would have received a new posting in 1898, but an exception was made – possibly because of his concern for the convicted woman – and his term extended for a year. A dynamic individual with boundless energy, a strong physique and a commanding voice, he understood the merits of a grass–roots approach to any problem. Foote talked to anyone willing to listen about the need to win a new trial for Olive. He likely expounded about it from the pulpit as well, for James Foote was an old–time preacher, who thoroughly enjoyed revival services and who would rather preach than eat.

At first, Olive's champions fought an uphill battle. As an editorial in the *Toronto Daily Mail and Empire* pointed out, Canada had experienced "a wave of murder" during 1897, and now three people, including Olive Sternaman, were awaiting execution.

> Those who doom to death by poison some friend or relative in order that they may enrich themselves through the medium of life assurance only carry a little further the avarice which in thousands of cases is impelling people to get something for nothing. The man who slays in deadly hate and anger only carries out to their extreme feelings that are writhing like snakes in many a breast ...

> It is a fact that for a convicted man there is always a measure of public sympathy. Perhaps the feeling is prompted by pity. However stern and cruel humanity may have been in the old days, it certainly derives no pleasure now from the sufferings of a fellow–mortal. Indeed, many of us pass over the details of a murder or execution to avoid the pain which the perusal of the horrible facts may inflict. But this sort of feeling should by no means stand in the way of the state carrying out to the full its solemn responsibility in the protection of the life and liberty of the [innocent]

Few would disagree with the argument that convicted felons should receive the full penalty of the law. Although there was some support for the abolition of capital punishment, Canadians were still

a cautious breed. The widespread coverage of the Sternaman case
had thrown into sharp contrast the American and the British systems of justice, and few Canadians were willing to advocate the merits of a system often derisively described as little more than mob
rule. At the same time, many socially–conscious Canadians were
caught in the spirit of progressive reform that had swept the country
in the 1880s and 1890s. That movement led to the establishment of
countless social institutions from the Children's Aid Society to the
National Council of Women. Thinking people knew that injustices
existed in Canada and that, with hard work and effective publicity,
some of the worst abuses could be corrected or prevented. They
made it their business to point out the flaws in the case against
Olive and to argue that a second trial was essential.

On December 6, journalist Phillips Thompson wrote "A Letter
on Behalf of Mrs Sternaman" which was published in the *Globe* five
days later. Thomas Phillips Thompson was born in 1843, and spent
most of his life as a journalist and writer. A socialist and advocate of
labour, he abhorred the class system and was well–known for his
sympathy to unpopular causes. Widowed in 1897, Thompson was at
a vulnerable stage of his life, and that, together with his inherent ro-
manticism, made him, perhaps more sensitive than most to Olive's
plight.

His letter began on a disappointed note.

> I have been hoping for some time to hear of some move-
> ment in favor of the commutation of the death sentence
> passed upon Mrs. Sternaman, which, unless clemency is
> extended, will be carried into effect on the 20th of January.
> Surely the heat of political conflict and the pressure of ma-
> terial interests have not so completely engrossed public
> opinion as to exclude the claim of justice and humanity.

He went on to argue that if murder convictions were to be handed
down on circumstantial evidence alone, "such testimony ought at
least to be clear, overwhelming, and lacking in no important detail."
The Sternaman case was sadly lacking in such clear and overwhelming evidence; for instance, he pointed out, no proof existed that
Olive had ever possessed poison or had attempted to obtain it. Then
he spelled out his most profound concerns:

> (1) Mrs. Sternaman was practically tried and convicted in
> the newspapers before a word of the evidence was heard.
> Long accounts of the tragedy were published, and re-

peated references made to it at every stage of the pro-
tracted extradition proceedings, generally in a tone of an-
tagonism to the prisoner, whose guilt was assumed
throughout.

(2) The object of the detectives in this, as well as in other
cases, appears to have been rather to assure a conviction
and make a record than to get at the truth. Our courts are
often made the instruments of injustice by reason of the
close association of the detectives and the newspaper reporters. The latter, anxious for items, often play into the
hands of the detectives, conceal their blunders, exalt their
achievements, endorse their theories, and, in fact, bind
themselves in every way to the work of impressing the detectives' views upon the public and hounding down anyone whom, rightly or wrongly, the detective has marked
as his prey.

Anyone who had followed Murray's exploits in the press would automatically recognize him as the target of Thompson's criticism. But
the journalist apparently wanted to make sure Murray was singled
out. He criticized a *Mail and Empire* report of November 20th, which,
after providing details of the trial, congratulated Detective John
Wilson Murray for his part in the case. The implication, clearly, was
that by congratulating Murray the reporter was also accepting the
detective's assumption that Olive was guilty.

Thompson also objected to another report in the same paper
and quoted one passage in which Olive threw herself on the floor
and wept. "It was not an hysterical attack, but one of genuine remorse," the reporter had commented. "Note the animus of the con-
cluding phrase," Thompson bristled. And, lest readers get the wrong
idea, he stressed that the *Mail and Empire* was not the only offender.
Thompson raised other objections:

The practice of securing the very best forensic talent for the
prosecution, leaving the defence to be conducted by counsel much less gifted in the art of convincing juries, heavily
handicaps a prisoner. I do not desire to cast any slur upon
the ability of Mr. German, who acted as counsel for the
prisoner. But it is no disparagement to his professional
standing to point out that Mr. Osler is a specialist in this
particular line of getting juries to adopt his point of view.

Thompson, in effect, was summarizing the main concerns

voiced by the Canadian public in the letters they had written to newspaper editors.

But, ever the reformer, he also targeted "The Pharisaical Canadian assumption of superior morality and stricter enjoyment of law to that obtaining in the United States," which, he said:

> tends to make convictions easy on evidence which would elsewhere be scorned as non-conclusive. Because in some American communities law is loosely enforced the oppo- site extreme of vigor is exalted into a virtue by a numer- ous class of jingoes ... Because some ill-judged exhibitions of sentimentality have been witnessed in American crimi- nal cases they sedulously encourage a spirit of brutality and Draconian severity in the treatment of accused per- sons, under the impression that they thereby demonstrate their loyalty to British institutions. This sentiment came largely into play in the Sternaman trial.

A week later, Ambrose K. Goodman, the Cayuga lawyer who had first persuaded George Sternaman to buy life insurance, pub- lished another letter in the *Globe*. This one began:

> I belong to the majority in this county who did believe in the guilt of Mrs. Sternaman, but at the same time I re- spected the opinion of the minority who felt that the case had not been proven beyond the possibility of a doubt, and I have also, in sympathy with the movements set on foot by that minority, signed the petition asking that the sentence be commuted. These petitions are being largely signed all over the county, and I now think it my duty to say where I believe there may be a doubt as to her guilt.

With careful logic, he listed seven reasons. First, why had not Park analyzed the medicine George was taking, which might have con- tained arsenic? Secondly,

> I have been personally told by ratepayer from South Cayuga that they knew it was Sternaman's intention to do away with himself. Mrs. Chipman and her daughter still persist in the innocence of Mrs. Sternaman. They contend that Sternaman's infatuation for Mrs. Sternaman was such that during the lifetime of her first husband it often over- came his reasonable conduct ...

Thirdly, insurance could not have been Olive's motive because evidence at the trial strongly suggested her indifference to it. George, however, was not and Goodman pointed out that he had personally probated the will of David Sternaman. His insurance was enough to pay off debts, "and start life anew. George Sternaman was so impressed with the importance of insurance that he told me he intended to insure his life at once."

Then there was Olive's own personality. "All who have come in contact with the prisoner about the court house (with few exceptions) believe her innocent," Goodman declared. He also pointed out that the medicine prescribed by the last Buffalo doctor to attend George had contained arsenic. Goodman further suggested that, perhaps, George had taken arsenic on his own, at least at first. Later, the medicine with arsenic was prepared improperly, with enough arsenic to kill him. Regarding Chipman's death, Goodman believed it was not proper to draw parallels, because the body had not been examined. Furthermore, "the case for the Crown rested upon medical theory only." And, "every theory," Goodman thought, "may be found inaccurate at times." Finally, he concluded with an appeal to common sense:

> ... a guilty woman would not have brought the deceased home among his friends, that this would be simply entering a trap. Altogether the case is one of such difficulty as to lead many to the conclusion that the present sentence of death is not the outcome of a judgement that is at present exhaustive, logical and convincing.

Meanwhile, others were pointing to omissions in Mr. Justice Armour's charge to the jury as sufficient reason for commutation. A Toronto barrister's anonymous letter in the *Globe* addressed both Thompson's reasoning and Armour's competence:

> Here let it be said that Chief Justice Armour is one of the shrewdest and most consummate Judges of human nature that can be found either on or off the bench. He is essentially a strong man. It is impossible to sway him by sentimental considerations. The moment a conviction fastens itself upon his mind he will soon let it be known. Let me here recall one sentence in his charge to the jury in the Sternaman case: "If she is innocent she requires no sympathy; if she is guilty she deserves none.

"Barrister" also raised a question that many were asking. Why was not Olive called as a witness? "She is a clever woman, with courage enough to face the gallows, if need be, and to die game, but the inexorable logic of facts was against her, and she knew it." Although he did elaborate, "Barrister" was apparently convinced that Olive had not been kept from testifying out of consideration for sex but because of the risk that – clever or not – she would incriminate herself.

Meanwhile, Adam Davis, a Cayuga justice of the peace, wrote to the Minister of Justice, David Mills, enclosing a statement expressing the sentiments of a large number of county residents. In his letter, Davis explained:

> There is no politics directly or indirectly in this matter, all who speak of it express themselves shocked at the idea of having a Woman executed in the County. They say justice should be done and would be amply satisfied if the sentence was commuted to life imprisonment.

This letter captured the feelings of the populace and the fact that petitions were being circulated throughout the region asking for commutation of the death sentence. Davis also included a warning:

> I trust you will pardon me if I bring to your notice this point that in refusing to grant the prayer of the petition and thus opposing public sentiment, it may seriously interfere with the due administration of Criminal Justice in future in this County.

Davis was referring to a growing belief that if Olive hanged, juries would be extremely reluctant to convict any woman of murder in the future.

Meanwhile, more letters to newspaper editors kept the case before the public. One, signed "British Subject," supported Thompson.

> British justice does not insist on the engagement of bloodhounds, so to speak men whose whole ambition is to secure conviction whether by fair or foul means, it does not insist on engaging by the Crown the best talent in the land to gain a verdict from the illiterate jury. If this able talent had been on the defence, other results would have happened.

It went without saying that "British Subject" believed the British system of justice was the best in the world. However, inherent in that system was a notion of fair play, and using government funds to hire the very best detective and prosecutor was eminently unfair when the defence could not afford equally skilled talent. Stacking the deck so heavily in favour of the Crown was itself a miscarriage of justice, "Subject" implied: it undermined a system designed to discover truth regardless of wealth or status.

That letter appeared on Christmas day – for Olive, the second Christmas spent in a county jail and the third unhappy holiday in four years. But not all the letters which made it to the newspapers were written in a spirit in keeping with the season. "Husband" wrote,

> Convicts undergoing punishment fare better in many respects than the average honest toilers [now] that scoundrelism is rampant, for it leads to comfortable living, with nothing to do, at the expense of the community. Then influential pressure or maudlin sentimentality, or both combined, has led to something like a general jail delivery of late. Heavy pressure was brought to bear to have liberated even that cold-blooded murderer [Valentine] Shortiss, who was so well fitted to adorn a rope. But Shortiss' criminality pales before that of the heartless deviltry that coos with the loving words of connubial tenderness while engaged in the detestably heartless game of the insidious poisoner. Mr. Thompson, I fear, is one of those who allow their sympathies to run away with their judgement ... Criminals of the class of Mrs. Sternaman only be hunted down by unerring and relentless pursuit on the part of officers of the law.

The reference to Valentine Shortis, who had killed two men during a robbery in Valleyfield, Quebec, a year or so earlier, was not surprising. The case had been widely publicized. Shortis, who was found guilty and sentenced to hang despite a plea of insanity, later had his sentence commuted to life in prison.

"Husband's" tough-minded letter was one of the milder condemnations written about Olive. A short time later, the well-known journalist, Kit Coleman, made this observation in the *Mail & Empire*:

> There is something shocking in the fact that daily I receive letters absolutely glorying in the fact that a woman is about to be hanged in Canada, heaping contumely on the

poor creature who lies in gaol under the heaviest condemnation any human being can lie under. Up to this I have studiously – for reasons that concern myself alone – refrained from uttering a word regarding Mrs. Sternaman's case, but when, daily, I see venom pursuing and hunting her down, I cannot refrain from pleading, at least – silence. I was always taught that the meanest villainy in the world is to kick the under dog. When a man's down, if you cannot lend a helping hand, at least let him lie without insult … Her life – were it granted – would not hurt you nor me, friend. It would be passed forever in the shadow of the prison. Why shriek for its passage through the rope and the gallows? Why "wish," as one woman does, "that the wretch could be hanged, drawn and quartered." God help her! She has only Him now. In no sense writing in a sentimental way, I hope the Minister of Justice will find it in his heart and conscience to grant the poor erring creature her poor life.

Coleman's hope was shared by most. Those who believed her innocent realized commutation would provide time to uncover new evidence or lobby for a new trial. Many of those who believed her guilty could not condone the execution of a woman; some of them opposed capital punishment for men as well. A small but vocal minority was crying for blood, but the majority who wrote to the newspapers of the day made it clear that neither the trial nor the sentence met their standards of justice. However, bowing too quickly to public opinion might result in accusations of mob rule or American-style justice. And so, Canadian authorities watched and waited.

"The prisoner has always lived a virtuous life."

A few days after Christmas, William German took the train to Toronto. Before Chancellor J.A. Boyd at Osgoode Hall, he argued that the evidence regarding the death of Elon Chipman had been admitted illegally. Then it was a matter of waiting as 1897 slipped into 1898, bringing the date of Olive's execution inexorably nearer.

On January 1, the *Globe* printed a letter from Wallace Thayer, who pointed out that he had worked for more than a year – without compensation – in an effort to get Olive acquitted.

During this long period I have naturally had abundant opportunity to examine all of the facts concerning the case and to test her character. I have talked extensively and confidentially with her and her first husband's mother and father, who are her chief supporters in this terrible ordeal. To say that I am convinced that she is innocent is to express it mildly. I am as certain that she has had no hand in the commission of this crime as I am certain that you have not.

Consider first that the prisoner has always lived a virtuous life; that for ten years she was a loving and faithful wife to her first husband and that she bore to him two children whom she leaves behind, two boys of whom she is so fond that the thought of being separated from them forever is the only grief which she cannot now bear up under.

I say the only grief which she cannot now bear up under advisedly, for her Christian fortitude and her absolute reliance upon the goodness of God, and her conviction that she suffers for Him and will have her reward hereafter, is indeed marvellous. Her hymns and prayers and Bible have been an abundant consolation to her, and they seem to make her oblivious to her fearful position.

The public has wondered that she could bear up so—that she could seemingly treat the matter so lightly. The explanation is that she is a simple, emotional, deeply spiritual and religious, unworldly woman. She has not a high nervous organization and she has the deepest religious trust that I have ever seen in any human being.

Thayer argued that one of the major points against Olive was her secrecy regarding the Buffalo doctor's diagnosis of poison. "That doctor testified that he told her if anybody ever heard about the suspicion it would be from her lips, not his. She construed this as an invitation to secrecy, and who would not?" Furthermore, it was not Olive who had obtained the insurance policies on her husbands' lives. Moreover, all testimony indicated that she had been happily married in both cases.

The only other suspicious fact pointed out against the

prisoner was her refusing to give her consent that Sternaman be taken to a hospital. Do we not, all of us, know many loving wives who will not permit their loved ones, when they lie low, to be cared for in strange places by strangers' hands?

Thayer also played up George's emotional state.

After the most extended consideration of all the evidence and facts I have come to the conclusion [that Sternaman] did die of chronic arsenical poisoning and that it was [done] by several doses which he gave to himself in the first month of his illness while he was up and around the house. The diseased condition of his mind, and his strange, excitable and morbid nature is clearly in evidence. He wished to save his wife from his suspicious-minded mother, who had accused her of murdering Chipman, and he wrote the letter "to whom it may concern" for that purpose. The letter is absolutely inexplicable on[?] any other theory. That the letter is in his own handwriting and contains his thoughts and words no one can [unclear] gainsay. He was desperately in love with the prisoner; he did not fear a painless sickness and death. You may say that this theory is a guess. I admit that it is, but is not the theory that she gave arsenic to him a guess? And which is the more probable guess? But, above all, is a person to be hanged upon a guess? ... I think the Crown established beyond a reasonable doubt that Sternaman died of chronic arsenical poisoning, but there was absolutely no evidence as to how he got the poison, and the facts seem to point to self-administration with far more likelihood than to administration by the prisoner.

Consider that the prisoner had no knowledge of drugs, never had arsenic or any reason to buy [unclear] or any other poison, and that she was uneducated and simple-minded and made tactless answers in her testimony, which no guilty person capable of plotting the crime attributed to her could possibly have made, that she would not help her attorneys to [?] the theory of suicide, and that she never has believed that the second husband killed the first.

> Conceive a designing murderess taking her dying husband
> and two children to her mother–in–law, who had been ac-
> cusing her of murdering her first husband, leaving the in-
> surance premiums unpaid, so that the insurance would be
> forfeited, and giving her second husband poison, almost
> under the eyes of his mother, when he was at death's door
> and probably would have died anyway, as the physicians
> think? Is this not too strange to credit? Yet upon this the-
> ory she has been convicted.

Thayer's continued involvement in the case indicates he was thoroughly convinced of Olive's innocence. Profit might have been a motive, since Olive had agreed to pay him out of the insurance money. But Thayer could have written off the case as a loss and saved himself the trouble of writing to Canadian newspapers and authorities. It is even less likely that he was motivated by dreams of glory. In the event of an acquittal, Olive's Canadian lawyer would get the credit. The passion of his argument suggests Thayer had gone beyond the lawyer–client relationship and was crusading in the cause of justice. His depiction of Olive as "simple–minded" and "tact-less" might have been exaggerated for effect. None of the reporters who interviewed her left that impression, although it is fair to say that she was unsophisticated and did not always consider the impact her statements would have in a court-room. Still, the overall effect Thayer created was that of an innocent woman of humble circum-stances caught in a cruel web of political and legal machinations.

Two days later, Chancellor Boyd and two other justices pre-sented a unanimous ruling on the appeal. Citing several precedents, they ruled that the evidence regarding Chipman's death was admis-sible. Although Boyd conceded that a "a prisoner on trial does not come to justify his whole past life," the fact that the Elon had died a relatively short time before George was suggestive. "Unless Chipman's death had been 20 years earlier, there was no reason to deny evidence," Mr. Justice Rose stated. With this avenue closed, German had one chance left to save Olive's life – an appeal to Ottawa.

"It is so hard."

In Cayuga, Olive was bearing up well, her phlegmatic stoicism still intact. On January 2, however, the first cracks began to appear. Perhaps it was the new year, or the realization that her execution

date was now less than three weeks away. She became nervous and
restless, especially at night when she would wake up, sobbing and
moaning.

On January 5, 1898, John Murphy told Olive that her appeal for
a new trial had been denied. "I would like to see the Sheriff," she said
quietly. Then, picking up her Bible, she moved from the sitting room
to the smaller cell and wept.

Other business kept Sheriff John Farrell away from the jail
house throughout the day. Although many visitors, some of them
influential, requested permission to spend time with Olive, all were
refused. Still, the curious sometimes caught a glimpse of her, standing at the small window on the north wall of the cell. In the yard,
she could see two men working with a hammer and a saw. It was
too soon to begin the scaffold, but little imagination was needed to
envision what they might be doing a day or two down the road.

At 4:30, Farrell's business was done. He left the court–house,
strode to the jail and up the stairs to Olive's cell. With him was a reporter from the *Daily Mail and Empire*, who provided newspaper readers with yet another description of Olive.

> She is tall, perhaps three inches above a medium–statured
> woman. She is slim almost to leanness, but her frame is
> well–proportioned, and shows few if any angular lines. She
> has slender hands, pretty hands, and they are very white.
> Her face is oval, with a high forehead, prominent cheek
> bones, sharp–pointed nose, and ample pointed chin. The
> mouth spoils the face, for the teeth protrude even when
> she is not smiling or sobbing, and suggest hunger or civi-
> lized ferocity. Her eyes are a bit too small, and are quite
> grey. They are shrewd eyes, and despite the whole sea of
> sorrow that seems surging and heaving in their depths,
> they flash out a quick sharp gleam that catches you un-
> awares and almost makes you blink. She has brown hair,
> ordinary light brown hair, brushed back plainly.

She was also unusually pale. Until the cold winter set in, she walked
in the little courtyard behind the jail three days a week. When she
was tired of moving about, there was a wooden chair against one
wall where she could sit. Now, with snow on the ground and the
chair covered with ice, it was too cold to walk in the yard, even if
she had been so inclined. But Olive's stoicism failed at the thought of
walking over ground that might soon be the site of her death.

When Farrell entered the cell, Olive looked drawn but deter-

mined. She was also nervously twining and untwining her
fingers.

"Mr. Murphy has told you."

"Yes."

There was an awkward pause. Olive sighed. Farrell coughed
and cleared his throat. "It is true, Mrs. Sternaman. But you still have
a hope of commutation."

Olive looked away, glancing out the window. "It is hard. Oh, it
is so hard." She moved back toward her cell, crying. "Why doesn't
Mr. German write to me?" she asked fretfully. I have not heard from
[him] since I – I –since I was –" She struggled for control. "He is an
awful man. It makes it so hard. Why did he not take the other line of
defence, the one I urged, the one I wanted, the true one, that would
have cleared me?" Ever since her conviction, Olive had complained
of German's handling of the defense. No reporter explored her accu-
sation that German had disregarded her wishes, however.
Consequently, it is impossible to determine whether Olive's lack of
confidence was justified, or appeared only after she had been found
guilty.

"But Mr. German is working hard for you," Farrell reminded
her.

"But he has not written to me."

"He has written."

"But not to me."

"And he says that he will go to the Minister of Justice for you
now."

But Olive, it appeared, had lost hope.

Soon afterwards, the death watch began. Someone had to be
with her at all times. One of the women appointed to the watch was
a Mrs. Farrell, presumably the Sheriff's wife. "I am glad some one will
always be awake with me while I am here," she told a reporter who
visited her on January 7.

At 11 a.m. that morning, Olive was sitting in a yellow chair beside one window in the western wall in the "sitting room" or larger
cell. Beside the other window sat Mrs. Lattimer, another woman appointed to be with her. Between them was a wooden table, painted
yellow, on which were some inspirational books on Christian living
which Wallace Thayer had sent to Olive. Scattered beside them were
newspapers, an orange, an apple, a box of cream soda wafers, pen,
paper and ink. On the window sill behind Olive was a gold watch,
its case opened, and a half-finished handkerchief which she had
been embroidering.

Olive was reading a small Bible until she heard footsteps on the landing. At the sound, she bolted for the smaller cell, determined not to be seen by prying eyes. Mrs. Lattimer watched her steadily, but made no effort to coax her out. Olive refused to speak to the reporter. The staff, however, provided some insight into her daily routine. Each morning, she rose at about 10 a.m., breakfasted at 10:30, lunched at 1:30 and ate supper around 6. To augment the prison diet, friends brought gifts of food. In between meals and visits, she read or sewed. Sometimes, she cried and, every now and then, she would stand up and look through the arched windows to the gentle hills beyond the river. On occasion she must have looked down at the jail yard, where, if German was unsuccessful, she would soon be buried. For the most part, she showed little sign of agitation.

A few visitors saw her regularly. Their access gave a touch of credibility to an astounding piece of gossip. According to the *Globe*:

> A rumour was rife for a time that an unexpected and surprising event personal to the prisoner would intervene and arrest the arm of death, because the law would be punishing the innocent with the guilty. This rumour was finally set at rest when the Hon. Jacob Baxter, late Speaker of the Legislative Assembly, and a member of the Provincial Parliament from Haldimand county, denied it absolutely. Dr. Baxter is the gaol surgeon and is Mrs. Sternaman's medical adviser.

The rumour, of course, was sheer fabrication. By this time, George had been dead for 16 months, and Olive had been in custody for 14. The idea that the jail staff would allow a widow suspected of murder to carry on a clandestine affair was highly improbable. Besides, Olive had other things to think about. Among them were her funeral arrangements.

As January 20 approached, she decided to attend to practical matters. She wrote to the Order of Rebekahs in Buffalo asking them to handle funeral arrangements, and requesting them to bury her in Forest Lawn Cemetery. Forest Lawn was close to the neighbourhoods in which Olive had lived, and, perhaps, it gave her comfort to think of resting in familiar surroundings.

Far more painful were the arrangements for her children's welfare. Always a protective mother, she had sent the boys back to Buffalo to live with their paternal grandmother in a quiet part of the town. As the date of her execution approached, Olive arranged for guardianship of the boys. Barrister T.A. Snider drew up the documents in the presence of two local ministers who had brought her considerable spiritual comfort, J.D. Edgar and J.G. Foote. Their encouragement was necessary because Olive was reluctant to sign, as though in doing so she was giving up the last bit of hope.

"A mountain of justification for leniency"

While Olive tried to resign herself to death, efforts continued on her behalf. The day after German's appeal was denied, Wallace Thayer wrote to the Minister of Justice, David Mills, petitioning for a new trial under Section 748 of the Criminal Code. He quoted it, underlining two phrases to emphasise his point:

> If, upon any application for the mercy of the Crown, on behalf of any person convicted of an indictable offense, the Minister of Justice entertains a doubt whether such person ought to have been convicted, he may, instead of advising Her Majesty to remit or commuted the sentence, after such inquiry as he thinks proper, by an order in writing, direct a new trial, at such time and before such court as he may think proper.

Thayer was positive that Olive's conviction had not been warranted. "The terrible speed at which the case was rushed through and the judge's most biased summing up against the prisoner, struck me so strongly that I cannot see how anyone could regard it as a fair trial." In addition, Thayer argued that no crime had been committed in Canada. Citing British precedents, he concluded that Canadian authorities had no jurisdiction in this case. "The true doctrine of the law is that the death is no part of a murder, which is wholly committed at the time and place of the blow or administering of the poison, though the death is subsequent and elsewhere."

The deputy–minister responded on Mills's behalf in a letter on January 5. Regarding Section 748, he wrote,

> … the section referred to has never been considered by the Department to be an alternative available to a prisoner where an application for a new trial or for leave to appeal would like, but rather as a remedy to be used by the Minister of Justice of his own motion when, in his judgment, exceptional circumstances may call for its use.

No new trial had ever been granted under the provisions of this section. As for Thayer's argument about jurisdiction, Mills promised to examine it.

By now, Mills was thoroughly familiar with Olive's case. A studious and thoughtful man, he was an expert in constitutional and international law, and had taught at the University of Toronto. One of his first actions as minister of justice had been to commute the death sentence of Valentine Shortis. Many thought him far less deserving of clemency than Olive Sternaman, and made Mills aware of their opinion, especially after it was rumoured that Shortis's wealthy parents had used their money, power and connections with both the governor–general and the Roman Catholic church to stop the execution. At the same time, however, others made it clear to Mills that Olive was either guilty or innocent and, if guilty, she should hang for it, female or not. Aware of the political repercussions that had resulted from the Shortis case, Mills proceeded cautiously.

Mills could not afford to ignore public opinion, especially when it was transmitted through fellow politicians. On January 3, Jacob Baxter warned him that the people of Haldimand overwhelmingly favoured commutation. While he himself refused to express a personal opinion as to Olive's guilt or innocence, Baxter said, "Considering all the circumstances of the case, I am of opinion, that you will not err in advising a commutation of sentence." Another Liberal politician concurred. After visiting Baxter in Cayuga, Norfolk MP John Charlton wrote from his home in Lynedoch on January 5, 1898:

> I think that the universal feeling ... is in favour of the commutation of the sentence of Mrs. Sternaman ... [it was rumoured] the Judge believed from the outset, that she was guilty and was insensibly influenced by that belief in the course of the trial. Not more than two of the jury would have consented to a verdict of guilty except under the belief that their recommendation to mercy would be accepted. I would be sorry to see the first execution during your official career as Minister of Justice, that of a woman and I am decidedly of opinion that the sentence should be commuted.

David Mills responded on January 7, declining to comment on the specifics of the case without prior examination. He was willing, however, to express his views on the public demand for commutation.

I have heard like representations from other quarters. Of course, one could not be governed in a matter of this sort by the feeling of the community or by such expressions of opinion as you[r?] jurymen are making. It is the duty of a juryman in accordance with his oath to find those guilty who according to the evidence have committed the offence, and if there is no ground of reasonable doubt a juryman according to this oath ought to acquit, but a juryman has nothing in the world to do with the consequences in the sense of making his verdict depend upon them. If there was reasonable ground of doubt the verdict ought to have been one of acquittal. If there is no reasonable ground of doubt and the woman is guilty, then the murder was a most atrocious and heartless one. At this moment, I have no opinion whatever upon the subject, beyond that which the verdict creates.

In response to Baxter, Mills noted the doctor had refrained from stating his own opinion on Olive's guilt or innocence.

You inform me of what the state of public feeling is in the locality ... Mrs. Sternaman seems to have evoked a good deal of sympathy form the community in the vicinity of Cayuga, but I have been unable to discover so far its origin; whether it is because they suppose her innocent of the crime of which she was convicted or whether because they are reluctant that a woman should be executed. In the first case the desire for the non-execution of the law is legitimate and proper. In the other case it points rather to the amendment of the law than to its administration. The Executive department of Government could hardly undertake to administer the law in such a way as practically to repeal it with regard to one-half of the community. Whenever this is done of course it must be done by Parliament.

It was Mills's duty to be fair and unbiased, and he was a man who believed firmly in fulfilling his obligations. But so did another man, who believed his responsibility lay in quite a different direction. J.G. Foote had apparently convinced his congregation, with, undoubtedly, the exception of Charles Wesley Colter, that his public defense of the convicted woman was the Christian thing to do. Foote went beyond his own congregation, too, writing letters to newspa-

pers and to the authorities on Olive's behalf. On January 5, he wrote
to Mills, pleading for a new trial, or, at the very least, commutation
to life imprisonment. He began with the "evidence" that George had
poisoned himself:

> ... she declares that he so stated to her but bound her not
> to reveal it under an oath unless to save her life because
> of his mother as he did not want her to know. Of course
> her word is at a discount now but still when you listen to
> the simple story of her life, presented in a simple transpar-
> ent way you realize that what she says is true. She main-
> tains her innocence unwaveringly and unquestionably. If
> she is not innocent I admit that she is a wonderful
> woman. My conviction has deepened as I have come in
> contact with her...

Foote then turned to the jury's admitted confusion and the fact
that jurors had entertained reasonable doubts as to Olive's guilt, but
found against her nevertheless. He argued that this confusion resulted directly from Armour's failure to instruct the jury clearly as to
its proper course if doubt existed. Then, Foote cited undertaker John
Snider's dubious testimony, shoring it up in a strikingly unchristian
display with a rumour about "some very suspicious transactions"
then circulating in Haldimand:

> He paid after [the] inquest $200 silver dollars on Mortgage
> on his property, which before he could not even pay in-
> terest.

Foote concluded with a plea for mercy:

> Better to let one guilty one go free than to destroy one in-
> nocent one. better if we err to err on the side of mercy.

Failing that he hoped that Mills "may commute her sentence."

Three days later, Olive's other champion, Phillips Thompson,
sent a collection of petitions to David Mills along with letters that had
appeared in Toronto papers. The petitions, he pointed out, had been
signed in Toronto. Possibly Thompson hoped to convince Mills that
the signatures represented only the tip of the iceberg, for he stressed:

> there has been no systematic or organized attempt to

bring the matter before the citizens generally, the procuring of such signatures as have been obtained being the work of a very few, who have presented the petitions as occasion offered to those with whom they come in contact. There is a general disposition since the publication of the petition of the jurors asking for commutation, to regard the matter as practically settled. I can assure you that if the public believed that there was any likelihood of the sentence being carried out a very strong movement would be set on foot to urge commutation.

Despite Thompson's declaration that signatures had been gathered in haphazard fashion, he stated that some petitions were still being circulated by canvassers, and these Thompson promised to send along later.

Drafted in early December, the petitions were typed and sent to various areas. Each was addressed to the governor-general and through him to Mills:

> The petition of the undersigned humbly sheweth,- That Olive A. Sternaman was on the 19th day of November 1897 convicted before his Lordship, Chief Justice Armour, at the Court of Assize at Cayuga Ont. of having murdered her husband George H. Sternaman by poison.
>
> That the jury in rendering their verdict of guilty recommended the prisoner to mercy.
>
> That the document annexed to this petition is a petition signed by such of the twelve jurors, who rendered the verdict as are available.
>
> That the prisoner is the mother of a family.
>
> That the execution of the death sentence of the law upon women is a proceeding, happily rare in Canada and almost generally repugnant to natural feelings and to Christian Civilization.
>
> Now therefore your petitioners most humbly implore that you Excellency would be most graciously pleased to commute the sentence of death passed upon the unfortunate prisoner to one of imprisonment.

The surviving petitions contain mostly men's signatures, although the signatures of a few women do appear. In Rainham, were the Sternamans lived, 50 people signed. In neighbouring South Cayuga, the number was 58. Dunnville, the county's most populous town, produced 284 signatures, beginning with that of Reeve Frank J. Ramsey and Deputy-reeve Robert Bennett. Former coroner David Thompson headed the list of 82 names from Cayuga, and three dozen signatures appeared on the petition from Caledonia, a few miles up river.

Altogether, 608 people signed the Haldimand petitions. Forty-seven – just under 8% – were women. The largest occupational group represented was farmers, followed by small tradesmen and artisans. Together, they made up more than 50% of the petitioners. Merchants and small businessmen accounted for another 16%.

Olive's support among these groups is hardly surprising. First, they reflected the demographical breakdown of the county. It was still very much an agricultural region, with a number of independent tradesmen and merchants, and some wage-earners. Moreover, many of the petitioners came from backgrounds similar to Olive's own. Even merchants and small businessmen could be included in this category, because many or most would be just a few years removed from the farm.

Together, government officials, politicians, professionals and those involved in the justice system represented just 16% of the petitioners. Again, this reflects the social structure of the county, but there may have been other motives at work within this group. Traditionally, better-educated people tend to be more liberal. Presumably this group should have been among Olive's strongest supporters and more heavily represented than they were. Perhaps the professionals and politicians of Haldimand County had greater faith in the justice system run by members of their own class than did the members of the working class.

Economics may explain the absence of some signatures. Men whose jobs depended on the good will of others are notably absent: there are almost no politicians' signatures (except in Dunnville) and only two teachers'. Interestingly, there are a significant number of members of the legal or law enforcement profession including several men directly involved with the case: Coroner David Thompson, jail physician and MPP Jacob Baxter, barristers Andrew Thompson and Ambrose Goodman, Sheriff Robert A. Davis, jailer J.A. Murphy and turnkey Thomas Walsh, clerk of assize James Mitchell, and justice of the peace A.A. Davis, who added next to his signature, "by me committed for trial." It is almost as if, having considered the trial in retrospect, they had come to the conclusion that justice had not been served and were doing what they could to correct the situation.

In Toronto, where a few hundred signatures were obtained, again most were from men. They, after all, had the political power to pressure government – although women's organizations frequently used petitions, too. Of the 237 signatures on Toronto petitions, only 18, or 7.6% were women's.

One exceptional petition from Lindsay, Ontario, reached Ottawa on January 13. All 29 signatories were women, who called Olive's death sentence "a shock to the humane throughout Canada" and requested commutation. A note at the bottom of the petition explained that the names "were obtained within less than two hours in a visit mostly from house to house." The noted added that, "double the number could be readily obtained were it not that haste to forward it [to] Ottawa was considered necessary."

On the day the Lindsay petition reached Ottawa, Thayer again wrote to Mills. Apologizing for "the informality and fragmentary character of my arguments," the American attorney pointed out that William German had defended Olive "on a totally false theory – the theory that the deceased did not die from arsenical poisoning, when in fact he did." Although careful not to use the word, Thayer contended that German's mismanagement of the case was directly responsible for Olive's death sentence. He further argued that no evidence had been submitted to the Canadian courts to suggest George's possible criminal intent. "The record before our Judge Fairchild is full of such evidence," he stated, "and I ask you to read it."

Thayer returned to the supposition that George had poisoned his own father, pointing out that David had died of stomach trouble while George was visiting. Three months later Elon died. "He disposed of Chipman for love the defendant," Thayer claimed. "He then developed this strange frenzy and final disposed of himself." Not only had German failed to use these circumstances in his defence, but he had also ignored medical evidence which Thayer considered crucial. He pointed out to Mills that Dr. Ellis had been asked how long arsenic might remain in the liquid contents of the stomach. Ellis replied that two or three days was normal, but he could draw no conclusion in George's case because both the stomach and the intestines were put in the same bottle. "Mr. German did not notice the testimony," Thayer wrote. "I conclude that the deceased gave the doses to himself early in his illness and no evidence conflicts with my belief."

Having stressed what he believed was significant evidence, Thayer returned to Olive's character.

I earnestly advised Mr. German to allow the defendant to
tell her story as she had told it before Fairchild. She is so
simple and sincere that no one could disbelieve her and
he refused against her and my own earnest plea. If she
had been allowed to testify, I think she would still have
been saved.

Thayer forgot that, despite Olive's testimony on her own behalf in
Buffalo, she had been extradited to Canada. He was also apparently
ill at ease with his judgement of German's defense. "These criticisms
of a brother lawyer are confidential and for you alone, but where
human life is at stake, I can not refrain from speaking what I feel."

Then, to add weight to his argument, Thayer enclosed affidavits
from two of George Sternaman's acquaintances. He knew that they
had no legal validity in Canada, yet at the same time calculated that
their very existence might add to whatever doubts Mills had about
the justice of Olive's sentence.

Frederick H. Wurster, a Buffalo contractor and builder, stated:

I knew George H. Sternaman, now deceased; he was in my
employ for two and one-half years steady, working for me
as a carpenter; he worked for me part of 1893, 1894, and
until about the spring of 1895. I knew him shortly after he
came from Canada and I knew that he was boarding with
Mr. Elon Chipman, who was at that time employed by me
as foreman. During the fore part of my acquaintance with
him he seemed to be a jovial young man and nothing
ever seemed to worry him very much, and I noticed that
after the spring of 1895, and after he had left me for some
time and came back to be re-employed, that he seemed to
be very much worried and a sort of absent minded; he
asked me for employment and I told him he might begin
work that day at noon, and he went away to get his tools
and I did not seem him again for two or three days. After
about three days he returned and at that time I had all of
the help I wanted, and he seemed very nervous and irrita-
ble and said that he was sick. During the latter part of
George H. Sternaman's employment under me, said
Sternaman seemed to be careless in his work, and would
make mistakes, and in my opinion, he appeared to me as
though his mind drifted from his work, and he would at
times go off to the attic or other secluded parts of the
building, and neglect his work ...

After leaving Wurster's employ, George went to work for another contractor, William McClellan. For two weeks in the late spring of 1895, George Ward had worked alongside him. During that period, Ward claimed, Sternaman often complained about being sick, and:

> did not work steady; he would come to work in the morning and work probably until noon some days and would go home, this he did during the first part of his employment under me; later on he seemed to get better and would work all day ... as I observed him, he seemed to strike me as a man of restless disposition.

Thayer left it to Mills to speculate on any connection between George's behaviour at work and his domestic situation, including the death of Elon Chipman in January 1895, George's continued presence in Olive's house and his mother's disapproval of both Olive and the couple's living arrangements.

While Thayer's missive was on the way to Ottawa, Deputy Minister of Justice E.L. Howe sent a message to Armour in Toronto. Armour's report on the case had been mislaid and Howe asked for another. Armour replied promptly. As far as he was concerned, Olive was found guilty on conclusive evidence. "No objection was made to my charge and no objection was made to any of the evidence given on behalf of the Crown," he emphasized, except for the details surrounding the death of Elon Chipman. He had reserved decision on the admissibility of this evidence, he explained, not because he thought it was inadmissible, but "in order that it might not be said that any indulgence was denied by the court." And, he pointed out, the evidence had since been deemed admissible.

Reviewing the matter of commutation, Armour explained that when the jury returned to the court, the foreman had inquired whether it was possible to recommend mercy. When he said it was, the foreman turned over the written verdict, "guilty with a recommendation to mercy," to the clerk.

> I do not think that this recommendation is to be attributed to any doubt existing in the minds of the jury as to the guilt of the prisoner for if the evidence had left any loophole for a doubt the jury would undoubtedly have taken advantage of it and acquitted her, so reluctant are juries to find any one guilty of murder; but is rather to be attributed to that feeling which exists among jurymen of reluctant to have it thought that they have [assisted] in taking the life

of a fellow creature particularly when that fellow creature
is a woman.

Such "mistaken compassion," Armour declared, led to recommenda-
tions of mercy when guilt was an inevitability. He concluded with a
dramatic revelation.

> ... had I tried the convict without a jury I should have had
> no hesitation in finding her guilty and ... I know of no
> reason ... why the law should not be allowed to take its
> course.

On the evening of Saturday, January 15, German and the
Reverend Foote disembarked from a train in Ottawa. Along with
more petitions for commutation, they carried another document: an
affidavit, signed by David Thompson two days earlier. At the insis-
tence of Foote, Thompson reported:

> That at the inquest held by me upon the body of the said
> George H. Sternaman, I was personally present and saw
> the remains exhumed. That I was also presented at the
> post mortem made upon the said remains by Drs.
> Harrison and Park. That upon the thoracic cavity being
> opened I observed a quantity of serous fluid in the said
> cavity, which I believed amounted to about one quart,
> more or less.
>
> That none of the said fluid in the said thoracic cavity was
> removed for analysis, or for any other purpose.
>
> That I was not personally present during a great part of
> the examination of Dr. Harrison during the trial at which
> said Olive Adele Sternaman was convicted; and that as a
> consequence of my absence therefrom I did not hear the
> doctor swear that the thoracic cavity was quite dry, as I
> am informed he did swear. That under the circumstances I
> feel it my duty to communicate without a moment's delay
> with the honorable minister of justice.

It was a small, relatively unimportant detail, but Foote was leaving
no stone unturned. He prevailed upon Thompson to write to the
minister of justice, and the former coroner had complied.

As soon as they arrived in Ottawa, German and Foote hurried
to call on Mills. He was unavailable, but an appointment was

arranged for Monday afternoon. Meanwhile, Mills would review the details of the case.

Although he had served in the Canadian legislature since Confederation, some regarded him as an unusual choice for Justice Minister. According to the *Ottawa Citizen*, he was a man of "natural amiability and undoubted integrity" but lacking "the distinguished legal career and immense experience of his predecessors." Instead, Mills brought the attributes of a scholar to his position: "By nature and inclination a student, a thinker and a teacher." A native of Oxford Township, Kent County, he could trace his roots back to New England Puritans.

Canadians watched and waited to see what Mills would do. The general feeling was there was ample justification for leniency in the Sternaman case. As the *Ottawa Citizen* commented:

> If the Minister of Justice thinks that there was a molehill of justification for the leniency shown to Valentine Shortiss [sic], he ought to see a mountain of justification for leniency towards Mrs. Sternaman.

Before German's meeting with government representatives in the afternoon of January 17, Foote took the train back to Cayuga, presumably so he could be with Olive when the decision was reached. The morning before the meeting, another drama was played out in Buffalo and duly reported to the public. According to the *Buffalo Morning Express* a mysterious woman, dressed in black and heavily veiled, called at the Board of Health Office in Buffalo's municipal building. "Apparently, she was a woman of refinement, and even culture, for her language was perfect," the newspaper revealed. She asked for the Registrar of Vital Statistics, and was taken to see Dr. Gram, where she inquired about the law regarding removal of bodies from Canada to U.S. for burial. Gram replied that it was legal, providing, of course, the requisite paperwork had been completed and there was no danger of spreading a contagious disease.

"But suppose it is the body of a woman who has been hanged?" the veiled visitor asked.

The question startled Gram. "Is – is this woman you speak of already, ah, executed?"

"No, she is Mrs. Olive A. Sternaman."

"Oh, yes, I understand now, but she may not hang."

"I think she will."

"And if she does, you want the body brought to Buffalo for burial?"

"Yes sir. I wish to bury it in Forest Lawn. Mrs. Sternaman would not like to have her body left in Canada. It seems to me when she has been hanged, the Canadian Government ought to be satisfied. They cannot claim her body."

Gram explained that he would have to investigate Canadian regulations before he could say for certain whether Olive's body could be returned to the U.S. or not. When he warned the woman that the Canadian government could choose to dispose of the body as it wished, she seemed disappointed. She had been one of Olive's neighbours, she explained, and she had vowed that she would not rest if the body was left in Canada. There was no mention of the Order of Rebekahs, but, in all likelihood, the veiled woman was a member who was trying to fulfil Olive's wishes.

Still, there was as yet no body to bury and German was doing what he could to see that there would not be. During a three–hour meeting, he presented a resumé of the case to Mills and his fellow cabinet ministers Louis Davis and Richard W. Scott. German's basic argument was that there was no direct evidence of Olive's guilt – all the evidence was circumstantial. He also presented Thompson's affidavit.

Meanwhile, hangman John Radclive arrived in Cayuga to prepare for Thursday's execution. A former sailor with the British navy, Radclive apparently got his first experience as an executioner aboard ship. After emigrating to Canada in 1887, he worked at different jobs until 1892. After hearing of a botched hanging, he offered to serve as official Crown executioner. For several years he travelled throughout the Dominion to carry out executions.

One of the new breed of scientific executioners who took into account the weight of the prisoner and the qualities of the rope, Radclive seems to have borne no ill will towards condemned prisoners. In fact, he treated many with the kind of professional courtesy one might expect from a doctor called on to perform an unpleasant but necessary treatment. He was a man who saw his duty clearly: to uphold the justice system by carrying out the highest penalty the courts could impose. When he arrived in Cayuga, a crowd had gathered at the train station, anxious for telegraphed news from Ottawa. Radclive stepped off the train, a short, slightly–built man with a ruddy face and bushy brown mustache, carrying a black valise containing the ropes and tackle required in his trade. When people realized who he was, there were some hisses. The same reaction came from the crowd outside the court–house. Undeterred, Radclive inspected the gallows with Sheriff Farrell.

A preliminary examination was necessary to avoid problems

on hanging day. The last hanging in Haldimand County had occurred on September 22, 1876. As John Young, murderer of farmer
Abel McDonald, waited for the final plunge into oblivion, the trap
door jammed. It was necessary to hammer the bolt back into place
before making a second attempt. That kind of bungling was just
what Radclive wanted to avoid. First, it gave fuel to the superstitious,
who might interpret either hesitation on the part of the hangman or
mechanical failure as a divine sign of innocence. Secondly, it added
unnecessary torture to the convicted prisoner's final moments.
Radclive wanted his executions to be clean, quick and professional.
As he once said to reporter Hector Charlesworth, "if there 'as to be
'angin's the only merciful thing is to do 'em right!"

To assure this, Radclive had to meet Olive face to face, to calcu-
late her height and weight to prepare the rope correctly and to fix
the proper weight so that she would die quickly of a broken neck,
rather than of slow strangulation. It must have been a strained, awkward encounter, but Olive at least had some emotional support. In
addition to the women who took turns watching her day and night,
her sister and other female relatives spent as much time as they
could with her.

Mills was already familiar with the details of Olive's trial and
conviction. Moreover, he would make the decision only after consulting with his fellow cabinet members. Still, he had weighed and
considered the alternatives and was prepared for any eventuality.
On January 15 he drafted a letter to the governor–general, recom-
mending Olive's sentence be commuted to life imprisonment in
Kingston Penitentiary. The letter was not signed, however.

When German left, Mills, Davies and Scott discussed the case.
They sat until midnight, turning the facts over again and again, arguing the relative merits of the evidence and German's arguments.
On Tuesday morning, they delivered their report to the Cabinet.
Apparently, the committee decided to recommend no action. A letter
to the governor–general dated January 18 and signed by Mills ends,
"Upon careful consideration of the whole case the Undersigned has
the honour to submit that he does not see any sufficient ground to
interfere with the sentence pronounced by the Trial Judge."

Mills seemed confident that the Cabinet would agree to the
committee's recommendation. But the case had generated so much
controversy that more debate was necessary. For the next several
hours, Olive's fate rested in the hands of the most powerful men in
the land. In Cayuga, Olive and her friends vacillated between hope
and despair while crowds continued to wait outside the telegraph
office in the chill January air.

All day, the Cabinet debated. Several votes were taken, but no clear decision was reached. Night fell, and still Cayuga had no word. Finally, at 11 p.m. the line buzzed. The clerk took down the message from Scott, then relayed it to the crowd:

> Minister of Justice has directed a new trial in the case of Mrs. Sternaman. You will take no further action. Answer this telegram showing you understand the message.

Immediately, a loud cheer went up.

When the shouting died a little, someone posed the important question: who would tell Olive? The Reverend Foote, who had worked so hard, was a natural candidate. With the Reverend Edgar he hurried to the jail. They entered Murphy's office noisily. A floor above, Olive heard the voices but could make out no words, although she recognized the cadences. Moments later, the men reached her cell. They found her pale and haggard, with dark circles under her eyes. All day long she had waited for news, asking over and over again if any word had come. Now, she glanced anxiously from face to face, as Foote spoke. "Well, how would you like a commuted sentence?"

"I should like it!" Olive replied.

"How would a new trial suit you?" asked Edgar.

"That is what I want."

And that was what she was going to get. The men congratulated her. Overwhelmed by the sudden turn in her fortunes, Olive was momentarily speechless. Then she asked for her children. Foote, switching roles from that of messenger to minister, told Olive she should first thank God for her deliverance. Shortly afterwards, a reporter was allowed in to speak to her.

"Oh! I am so glad," Olive said, "that I am not going to be hung. Now I will have a chance to have all the facts brought out and clear myself. This is heaven to me. You do not know how glad I am, oh! I have suffered no one knows but thank God it is all right now."

Even Murphy and Radclive shared her enthusiasm. Jokingly, Olive told the jailer, "If you leave the door open tonight I would not walk out. I would rather stay here till spring and receive a new trial, when everything will be brought out, and I shall then be able to go out and face the world, having the satisfaction of being an innocent woman."

While the news spread across the country, officers of the court were busy handling the paperwork. At 8:50 a.m on Wednesday morning, Sheriff Davis telegraphed his receipt of Scott's message. "All preparations & execution stopped. Many thanks." That same day, Joseph Pope, under-secretary of state, sent a certificate to Davis, confirming that a new trial had been ordered.

Not everyone was pleased with the turn of events. In fact, Detective John Wilson Murray was furious.

> If the report is true, I think it is a mistake. Never in the history of this country has there been a fairer trial than that of Mrs. Sternaman, with a respectable jury and witness composed of a good class of intelligent people.

As for Thompson's affidavit, Murray felt personally betrayed.

> I do not think there is anything in them [*sic*], for to my knowledge Dr. Thompson was present on more than one occasion when Doctors Harrison and Park were giving evidence. Dr. Thompson had himself given evidence on two occasions, as I am personally aware, and it is the first time I have heard either from him or anyone else anything about the fluid having been found in the throat of the deceased.

He further explained that Thompson had not mentioned his misgivings to him during either the investigation or the trial. As far as Murray was concerned, had Thompson considered this piece of information important, he would have mentioned it; certainly he had many opportunities.

"Do you then think that there is good reason for the decision arrived at in Ottawa?" the reporter asked.

"I do not think so at all," Murray replied. "I am afraid it is establishing a bad precedent, although I might say for myself personally, that I am not in favour of capital punishment as a rule."

There were others who agreed with Murray, although the roar of sentiment applauding a second trial made it difficult for them to be heard. Perhaps the *Ottawa Citizen*'s commentary captured their view best. Recounting another newspaper's approval of a new trial because there was so much doubt in the public's mind, the *Citizen* retorted that Olive had not been tried by the public, but by a jury. "It would never do to disturb the process of law simply because the 'public mind' would thereby be relieved." Again, the inference was that British justice was superior to American, because it was less likely to be affected by public sentiment.

Significantly, similar sentiments were echoed in Mills's statement describing the decision to grant a second trial:

although I entertain no doubt as to the propriety of the said conviction of said Olive Sternaman ... yet inasmuch as representations have been made upon the said application for clemency, and evidence and circumstances called to my attention which were not presented at the trial, or considered by the learned Chief Justice of the jury, which throw doubt on the propriety of the said conviction, and on account of which I entertain a doubt ...

Regardless of Mills's opinion or public debate, Olive had got what she wanted. She would be tried at the spring assizes in Cayuga. Originally, German had tried to get a change of venue, suggesting Welland as a possible alternative if it seemed Olive would not get a fair trial in Haldimand County. By the time German conferred with Mills during the last week of January, he was sure that popular opinion had swung around so much in Olive's favour that Cayuga would be the best setting for the second trial. And so Olive sat down to wait for spring and one more set of courtroom appearances.

PART FIVE

THE POWER OF PUBLIC OPINION

"The right of giving to each and every person a fair and impartial trial ..."

A few days after Olive was granted a new trial, a letter appeared in the *Toronto World*. Written by assistant U.S. District Attorney W.A. Mackey, it was addressed to John Wilson Murray. Who sent a copy of the letter to the newspaper is not known, although it might have been Murray himself. As an officer of the court, Murray could not comment publicly on a pending case. Anger at Mills's decision may have overcome his judgment, however. And he certainly had a working relationship with the press, who celebrated his exploits at every opportunity.

In the letter, Mackey expressed astonishment at the granting of a second trial, and at the new evidence David Thompson referred to in his affidavit. He declared himself surprised that Thompson

> should have suppressed his knowledge, or pretended knowledge, of the presence of embalming fluid, and have waited to disclose the fact until the 11th hour.

> I do not know, of course, anything more than what I have seen in the papers, but it strikes me that the coroner is either lying or is a knave, and wholly unfit to hold the important office which he does.

An angry David Thompson replied immediately, stating that the entire case rested on the issue of embalming fluid, but that his affidavit did not refer to it. Furthermore, he was certain the new trial had not been granted on the strength of his statement. Mackey's letter he dismissed as a "tissue of lies." Thompson's analysis was not exactly on target, either, because the embalming issue was only one of several crucial aspects of the case.

Meanwhile, Dr. T.T.S. Harrison followed the proceedings and felt compelled to add his voice to the argument. In a letter to the *Dunnville Chronicle*, he claimed never to have stated there was no fluid in the body. He had stated, however, that there was no evidence of embalming. After the inquest, he had also discussed the dryness of the organs in general and, at that point, Thompson told Harrison he had seen some fluid in the thorax, which he supposed came from the blood vessels. Harrison agreed. In his letter, Harrison took issue with Thompson's statement that there might have been as much as a quart of fluid. As far as the elderly physician was concerned, there was only a few ounces of "bloody serum." What everyone but David Thompson seemed to have forgotten was that Thompson himself did not think the fluid significant.

As Ontarians waited for spring, there was a certain amount of speculation as to the outcome of Olive's second trial. On February 18, a letter from "Observer" in Cayuga appeared in the *Dunnville Chronicle* predicting an acquittal:

> Any jury that may be brought together on the second trial of Mrs. Sternaman, no matter if the evidence against her should be even more conclusive than on the first, will fail to bring in a verdict of guilty, so great will be the repug-nance of some of them at least to the thought of hanging a woman. The presiding judge at the murder trial ought to be allowed to pronounce sentence of imprisonment for life at the conviction, whenever in his discretion such a course would be in the interest of justice.

Presumably, "Observer" believed Olive was guilty. Whether this was so was a matter for the court to decide, but this time her supporters decided she deserved a fighting chance.

Before the end of February, a move was afoot to hire E.F.B. Johnston to defend her. Johnston, as the *Chronicle* reported, "is a peer of Osler in criminal trials." In fact, the two lawyers were arch–rivals. Johnston was probably the only lawyer in Ontario who could hope to best Osler. But anyone who expected to hire Johnston had to be ready to meet his $500 fee. Olive's supporters decided to raise the money to do just that.

The flurry of campaigning surrounding the provincial election on March 1 slowed efforts down somewhat, but on the afternoon of Monday, March 14, the inaugural meeting of the Sternaman Fund Committee was held at the Mental Science Institute on the corner of Spadina Avenue and Cecil Street in Toronto. Press coverage did not indicate how the committee had come into being, but Phillips Thompson's involvement indicates that he may have been a prime mover. The Reverend Charles Harper Shortt was appointed chairman, while Thompson served as secretary. One of his first official duties was to read a letter from the Reverend Foote in Cayuga. In it, the minister revealed that a similar committee had been formed in Buffalo, and that he had been made treasurer.

The crucial business of the afternoon was the passing of a resolution:

> That whereas a new trial has been granted to Mrs. Olive A. Sternaman, charged with murder, and it is desirable in the interests of justice and humanity that her case should be fully and fairly presented, and whereas, while the resources of the Crown are available for the prosecution, she is without adequate means to engage counsel and secure witnesses, it is hereby resolved that an appeal be made through the press to the public for contributions to and in her defence, and that all in sympathy with this object are requested to forward their subscriptions to Rev. J.G. Foote, Cayuga.

The motion was made by 43–year–old James Mavor, a Scottish–born economist with socialist leanings who taught at the University of Toronto. Mrs. Mary McDonnell seconded it. The resolution passed easily, and the meeting adjourned.

The Buffalo campaign was shaping up along similar lines. In a report reprinted from the *Buffalo Evening News*, the *Dunnville Chronicle* quoted a statement signed by "prominent" but anonymous women of the Queen City.

> As the acquaintances of Mrs. Olive A. Sternaman, who believe that she should have a fair trial for her life, and who believe that at her former trial she did not have the opportunity for proving her case, which justice requires, we make this appeal to the public:
>
> The counsel, both American and Canadian, have fought her cause without compensation or the hope of compensation. The total failure of her counsel to bring out the facts and to make the points of law as widely known, are generally conceded. It is generally agreed that had the Crown's counsel been her attorney, she would have been acquitted. She has suffered more than death and we are determined to do what we can to secure for her a new counsel, and such expert evidence as she needs at her

approaching trial. Mr. German has consented that another counsel be associated with him, who should have charge of the case. The expense will be $500, of which we must raise at least $300. If every person who believes in fair play, whatever doubts they may have, and who believes that no one should be convicted upon guess, will send to the Rev. J.G. Foote, the sum of $1, or a lesser sum if they cannot afford the full amount, a sufficient fund will be raised to provide our fellow citizen a fair trial in a foreign country.

We feel that as Americans and as Christians, we are called upon to make this appeal.

No one can know or really be possessed of enough data to say that they think the prisoner is guilty, and we, as individuals, feel that we should not neglect a human being in distress. The public was never called upon for aid for a woman forced to confront without means, or the possibility of getting suitable counsel, so terrible an ordeal. She has to meet death twice absolutely alone, unbefriended, and her fellow men can provide her with the weapons to establish her innocence. We believe that this appeal will not be in vain.

German's decision to step aside in favour of another counsel was not surprising. Reports that he had mismanaged the case put him in a precarious position, particularly if Olive lost her second trial while he was acting as her defense lawyer. Olive was completely disillusioned with him, convinced that he believed her guilty. Furthermore, German was fighting a professional battle of his own. Following the Ontario election, rumours were circulating that the affable lawyer had bribed a voter in order to ensure victory at the polls. Furthermore, although there is no conclusive evidence, it is possible that German took the case in the first place to raise his profile as a lawyer and as a politician. The money for Olive's defense came in dribs and drabs from various sources. The progress of the fund-raising campaign in Dunnville was perhaps typical. After hearing about the campaign, music store proprietor W.S. Moote decided to do his part to ensure its success. He set out a sheet of paper in his store, headed by the statement:

We, as citizens, believing in the right of giving to each and

every person a fair and impartial trial, and finding that
Mrs. Sternaman, now confined in Cayuga gaol on the
charge of murdering her husband claims that she has not
the money necessary to procure counsel and witnesses to
make her defence, do set aside our own opinion as to her
guilt or innocence and cheerfully pay the amounts oppo-
site our names to assist her in procuring the necessary assistance to a fair, impartial trial.

By the end of the month, the store had raised $5.20. The money was
sent to Foote in Cayuga and acknowledged by a letter which appeared in the *Chronicle* on April 8 listing the following donors:

Mrs. W.S. Moote	50c
M.M. Moote	50c
W.S. Moote	50c
Paul Honsberger	50c
Levi Werner	$1.00
J.H. Smith	50c
Mrs. J.G. Winslow	$1.00
A. Couper	25c
E. Furry	20c
Geo. H. Werner	25c

In his response to the Dunnville collection, Foote revealed that
Johnston had agreed to defend Olive at the upcoming trial. The minister also congratulated Moote and his fellow subscribers, assuring
them that they were:

engaging in a noble work. I believe God is fighting for this
woman ... You may not know all now, but I want to say
that as certain as I live the future will vindicate your
course and mine, for as I live I am convinced of this woman's innocence. I know, Mr. Moote, more about this woman's life and this case, I believe, than any living man. I
have approached it from every standpoint; I have weighed
the evidence; I have watched the woman; I have been
with her on my knees before God until her cell was a perfect Bethel; and I have risen in the tremendous conviction
clear as sunlight that she was an innocent woman. If some
of her traducers had gone into the case as [I] have, they
would find this as I did, but because of ignorance of the
case and newspaper influence they have condemned this

woman and are prejudiced. I do not blame them, but tell them to get down on their knees and ask God to get the prejudice out of their minds and they will believe as I do if they know as I do. The future will reveal something. I have wrestled with this case through the long weary hours of the night, until my brain reeled – until the awful conviction came upon me that to allow this woman to die undefended would be a legal tragedy and her blood would be upon me.

Dear friend, work for all you can – get what you can – to help us, and tell the people to reserve their judgement as to her built, but give her a fair trial. Every mother, every Briton, every true man, will give her a proper defence if he can. May our common Father help us, and God speed the right. I will be glad to hear from you again.

By this time, the defense fund had raised nearly $300. Because of Johnston's reputation, most of Olive's supporters felt it was money well spent.

Meanwhile, those who believed her guilty were generally silent, perhaps sensing that public sentiment was against them. However, there had been an effort in the House of Commons to make sure that no other convicted murderer would have the same opportunity given to Olive. On March 10, flamboyant MP Nicholas Flood Davin introduced Bill No. 65, which called for an amendment to the Criminal Code. It included the repeal of Section 748. "I have never heard a jurist of any standing who did not think that it was a mistake to introduce that clause into the Criminal Act, and therefore I propose that it shall be repealed," Davin stated. Initially, he had some support, but it died in the House within a few weeks.

By this time, Foote could report that Haldimand County had subscribed a total of $32 towards the Sternaman fund. Meanwhile, some people were calling for the government to pick up the bill for Olive's defense. An editorial in the *London News* asked provocatively if there were any good reason why the government should not pay the expenses, not only for Olive, but also for "every accused person." Referring to the London article, *Dunnville Chronicle* editor Bill Fry argued that it was a hard decision. Money was no object when government forces, such as the provincial detectives, were investigating the case. And money was no object in procuring the very best legal minds for the prosecution. Under those circumstances, Fry said, if the Crown failed to get a conviction, it deserved to.

On the other hand, a fairly strong circumstantial case is usually made out before an arrest is made, and as in many cases the accused are well enough off that they are enabled to put up a first-class defence, it would be uncalled for if the Government were to pay the expenses as The News suggests. But there are cases – such as Mrs. Sternaman's – where circumstances are different. This woman never was well to do, and her parents are known by the neighbors to be unable to help her. She was arrested and clapped into jail almost before she knew that murder was suspected. She was obliged to accept the services of such lawyers as were generous enough to take up her defence without remuneration – and it is not usually the best who do this. As everyone knows she was convicted, and by a prerogative of the Minister of Justice has been granted a new trial. Nearly all have made up their minds by this time as to the guilt or innocence of the accused. These opinions are deep set, but British fair play is not a myth, and although in the opinion of many who subscribed to the defence fund Mrs. Sternaman had a fair trial, they wish her to have a fair trial again. The Government, we believe, should assist the defence cases where it can be ascertained that no funds are available, and the public would back up the action.

By April 29, Haldimand County had subscribed a total of $73.50 towards the Sternaman fund. As the date for the trial approached, the case again dominated conversation, both in the county and elsewhere. Seeing an opportunity to tip the balance a little more in Olive's favour, reporter Phillips Thompson visited the Haldimand County Jail on April 27. In his report for *The World*, Thompson reviewed the case, noting that it had created great excitement:

> ... there is no question that the idea of a double crime intensified greatly the feeling against the prisoner and rendered the jury more ready to put the worst construction upon any points in evidence which appeared to tell against her than if the charge on which she was arraigned had only been considered ...

After describing Cayuga, the court-house and jail, Thompson relayed jailer Murphy's remarks. Olive, Murphy said, was an "exemplary prisoner," who tried to make herself useful "in any way she can." She was also quite different from other prisoners he had known.

> Generally prisoners don't talk much. They are apt to be re-
> served and sullen. With her, now, it is not so at all. To
> those in whom she has confidence she is very commu-
> nicative about herself, and wishes to discuss the whole
> case in all its details.

Olive was not quite so communicative with casual visitors and the press. She preferred to see only intimate friends, and, as for reporters, she would just as soon live without them. "They have come [and] in-terviewed her – or perhaps not seen [her] at all and written up inter-views without a word of truth in them," Murphy explained.

She willingly made an exception for Thompson, however, real-izing how vital a role his sympathetic reports had played in giving her a second chance for survival. So Thompson followed Murphy up the stairs, where the jailer unlocked the door leading to the second floor with one of his heavy keys. Then he stepped up to the bars of Olive's cell. Since the second trial had been granted, no visitors were allowed in her cell.

Olive was crotcheting when Thompson arrived. The Reverend Foote sat nearby. The reporter found the prisoner attractive, slim, "almost girlish," with a clear complexion and full lips. Possessed of a "lively and vivacious disposition," Olive seemed, in Thompson's opinion, to look as though her background were Irish, rather than German. To win her over, Thompson first asked Olive if there were any erroneous newspaper reports she wished to correct. "Yes," she replied promptly.

> There was a report in a Buffalo paper, which was copied
> all over Canada, that made me say if there was any loop-
> hole through which I could crawl I intended to do so. Now
> I never made use of any such expression. I am not looking
> for loopholes. I want everything to come out. I have noth-
> ing to conceal.

With Thompson's prompting, she explained that she had been eager to face Canadian authorities following her arrest in Buffalo but instead, on the advice of lawyers Duckwitz and Thayer and Commissioner Fairchild, she had fought extradition. She also stated that she was optimistic about the outcome of the new trial:

> They said it wouldn't be possible to get a new trial – that
> the law wouldn't permit it, but something told me that it
> would be so. Just after the trial I said to Judge Armour that
> I would have a new trial and prove my innocence and I
> held to that conviction all along. The only time I wavered
> an instant was when the good news was telegraphed from
> Ottawa and I heard Mr. Foote coming up the stairs so
> softly and quietly that I began to fear the worse. But as
> soon as I saw him I knew it was all right. Indeed, if it had-
> n't been for Mr. Foote I shouldn't be here now.

As she glanced at the minister, he explained that he had been afraid
to break the news too suddenly.

"You needn't have been," Olive said. "I was expecting it all
along."

Thompson turned to the subject of Olive's religious faith.
Quietly, she admitted that it had been a great support to her during
the ordeal, but she did not discuss it at length. For theosophist
Thompson, it was a perfect response, and his report went on at
length comparing Olive's silence on her faith to prisoners who made
a great display of religion as evidence that they had changed their
ways. But Olive had a human as well as spiritual side, and she confessed to Thompson that since January she had rarely been out in
the jail yard.

> When I thought of what might have been my fate there I
> just felt as if I never could go into that jail yard again. But
> I mustered up courage and I was glad to be out in the
> fresh air. I thought to myself if it feels so pleasant even
> being in a jail yard, what must liberty be? But I'm well
> treated here. I have nothing to complain of, and Mrs.
> Murphy is just as nice a woman as ever I saw.

"Why that's just what I thought," agreed Murphy, touching off
a wave of laughter. The interview ended pleasantly.

The *Dunnville Chronicle* reprinted Thompson's report on May 6.
That same day, a letter to the editor appeared in the newspaper.
"Candor" took issue with the circumstantial evidence and "so-called
expert testimony." Although medical experts and juries might believe such testimony, he wrote, in too many cases it was "notoriously
fallible, misleading and unreliable." He also suggested that the latest
tests would indicate that arsenic was not eliminated from the body
as quickly as testimony at the trial had alleged.

He censured the Buffalo doctors for not protecting their patient better, implying that a doctor might well have been responsible for George's demise. According to "Candor," one Buffalo druggist had told him of an incident where a doctor wrote a lethal prescription, and only the druggist's refusal to fill it had saved the patient's life. Testimony at the trial revealed that one of the doctor's prescriptions had contained a "trace" of arsenic. "Of course, we would not expect them to say enough to kill, but all the same they might kill through the mistake of a druggist or doctor – but doctors' mistakes are all buried."

Given the writer's knowledge of doctors and druggists, it is possible that the writer was himself a druggist. The letter indicates contact with Buffalo druggists, likely in a professional capacity. Furthermore, there is no hint of the town where the letter originated. The diction suggests a man of some education, and the reference to latest research into poisoning points towards someone who read scientific journals. Possibly the writer was a Dunnville druggist, either J.H. Smith or R.A. Harrison. Smith, it should be noted, had been one of Dunnville's first contributors to the Sternaman defense fund. Whether it was Smith or not, his comments were the last local reference to the case before the trial got underway.

"I have never seen the constructive talents of Mr. Johnston … more ably employed."

Olive's second trial began on May 4. Again, Britton Osler was Crown Prosecutor, but Judge Armour had been replaced by Chancellor John Boyd, one of the jurists who had turned down William German's appeal at Osgoode Hall. "A brilliant legal technician," according to reporter Hector Charlesworth, he, none the less had relatively little experience in criminal prosecution. By contrast, Olive's new defense attorney, E.F.B. Johnston, had plenty.

Ebenezer Forsyth Blackie Johnston was born in Berwickshire, Scotland in December 1850. After emigrating to Canada, he farmed for a period of time, then taught school. For a little while he also ran a newspaper, *The Critic*, in Guelph. Finally, he settled into a law career. Called to the Ontario bar in 1880, he practised in Guelph for a period, then moved to Toronto. During the Mowat administration, he was Deputy Attorney General for four years.

"A man of very acute intellect," according to Charlesworth, Johnston was a rather nervous character possessed of a "Scottish metaphysical mind." Technically brilliant, he hated to have legal issues clouded by personalities. Consequently, he rarely spoke to any of the people he defended in murder trials, or their close relatives. Instead, he relayed questions and instructions through solicitors. Again, according to Charlesworth:

> He would take the facts of the case and with the coolness of a mathematician work out a theory of possible innocence, on which he would frame a defence, and direct every question toward that end. Sometimes questions which seemed trivial and irrelevant would take on significance in the final argument. The minutiae of his defences were amazing.

In the 1890s, Johnston emerged as Brick Osler's chief rival. Johnston, who lacked the presence and authority Osler commanded, was a great admirer of his rival. Ever the cool intellectual, he turned Osler's awesome reputation to his own advantage by complimenting the older man in the courtroom. Charlesworth, who watched him at several murder trials, described this tactic:

> ... Johnston used to irritate Osler extremely by expressing admiration under conditions when it was likely to benefit his own side rather than that of his great opponent. In addressing a jury he would pay glowing tribute to the superlative abilities of the Crown Prosecutor; and plead sympathy for his client on the ground that his own humble abilities were, he feared, inadequate to secure justice. This used to make Osler furious, for it was the kind of plea he could not answer except by growls of deprecation.

With a significant segment of the public complaining that the Crown's ability to pay for the best lawyers put defendants at an unfair advantage, Johnston's tactic almost always gained sympathy for his case.

Shortly before proceedings got underway, reporters spoke to Johnston, Detective Murray, and possibly to Osler. Although no attribution was made, one report stated that the court officers were irritated by the public sympathy that had been generated for the case, and particularly by the part the Reverend Foote had played. There was also a suggestion that Johnston would object to the admissibility of the deposition taken in Buffalo during Olive's extradition hearing. Rumour was that he would put Olive on the stand to speak in her own defense, and that she was anxious to do so.

Everyone who could spare the time from farm chores or work turned out for the trial. Early in the morning, the court-house was packed. Men and boys climbed to the roof to sit on the window ledges of the cupola with their feet dangling inside the building. Some bicycled from as far away as Attercliffe Station, 25 miles distant. By the time proceedings started, several people had to be turned away.

Olive arrived, looking calm and reasonably healthy, with no hint of prison pallor, thanks to the resumption of walks in the jail yard, and no evidence of embarrassment. She took her seat in the prisoner's dock, quietly looked over the crowd, nodding and smiling when she saw an acquaintance.

The selection of the jury was far more painstaking than at the first trial. The Crown lodged 24 challenges, the defense 20. As had been predicted, Johnston opened by stating that he would challenge the admissibility of the Buffalo deposition. He requested that Osler avoid discussion of this evidence until he presented his arguments, and Osler agreed.

Osler then began his opening argument. First, he pointed out that the jury had to assume Olive was innocent. They must wipe from memory all they had heard about the previous case, all rumours, all reports of Olive's character, and focus their attention on the evidence they would hear in the court room. Based on that evidence, and that evidence alone, they must render a verdict. If it was a verdict of guilty, they must be absolutely certain of the accused's guilt. The burden of proof was upon the Crown, he reminded them.

After informing the jurors that reasonable certainty was necessary to render a guilty verdict, he warned that they must also give reasonable consideration to the facts presented by the Crown. The evidence could not be rejected solely because of its circumstantial nature. If all circumstantial evidence was ruled out, he argued, "all skilled and premeditated crime" would go unpunished.

Osler also cautioned jurors about their own views on capital punishment. Whether or not executions were justified was not the issue. Instead, they were "to administer the laws as they found them, and to decide in accordance with the evidence." He also warned them about the sympathy they might feel for Olive because she was a woman. To counter this influence, they had to keep in mind their duty and privilege as jurors to fix the standard of morals in the community. This, Osler conceded, was a great responsibility, because the lives of other people, as well as their morals, depended upon the jury's own inflexibility and uprightness.

Osler then recounted the details of George's illness and death.

He pointed out that, during part of his illness, George had been unable to feed himself or tend to any of his other needs. How, then, could he have taken poison? The irresistible conclusion was that he had been given it by the prisoner. Osler contended that accidental poisoning had to be ruled out, suggesting that Olive had planned the murder carefully. Her motive, of course, was insurance money.

Eliza Sternaman was the first Crown witness called. Just as she had done at the previous trial and hearings, she recounted the details of George's marriage, illness and death. This time, however, Johnston extracted some revealing admissions. Eliza confessed she had seen no evidence of "unwifely conduct," and that, in fact, she and Olive had been on friendly terms during George's illness. Furthermore, despite her suspicions regarding poison, Eliza had made no attempt to remove her son from Olive's care. Her daughter-in-law, she admitted, was faithful and attentive. And, given all her suspicions and her son's premature demise, she had sworn the complaint against Olive only after she had written to Olive "in a friendly spirit" asking for $25.

Dr. Philip Park was next. Again, George's symptoms were reviewed, but this time Park admitted to Johnston that he would not have been able to maintain the arsenic poison theory if no arsenic had been found in the body after exhumation. Park's admission was undoubtedly more reflective of his own inexperience with poison than with the facts. Nevertheless, his testimony further confused the jury as to whether or not George had been poisoned.

Following Philip Hartwick's testimony about Eliza and Olive's conversation concerning insurance, Johnston asked that Olive's Buffalo deposition be declared inadmissible. Perhaps his plan was to put Olive on the stand so that jurors could assess their veracity for themselves. If the Buffalo deposition was inadmissible, he would, in effect, be starting with a clean slate. Boyd, however, refused to grant the request, and court adjourned for lunch.

In the afternoon, Dr. T.T. S. Harrison reiterated his evidence from the first trial. This time, however, the fluid mentioned in David Thompson's affidavit came under close scrutiny and Harrison stated, as he had in the letter to the editor of the *Chronicle*, that he believed it to be bloody serum, not embalming fluid.

At 2 p.m., Dr. Edward Frost took the stand. Again, he recounted the details of George's illness. He described George as an emotional and neurotic individual. He also stated that the letters George had written were just what he would have expected from such a man, given his emotional and mental health. As for Olive's objection to hospitalization, it did not surprise him, considering the long walk it would have entailed for her with two young children in tow.

Dr. Phelps and Annie Franklin followed. Annie, now recovered from the effects of her most recent pregnancy, first said Olive had given George his medicine after midnight on the night of his death. Under close questioning, she changed her testimony, claiming the medicine had been administered between 9 p.m. and midnight.

Then Drs. Rich and Parmenter went over the details of Elon Chipman's death. Both agreed that his symptoms were consistent with arsenic poisoning, and that they were similar to those George had experienced. Testimony regarding the insurance policies followed. The day ended with the reading of Olive's deposition into the record.

Witnesses called the next day included Dr. David Thompson, who told the court that the fluid found in George's thoracic cavity was not at all unusual. He added that he had sworn out an affidavit because the Reverend Foote seemed to think it was important. Dr. Ellis and his assistant, Edith Curzon, both reported on the analyses they had made. In addition to searching for arsenic, they had tested for lead and zinc, but found neither.

The undertakers, John and Abraham Snider, were called to the stand as well. This time, Abraham was first. He attested that there could not have been any embalming done because his father's account book would shown the charges. John Snider took the stand after lunch. He was questioned closely regarding his preparation of the body. Initially, he swore that he had only lifted George from the bed to the coffin. When reminded that he had testified at one of the hearings that he had punctured the intestines to let gases escape, he conceded that if he had made the statement, he supposed it was true. But it was pointed out to him that he had subsequently contradicted himself. After some tough re-examination by Osler, Snider finally admitted that the Sternaman funeral had not made an unusual impression on him, and that therefore there was no reason why he would recall any particular details vividly.

Olive's aunt, Olive Walker, and Olive's mother both took the stand. Their testimony centred on a visit to Snider, where he had admitted to embalming the body. Under Osler's questioning, however, Olive Walker changed her story. Snider had only shown the books to them, she said, to prove that he had not charged for embalming.

The final witness was a doctor from Toronto, Arthur Jukes Johnson, whose grandfather, Lieutenant-Colonel John Johnson, a former officer in the East India Company, had settled in the Dunnville area in 1836. Dr. Johnson's parents, William Arthur Johnson and Laura Jukes, were the first couple whose marriage was recorded in Dunn Township. William later became a prominent Anglican minister and friend of Dr. William Osler. Johnson was an expert on poisons who, on many occasions, had served as an expert witness for the Crown and a consultant for B.B. Osler. He told the court that he had listened carefully to all the testimony, and, based on what he had heard, he was convinced that George had indeed died of arsenic poisoning.

At this point, E.F.B. Johnston moved that the case should not be tried, because, if any crime had been committed, it had occurred in Buffalo. This may have been a diversionary tactic more than anything else. The matter of jurisdiction had been argued at length before the first trial took place. Perhaps Johnston was trying to create an impression that he was grasping at straws in order to lull Osler into a false sense of security. At any rate, Boyd rejected the motion. After a brief recess for dinner, the court resumed again. Johnston rose and said the Crown had no new evidence. Osler and several reporters now realized that Johnston's defense would consist of discrediting the testimony of Crown witnesses, a process he had already begun during his lengthy cross-examinations. Many years later, after Johnston had won all but one of a score of murder cases, Charlesworth would recall his performance in the Haldimand County Court-house:

> I have never seen the constructive talent of Mr. Johnston as a defence counsel more ably employed, for it was his task not only to give a new colouring to testimony in behalf of the Crown but also to that of several of his own witnesses, whose evidence at the first trial was a matter of record. When answers conflicted with those given a few months previously they asserted they would have made matters clearer if they had been questioned in the proper way. His subtlest move was to call the undertaker and induce him to refresh his memory to the extent of admitting that he might have squirted a little embalming fluid into the body ... He rode over Crown experts roughshod, and fought a drawn battle with Dr. Arthur Jukes Johnson and Dr. Harrison of Selkirk, unbreakable witnesses who had amazed the Buffalo doctors by their adroitness in the witness box and their knowledge of their subject.

In his characteristically slow and deliberate speech, Johnston proceeded to his summation, which one reporter described as a "strong, vigorous appeal." He played heavily on the emotions of the jurors, drawing attention to Olive's forlorn state and the strain imposed by the court proceedings of the past two years.

> Twice for her life. Twice within the shadow of the gallows, and of death. Twenty long months of imprisonment hanging over her head. Life is sweet to all of us, and doubly sweet because of those we love. Such is the life that I stand pleading for, not the life of a man, strong, vigorous, active and young, but the life of a poor, defenceless, lone woman, so defenceless that to make her defence she has to depend on the charity of the Crown to get the evidence she has produced here. So penniless that she has to depend on the pittance of charity of friends to bring me here to perform whatever feeble service I may have rendered ... I stand alone against terrible odds. From the Crown Counsel to the lowest detective, I feel that I cannot make a fair fight against such odds, I cannot cope with the strong pressure that has been brought to bear against this woman.

He described her as a woman prosecuted by her enemies, whose life had been exposed to the callous gaze of the public. And, as if that were not enough, the most brilliant criminal lawyer in the country had been enlisted to bring her to justice. All the machinery of the Crown had been put in motion to this end.

It was a classic appeal, and classic Johnston, based on sympathy and emotionalism, with Olive painted as the unfortunate female underdog. In rural Haldimand, women worked as hard as men in the fields and barns, but the Victorian illusion of female weakness and dependence persisted. In fact, Johnston was counting upon that illusion and the prevalent notion of "chivalric justice" to save Olive's neck. According to the popular mythology of the late–19th century, women not only lacked men's physical and mental power, but also were more likely to succumb to immorality, especially if they belonged to the working class. As champions of the weak, men were expected to show mercy, even in the dispensation of justice. Time and again, women had escaped the gallows because of chivalric justice. Now Olive Sternaman stood before the court, and, if she was an innocent woman, she had been doubly wronged: first, because she had been arrested for a crime she had not committed; secondly, because the full force of a powerful justice system had been brought to bear against her. It must have been nearly impossible for the jurors not to feel some pity for Olive as they listened to Johnston, particularly when the unfortunate woman sat a few feet away from them, handkerchief to her eyes, sometimes sobbing audibly.

But Johnston wanted an acquittal motivated by more than emotion. He wanted a decision that was legally sound. "I want no verdict of sympathy," he insisted. "I want a verdict of truth and justice. Though this woman be the guiltiest alive, I maintain that the Crown has not brought it home to her." To prove his point, he catalogued the Crown witnesses. Coroner David Thompson was "a blowhard," undertaker John Snider was "a perjurer," the insurance agents were "persecutors of a low type," and, as for Eliza Sternaman, she was Olive's arch-enemy.

It took Johnston 4 hours and 20 minutes to complete his address, which he ended with a plea to the jury to return Olive to her little children. The court adjourned for lunch, and then Osler had his turn. Typically, his arguments were cool and logical. "Anyone who kisses may also kill," he told the jury, calling to mind numerous instances of marital murder. He also maintained that it was the duty of the defense to prove that embalming had not been performed, not vice versa. His arguments were far more concise than Johnston's had been and he was finished in two hours.

For the most part, Osler's prosecution was as solid and compelling as it had been at the first trial. There might have been a little less enthusiasm at having to cover the same ground a second time. There was also an undercurrent of frustration as witness after witness avoided the unequivocal statements they had made during the first trial. In addition, Osler was perceptive enough to realize that, thanks to the public controversy, he could no longer play the role of society's avenging angel. That part now went to Johnston, whose brilliance alone might have bested Osler in a difficult trial. As it was, Johnston hardly needed to exercise his formidable skill at all. He only had to provide witnesses an opportunity to recant the damning testimony they had given at the first trial, to soften their position enough to persuade the jury that reasonable doubt existed. Most witnesses were eager to co-operate. After that, all that was required of Johnston was a summary of the defense and a final appeal to the jury's emotions.

Chancellor Boyd then addressed the jury. Befitting his position, he was impartial, touching on the important arguments presented by both parties, and pointing out biases. There was no evidence of persecution as Johnston had argued. The American insurance agents were simply doing their job. However, Boyd did stress that Johnston's questioning had raised some strong points especially about the presence or absence of embalming fluid. As far as the suicide theory went, though, Boyd had a hard time accepting this. It was difficult, he said, to understand why a suicide would call in a doctor, or go through the farce of consenting to hospitalization.

The jury retired at 5:30 p.m. Olive was taken back to her cell, while the crowd waited. At 7 p.m., the jury sent word it could not agree. Boyd sent back a note telling them to come to a decision. The debate continued in the jury chambers. Finally, at 9:30, the jurors reached a verdict. Olive was sent for, the judge took his place and the jury filed in, flanked on either side by the constables with their bright red badges.

A hush descended on the courtroom as the jury was polled, and the clerk asked the foreman if they had arrived at a verdict.

"Not guilty."

The courtroom broke into shouting and cheers. Moments later, when the noise subsided, Boyd ordered Olive to rise. For the first time, everyone in the courtroom could see how she had been affected. Her face was flushed, tears flowed down her cheeks and her legs seemed unable to hold her. Boyd told her she was free and the crowd surged forward to congratulate her. There were more cheers, more good wishes, and, somehow, Olive was escorted back to the jail house for the last time. Ten minutes later, a reporter slipped in to record her reaction.

"I can't realize it, I can't realize it," she was saying, her hands covering her face.

> It seems like a dream. I feel as if I would have to go back to the court room and be tried again to-morrow. I won't realize it for days! I felt sure I would get off, though, until the jury disagreed. Then I gave up. I didn't want to live. I'd just as soon have died as go through another trial. I thought that if the jury disagreed after all Mr. Johnston said I might as well give up. Mr. Johnston is the best lawyer in the world. At least I don't think there is any better lawyer in the world than him.

She talked volubly for some time and, eventually, referred to William German. For him, she had little praise. "He couldn't get me off because he wouldn't accept my word that I was innocent. I knew all the time he thought I was guilty."

Jailer Murphy, who was standing nearby, rebuked her, pointing out that German's efforts had won her a new trial. Undaunted, Olive continued, but the lack of gratitude towards her first defense lawyer left a bad impression with some of the people in the room, including Hector Charlesworth. German may have lost the first case, but his efforts had helped persuade authorities to grant a new trial, and Olive's criticism seemed singularly ungracious.

Asked about her plans, she replied, "I'm going to Buffalo next week, and I'm going to work there. I'm going to make it hot for those devils the insurance men. You'll see what I'll do." She also mentioned one of the witnesses, a Buffalo insurance man, by name, although his identity was not revealed in newspaper reports. "I'm going to go back with a witness and pay him back in a way he'll remember. I'm going to have articles put in the Buffalo papers about those insurance men."

"I supposed your means are exhausted?" one reporter asked.

"Yes, but I don't care about the means if I have my liberty."

Moments later, family helped her out of the court-house. Ecstatic with her new found freedom, she would not walk on the sidewalk, but kicked her feet in the dirt of the road instead. Then she climbed into a wagon and was driven home to Rainham.

"Mrs. Sternman looked calm and seemed to feel confident."

"She broke down completely and gave way to hysterical weeping"

Throughout the trial, newspaper reports had frequently commented upon Olive's composure. For many, her ability to face a murder trial calmly proved she had the coolness needed to commit a pre-meditated murder. Stereotyped as sensitive and emotional, women, supposedly, unable to hide their feelings under pressure. Paradoxically, on the occasions when Olive broke down and wept, some interpreted it as remorse, a certain sign of a guilty conscience.

Descriptions provided by Wallace Thayer, who knew Olive better than any reporter, suggest that she was calm, phlegmatic and definitely not the nervous type. But she was also depicted joking with friends, enjoying lighthearted conversation, or weeping bitterly. Like most humans, she was far more complex than words can describe. Underlying her apparent cool exterior there was a warm, vivacious nature, carefully kept in check.

There is a rural tradition of taciturnity. Sometimes interpreted as stupidity by outsiders, it arises from the knowledge that in a close-knit community almost everything one says is bound to be repeated to relatives, neighbours, friends and business associates. The Victorian adage that "children should be seen and not heard" was also applied to women. Voiceless in society, many women, especially working-class women, were not comfortable speaking outside their own circle of family and friends. In many situations, the ability to keep silent, to give no hint of one's feelings, was a definite asset. Certainly it was useful in domestic service, as Olive had no doubt learned. It was natural for her to fall back on years of habit and training, to drop a curtain of apparent indifference between herself and those who watched her every move. But, Olive was not indifferent. She, too, was watching, trying to guess at her fate in the reactions of the jurymen, court officers, reporters and spectators. Caught in a crisis few people ever experience, she was sometimes overwhelmed by emotion. But she usually recovered quickly and again slipped behind the stolid, silent facade she believed respectable women should present to the world.

For nearly two years, Olive Sternaman had felt the harsh glare of public attention focused on her. Her triumph at her acquittal did not mean the glare was about to diminish. Newspaper reporters and, presumably, the people for whom they wrote, were anxious to see the last chapter of the drama played out. Would she get her insurance? And what about romance? Soon after her release, rumours circulated that she would soon marry a businessman who had begun his courtship in the Haldimand County jail. Everyone waited to see what would happen next.

PART SIX

AFTERMATH

"The policy ... has been eaten up in the cost of her defence."

Olive spent two weeks visiting with family and friends in
Rainham and South Cayuga. Then, somewhat recovered from
her ordeal, she returned to Buffalo, passing through Dunnville
on Saturday, May 21. She went to live with Elon's sister, Dora
Bonestead, amid rumours that she was planning to marry for a third
time.

Shortly after her trial, when asked about the insurance policies,
Olive told a reporter that she would "refuse to touch a dollar of their
dirty money." As it turned out, she had little choice. Prior to her extradition hearing, she assigned part of the proceeds from the insurance to Wallace Thayer; later, she offered the remainder to William
German. German was not interested in the money, but Thayer, who
had worked above and beyond the call of duty to get Olive acquitted, was. He insisted on pursuing legal action against Metropolitan.

On May 28, Charles R. Roberts travelled to Toronto on behalf of
the Metropolitan Life Insurance Company. He spent some time with
the Deputy Attorney General discussing Olive's lawsuit for $1000 in-
surance on her late husband's life.

The first hearing in the Sternaman lawsuit was set for June 15,
under United States Supreme Court Justice Laughlin. According to a
Dunnville Chronicle report of June 10, the Company would argue that it
was justified in withholding payment, on the grounds that Olive had
murdered her husband:

> If she succeeds in beating the company this time, the case
> will, of course, be appealed and carried to the highest
> court, thus rolling up an immense bill of costs. Even
> should she succeed in the end, there will be nothing for
> her, for the greater part of the amount of the policy, $1800,
> has been eaten up in the costs of her defence on the
> charge of murder. It is a case where the lawyers benefit in
> any event.

Olive's lawsuit was dismissed in the Buffalo court. According to a witness called by the defense lawyer for Metropolitan, George had misrepresented his physical condition to the company doctor. Instead of being in good health, as he had claimed, he had a host of ailments, all of which had been well–documented in the two murder trials. Thayer did some quick legal backtracking, trying to amend his plea, but Mr. Justice Laughlin threw the case out. Thayer immediately began the process that would lead to a second trial.

This time, observers speculated that Metropolitan would take another tack. According to the *Hamilton Spectator*:

> the Metropolitan Insurance company will set up an ab–
> solute defense of murder if the case comes to court, which
> will mean that the question of Mrs. Sternaman's innocence
> or guilt will be practically tried over again in the civil
> courts at Buffalo. The Canadian verdict of 'Not guilty' does
> not preclude any such defense on the other side of the
> line.

With yet another legal battle looming before her, Olive tried to live as normally as possible. She could not avoid media attention, however. Her presence alone was enough to warrant mention in the newspapers, such as the *Dunnville Chronicle*, which reported she passed through that town on July 23.

Her journeys back and forth between Buffalo and Haldimand County may not have been newsworthy, but her third marriage certainly was. On October 28, 1898, she married Frank Crentzbourg of Buffalo in Niagara Falls, New York. Her willingness to contract a third marriage after the tragic consequences of her second suggests either blind optimism or economic necessity, probably more the latter than the former. Ellen Chipman was aging, and although Walter and Albert were now in school, they were still young enough to need a mother's attention. The results of her first brush with Metropolitan in civil court made it clear to Olive that she would probably spend a great deal of time involved in litigation over the next several months. It would be difficult to find and keep a job under such conditions, and perhaps she had already experienced a certain amount of prejudice from prospective employers. So she married Crentzbourg.

Little is known about him, although he may have been the businessman who had visited her in the Haldimand County jail. At any rate, it was an ill–starred union. By March 1900, Olive filed for separation papers, claiming her husband had a living wife. Years later, Charlesworth related another possible reason for the separation.

In *Candid Chronicles*, he wrote:

> ... she proved a good wife, but one day her husband had
> a severe attack of cramps. It was a paltry matter but he
> made the nonsensical accusation that she was trying to
> poison him. He was alleged to have said that if he ever
> had another attack of the kind he would not wait for the
> end but kill her on the instant. Not being able to control
> the forces of Nature sufficiently to guarantee him against
> an occasional attack of cramps she decided that the course
> of safety lay in leaving him, and whether she ever re-
> turned to him I cannot say.

She did not. She resumed the name of her first husband, Elon
Chipman, and never married again. Charlesworth's story, which he
attributed to a Haldimand MPP, may have been apocryphal, but it
was one of the most enduring legends surrounding the case, and a
version of it was still circulating in Haldimand County as late as
1990. Charlesworth also recorded another legend: that a railwayman
had seen Olive give George medicine as the train crossed the border
between the United States and Canada in August 1896. Her motive
was to confound authorities by administering poison in an area over
which neither Canada nor the U.S. had clear jurisdiction. No such
testimony was every admitted during either murder trial, however.

Metropolitan absolutely refused to settle out of court. The case
was appealed and, in early 1900, it was overturned again. Wallace
Thayer appealed once more on Olive's behalf. On February 26, 1902,
a Buffalo Court of Appeals ruled that she should receive payment
from Metropolitan.

The ruling in Olive's favour had been won on the questions of
whether a doctor in the pay of an insurance company could func-
tion as the agent of the applicant. As the applicant's agent, any errors
the doctor made in filling out an insurance application would be at-
tributable to the applicant. If information proved erroneous at a later
date, the applicant's claim could be disallowed. "The Court of
Appeals decided that by no use of English can an insurance company make its agent, selected, hired and paid by itself, the agent of
the insured, so that his alleged errors shall prevent recovery."

Metropolitan, one of the four largest insurance companies in
the United States by this time, had nearly limitless resources at its
disposal, and refused to let matters lie. The case went all the way to
the Supreme Court of the United States, with Metropolitan again
arguing that George had been murdered. On October 12 1903, the

ruling came down: Olive was awarded $1431.68 – the insurance plus costs.

A final appeal was launched by Metropolitan. This one was settled on March 23, 1905. Olive was awarded the insurance, plus court costs. Most of the money went to pay her lawyers.

"It is said that Sternaman was as likely to do it as she was."

Little is known about the rest of Olive's life. She did stay in Buffalo and raised her boys to adulthood. Walter and Albert eventually married, producing eight children between them, including one who remembered his paternal grandmother as his favourite family member. By the time Olive died in 1941, few people could recall the sensational murder trial that had fascinated two nations. For those who did remember, one nagging question would always remain – who killed George Sternaman?

The evidence generated by the trials and newspaper discussion suggests four possibilities: 1) George died of natural causes; 2) George was accidentally poisoned; 3) George was deliberately poisoned by someone; 4) George committed suicide. Early newspaper reports and German's arguments suggested death by disease was possible and that embalming was the only reason for the presence of arsenic in George's body. However, John Snider's testimony was so unreliable that it seems certain that George had not been embalmed. Neither Harrison nor Park found any evidence for it. And Dr. William Ellis, in response to a question posed by a juror, explained that if George had been embalmed, he would have expected to find comparatively higher traces on the outside of his liver than inside the organ. Ellis, however, found more poison inside. It seems, therefore, that the introduction of arsenic through the embalming process must be ruled out and with it any possibility that George died of disease.

"Candor" raised the question of accidental poisoning, something Olive herself had suggested. Dr. Frost did, indeed, prescribe medication containing arsenic, "Between the 20th and 30th June I used a few small doses of a mild arsenical preparation; very minute doses," he testified at the first trial. "The amount that he took altogether would not exceed one-thirtieth of a grain of the arsenite of copper." But the similarity of Elon's symptoms must also be considered. Was he accidentally poisoned, too? He and George were not treated by the same physician, so that it seems unlikely that a similar, lethal dosage was prescribed. Furthermore, in view of the publicity surrounding the case, if such a doctor was practising medicine in Buffalo in the late 1890s, he surely would have drawn attention to himself sooner or later.

Could an incompetent druggist have prepared the poison that killed George? Possibly. It is not clear whether the one druggist who testified, Dr. George W. Sales, was the one who filled the prescriptions written for either George or Elon. In fact, the druggist's involvement and the possibility of an accidental dosage was barely discussed at the trial. Again, the similarity between George's illness and Elon's suggest the same cause. The argument applicable to an incompetent doctor also applies here. If one druggist prepared the lethal medication for both men, he likely would have done so for others. Again, no mention of a deadly druggist has ever surfaced.

Of course, it is possible that Olive had George's prescription filled by a different druggist from the one who provided Elon's medicine. If she did, it seems logical to expect that that fact would have surfaced at the trial as yet one more link in the chain of damning circumstantial evidence. It did not.

George and Elon's similar occupations might also have led them to similar deaths. Arsenic is an ingredient in yellow and green paint and wallpaper. If food is contaminated by these items, or if an individual is exposed to them for long periods of time, arsenic poisoning might result. As carpenters, both Elon and George worked on job sites where paint and wallpaper were present. However, there is no evidence that they ever worked on the same site. Furthermore, if contaminants were present on the job, it seems other workers would have fallen ill. Had this happened, given the publicity surrounding the case, the authorities surely would have been notified. They were not, and it is highly unlikely that two men living in the same house should be the only victims of "accidental" poisoning.

It seems, therefore, that the arsenic in George's body was put there deliberately, leaving for consideration the third and fourth alternatives, murder and suicide.

If the circumstantial evidence presented in Buffalo and Cayuga is accepted, it seems certain that both Elon and George died of the same cause, arsenic poisoning. Eliminating Elon as a suspect, there are only two possible poisoners, George and Olive. No inquest was ever held into Elon Chipman's death, thus, many of the details will never be known. But there is no doubt that both George and Olive had equal opportunity to poison him. The one fragment of evidence that suggests otherwise is the report that Olive prepared lunches for both men. This testimony was considered important by both lawyers and jurors, all of whom seem to have accepted without question the traditional division of labour in Victorian households. It is almost as if each man who heard the evidence thought, "The arsenic was in the lunches, the lunches were prepared by the woman, therefore the woman must have poisoned the lunches."

But there was also evidence that both George and Elon helped with household chores. And, although Olive would certainly have handled most domestic work, the men must have had have access to the kitchen. There is also evidence that George avoided encounters with the Chipmans' family and friends, suggesting he could come and go pretty much as he pleased. Is it not possible, then, that George had the opportunity to tamper with Elon's lunch?

B.B. Osler himself noted that there was no indication of a sexual liaison between George and Olive prior to their marriage in February 1896. Under these circumstances, it seems unlikely that the pair plotted Elon's demise. One of them must have acted alone, and that one was George. Three pieces of testimony are particularly telling in this regard: his emotional reaction to Olive's life-threatening illness, his sudden interest in religion following Elon's death and his violent anger whenever the photograph of Elon was left uncovered.

Enough testimony was presented at the trials to convince many that George might have murdered Elon in order to marry Olive. What many, including Armour and Boyd, found difficult to accept was the possibility that George had also committed suicide. Boyd thought it farcical that a man attempting suicide would allow a doctor to examine him or agree to hospitalization. And, in his charge to the jury, Armour had commented,

> If a man commits suicide he generally does it by one impetuous, rash act. He may cut his throat; he may hang or drown himself; he may take poison; but he takes enough or intends to take enough to deprive him of life. We do not find a man taking poison and continuing to take it from time to time to put an end to himself.

Yet Armour must have encountered chronic alcoholics and drug addicts many times during his career. It requires little imagination to see that these individuals were slowly poisoning themselves.

Armour could not accept even the possibility that George was responsible for Elon's death. A short time earlier, he dismissed the idea:

> It is said that Sternaman was as likely to do it as she was.

> If Sternaman had known of it, if Sternaman had done it,
> he would have known what he did it with. He would have
> known the kind of poison he used and when he was get-
> ting the same sort of poison himself he would have
> known of it.

By inference, it appears that Armour and the first jury would easily have accepted George as the murderer of Elon Chipman, but only if they were convinced that George was capable of committing suicide by arsenic poisoning. Psychiatry was still in its infancy, although a few pioneers were active in Canada, and some had been expert witnesses at the Valentine Shortis trial. But a knowledge of mental disorders and their consequences was not a part of a typical 19th-century jurist's courtroom arsenal. After a century's exposure to Freudian theory and almost daily exposure to pop psychology, however, modern readers are apt to conclude, and rightly so, that George Sternaman was an exceedingly troubled young man. George's spells, which, by his own admission, often resulted when he was feeling downhearted and his tantrums indicate some form of mental illness, possibly schizophrenia or depression. Physical ailments, including stomach problems, sometimes accompany mental disorders. In addition, some mental illnesses – including schizophrenia – frequently shows up when the victim is in his late teens or early 20s.

From the distance of nearly a century it would be nearly impossible to make an accurate diagnosis of George's mental health. However, there are clues which indicate some of the stresses he suffered. His home environment was not a happy one. The letters and trial transcripts which survive portray Eliza Sternaman as a possessive, domineering woman, one who wanted to control her adult son, yet who resented leaving her household in order to visit him even during a serious illness. Her letter to Olive after George's death, in which she asked for $25, suggests parsimony and greed, as well as a notable lack of empathy. George's younger brothers gave little hint of any fraternal affection. One, Avery, was courting his future wife during George's final illness, and married her just as the investigation into the case began. And, by their own admission, both Avery and Freeman gave little thought to George's condition or their mother's suspicions.

The situation at home may have been one of the reasons George decided to move to Buffalo at the age of 20. Although he could shake the heavy Haldimand clay off his boots, he could not drop the burden of his upbringing and personality as easily. His possessiveness, his jealousy, his petulance and the mysterious spells went with him to the United States. And, if the rumours that floated around Haldimand County at the time of the trials are to be believed, so did a decided tendency towards self-destruction.

During the trials, old acquaintances of George said he had talked about suicide, presumably while still living in Canada. His sudden illness when it seemed Olive was dying is consistent with ingestion of poison. Why he would pick that particular method is open to speculation. Perhaps he considered it less prosaic or less violent than shooting himself, hanging or falling in front of a train. Perhaps he saw poisoning as a way to achieve a modicum of fame: suicides who took poison often received considerable space in the newspapers of the day.

George may have preferred poisoning for other reasons, too. First, it gave him greater control of his physical condition – he could ingest miniscule quantities without killing himself outright, an alternative that few other methods offered. Toying with poison also offered an element of excitement, akin to a modern young man's compulsion to drive at breakneck speeds regardless of danger.

Secondly, poison allowed George to have greater control of those around him. By ingesting just enough to become sick, he could put himself at the centre of attention and receive the sympathy and love he desperately desired. It was no accident that George became ill just when the honeymoon period of his marriage was ending. Hadn't he told Olive that he wanted to be sick for a long time so that she would never leave him? George, it seems, would go to great lengths to get what he wanted even to the extent of risking his life. As long as he lay suffering in bed, his wife hovered around him, devoting her entire attention to his needs, his whims, his comfort. For a time, the gamble paid off. George not only succeeded in keeping Olive by his side, but he also got himself back to his mother's house, where Eliza would also be touched by his condition. As she observed his suffering, perhaps her disapproval regarding his marriage would vanish, or so George might have reasoned. Most certainly she could not ignore him. As George undoubtedly realized, his return to Rainham under such unfortunate circumstances would be a favourite topic of local discussion for many days. Perhaps that was why, when Dr. Harrison first called on him, he found "his countenance good and hopeful." Harrison assumed it was because George expected to get better. Given George's character, however, what Harrison might have seen was a man who was ecstatically happy because his illness had made him the centre of attention.

Still, Harrison's remark raises yet another question. Did George expect to recover? If he had killed Elon, he knew how lethal arsenic was. The course of his own illness suggests that initially he received considerably less arsenic that Elon had. For a time, doctors actually believed George might recover. Although testimony does not offer enough information, it is possible that whenever George seemed to be recuperating, Olive's attention wandered to other, less pressing, concerns. It is equally possible that in order to stop this, George took another dose of arsenic, merely planning to prolong his illness. Eventually, however, the cumulative effects took their toll and re-covery became impossible. But even imminent death had its com-pensations: George might have reasoned that his picture would replace Elon's in Olive's parlour; in effect, he would have achieved a kind of domestic sainthood.

Of course, there was always the possibility that Olive might marry again, but George had taken steps to prevent this with the cu-rious letter requesting an autopsy, which he had composed early in his illness. His motivation, he stated, was to clear Olive because he knew of the suspicions directed at her following Elon's death. On the surface, the letter seems the work of an innocent man, a lovestruck young husband unable to imagine his wife as a murderess. But below the surface there is evidence of a cunning and twisted mind at work. The mere mention of the circumstances of Elon's death was enough to revive suspicions that Olive had murdered him. At the same time, by posing as a loving and unsuspecting husband, con-cerned only with his wife's welfare, George diverted suspicion away from himself. Almost automatically, those suspicions would land at Olive's door and, this time, George's letter would guarantee an in-vestigation – one that would find definite traces of arsenic. Then the law would take its course. Whatever the outcome, George would emerge triumphant: Olive's execution or life imprisonment would preclude a third marriage and, as Charlesworth's anecdote proves, acquittal would not restore her reputation to a point where she could live happily with another husband. The stakes were high, but George won. As long as any record of the murder trials survives, Olive and George are joined together forever.

APPENDIX A

A Selection of Letters to David Mills

*Written from Toronto, December 22, 1897, on stationery from the
Hartley House, Walkerton.*

Hon. David Mills, Senator
Ottawa

Dear Sir

There seems to be a growing sentimentality in this country against the Death penalty for murderers and notably just now in the case of those sentenced to be hanged in the months of January and Feby. And especially so in the case of Mrs. Sternaman.

Her friends are moving for a commutation = I think you will agree with me that she is either Innocent or Guilty = If innocent, commutation would be a wrong perpetrated against her & she should go free – If she is guilty, it was [one of] the most diabolical crimes ever perpetrated in this country. She slowly and by [poison] has murdered a man (her husband) in love with her who believed she was in Love with him.

These are the facts, if she is guilty and if guilty I do not see any reason for a commutation any more than in the case of any other murderer. It may be that the sympathy extended towards her is because she is a woman. But such was not considered in the case of Phoebe Campbell who was hanged in London for the murder of her husband with the supposed aid of an accomplice. In the Campbell case, she beat her husband to death in a few minutes.

In the Sternaman case he was poisoned slowly for weeks, deliberately poisoned by some one and as she was the only attendant all these weeks I suppose is the reason why the jury & judge believed her guilty.

I believe there was a miscarriage of justice in the commutation of Shortis the Murderer of Valleyfield. The great majority of the people believe he should have been hanged & believe the commutation was secured through the powerful influence of the Church & large expenditures of money. There was no doubt of his guilt–but that often set up plea of Insanity secured his commutation.

It is time this flimsy plea of Insanity had its quietus if we are going to adhere to the death penalty for murder, & especially so if there was a motive for the murder as in the Shortis case (viz money)

There seemed to many to have been a necessity for commutation in the Harvey case of Guelph, in as much as he had no motive for the murder of his family which he loved so much, except it was his pride which would not allow him to see his family come to want. But the then Minister of Justice did not interfere. The case of the young man Hammond, sentenced for the poisoning of Katie Tough his wife is on a par with the Sternaman case.

Do you not think that much of the reason for petitions & letters asking for the commutation of Mrs. S. is because she is a woman and also because a number of people do not believe in capital punishment for murder?

I am inclined to think that in many cases even jurymen hold out against the death penalty because they do not believe in it, and in several instances a guilty man goes free.

Yours &c

C.G. Scott

154 Rose Avenue

Toronto

St. Thomas   Jan 17/981

Hon. David Mills Q.C.
  Minister of Justice
  Ottawa

Dear Mr. Mills

  re Sternaman

In the interest of justice of the cause of humanity for the sake of my country's name I am impelled to write you to spare the life of this unfortunate woman, who if the arm of mercy does not rescue her will, in the minds of thousands of good Canadians, be, on the 20th of this month, the victim of a judicial murder.

There may have been a time when we were too lenient. We are living in a time when the blood thirsty detective, with his thousands of the people's money at his disposal and the bristling fame of a certain criminal lawyer are gloating and dancing at the verdict of "guilty" and becoming proud over the death sentences passed upon their victims. We are reaching a dangerous extreme.

I have read law but I am not a lawyer. I must however submit that this admission of the evidence as to the death of the first husband is in spirit unsound, is contrary to the general principle of our law inasmuch as it is a presumption of guilt instead of a presumption of innocence as is the guiding principle of British criminal law. The safe rule has been not to give evidence of bad character except to refute evidence as to character for the defence. Under a new name–to prove motive–the courts are laying down the rule that if a man commits one crime, the probabilities are clear th[at] he has committed all the similar crimes of which he may be subsequently charged. This new departure is a dangerous one in itself and should not be given an enlarged hearing.

In this case I submit that there are special reasons why as Minister of Justice you should rule against its application

(1) In the case followed by the learned judges the other offences charged against the prisoner were offences which could be made an issue in that very court. There was full jurisdiction. While I believe the whole principle is so unsound that if ever I am honored with a seat in the Canadian Parliament I will do my best to have it wiped out of our law, yet if judges must follow it at all, it should only be in cases which they either have the right to investigate or which have previously been investigated by a court of competent jurisdiction. In this case if the first husband was poisoned by the prisoner or by any one else the offence was committed in the United States, out of our jurisdiction. It was not proved against the prisoner there and it was not an offence against our statutes but against the statues of the United States, an offence which we had no jurisdiction over and consequently no legal proof could be offered upon it in our courts. I submit that an important point has either been overlooked or given a narrow construction, that viewed as a citizen or a legislator would view it the principle was improperly applied.

(2) That even if this dangerous law be unfortunately ours, the prisoner was placed at such a disadvantage owing to its application she had no change. The other offence charged occurred years before it occurred in a foreign state. The wealth of the crown was used to hunt up evidence which was ingeniously designed to show suspicion, while the prisoner was poor, could not spend the money necessary to met it and had every reason to expect that it would not have to be met. What chance has a poor prisoner against such odds?

(3) Viewing this matter broadly it seems to me that the American Government may have some objections to raise against our taking one of their citizens to the gallows on a verdict reached in the main by evidence proving an offence against their law & not against ours. When they surrendered Mrs. Sternaman under the Extradition treaty it was not to be tried for the murder of her first husband. That was their affair and the jurisdiction for its investigation lay in their courts.

(4) The weakness of the crown case is shown by their failure to prove the possession of poison by the prisoner. If she systematically used poison it could have been proved.

(5) If she intended murdering her husband she would not have brought him to the home of her mother–in–law.

(6) The most cruel argument was used that because of her close attention to him she poisoned him. What is a wife who holds insurance on her husband's life to do? Must she to clear herself of the charge of being a murderess turn away from his death bed be no more his watcher by day and night, leave him to the care of others or hang by the neck till she be dead?

I have watched with serious interest the progress of the detective and the newspaper combination in these cases. It is safer to say that the pandering to the detective force by the newspaper reporters for their material gain has decided more cases than the evidence given in the courts for the last five years. A Government detective wants convictions, newspapers want sensations. The detective and the reporters work hand in hand and communities are educated into a belief of guilt so that it is next to impossible to get a fair jury.

This woman an alien brings her sick husband home to his own friends they all [know] to die. If she had not watched by him she would have never been called and, since she watched by him she must hang.

If we were let it be on the side of mercy. If she be guilty of murder the Great God above will punish her. If she be innocent will we be her murderers?

I enter my humble plea for the life of this poor creature and I hope to hear that you have spared it. I know how trying these matters are to one who is kind of heart and just. I sympathise with you in the severe trials you undergo in determining these matters. I

would have spared you any interference but I cannot rest until I
have sent away this appeal.

Believe me
Dear Mr. Mills
Yours Sincerely

Alex T. Darroch

Toronto
January 17/1898

Hon. David Mills
Minister of Justice, Ottawa

Coming in contact a great deal with the public in my business I
beg to advise you that public opinion is strongly against the execution of Mrs. Sternaman, not so much on the grounds of her sex as
the opinion that the evidence contained such an element of doubt
that it did not justify the verdict, the [main] points being first, the absence of motive, it is generally agreed that the trivial amounts on the
lives of her husbands, her indifference as to the payment of premiums, in fact her indifference to the insurance generally did not show
that gain was her motive, if not what was it?
    The fact that the purchase of the poison that she gave to her
husband has not been proven in any shape or form, there is also
doubt as to whether the body was embalmed or not, it appears that
the undertaker stated at first he did embalm and again that he did
not, the fact that this woman brought her husband from among
comparative strangers to within a short distance of her mother in law
who disliked her, a most unlikely act if she was poisoning him, her
husbands letter exonerating her from all blame...on account of gossip, which in itself would have been enough to have prevented any
person of ordinary intelligence from going any farther with poisoning. The fact that she did not make the slightest attempt at escape in
Buffalo while under suspicion although she had ample chance, her
perfect confidence in the result of the trial notwithstanding her lack
of faith in the justice of a Canadian Court, is also stated by witnesses
of the trial that the judge never touched on this point that if there
was any reasonable doubt of guilt that the prisoner was entitled to

the same, this of course may have been an oversight and I am inclined to think it was as I have every faith in our system of justice, this omission may have conveyed to the minds of the jury coupled with the judges charge generally that there was no other course open than to bring in a verdict of guilty, evidently relying on their recommendation to mercy to save the prisoners life, it is a common rumor that a considerable number of the jury now deeply regret their verdict and are willing to do anything they can to right a wrong, the unproven charge that the prisoner poisoned her first husband had a bad effect on the minds of the jury and the general impression is that it was unfair to admit the evidence under such circumstances. I never saw Mrs. Sternaman or never heard of her until this trial but I think in the interests of justice you should know that public opinion is on this matter and I have heard it freely stated that if this woman is executed it will go a long way towards preventing juries from bringing in a verdict of guilty when there is any doubt then perhaps each verdict would be a righteous one as they would have no faith the recommendation to mercy being acted on, a result to be deplored I have very faith that you will grant a new trial.

    Reformer

APPENDIX B

PETITIONS*

Petitions circulated in Haldimand County
Geographic headings indicate places of residence, as reported on petitions.

BUFFALO
David Marks

BYNG
Jas. Gamble
Geo. Hanna
Elizabeth Main
William Main
John Mehlenbacker
Jane Murphy
J.E. Scott
Mrs. Alice Stephens

CAISTOR
James Blade

CALEDONIA
David Ashbaugh
Samuel Avery
James Bain
Henry Barrett
W.H. Brown
H.C. Clark
J.M. Clysdale
James Cochran
James Draper
Thomas Draper
Patrick Fagan
Robt. Ford
Alexis Gauthier
J.N. Grigsly
W.H. Hall

J. Aldridge Jr.
Edward Lewis
John McGarry
John McMillen
Peter McMullin
Lewis Mitchell
N. Mitchell
John Murphy
James Overend
Thos. Pattison
J. Smiley
Thom. Spratt
Robert Thompson
James Thorburn
Robert Weston
F.W. Yolliss

CANBOROUGH
Marlin Glenny
Thomas Glenny
S. Clifford Jr.
Jacob Kline
William Robinson
V.H. Wardell
J.D. Whitwell
G.S. Wilcox

CAYUGA
L. Anguish
William Arrell
L.L. Barber
W.A. Barnes

Chas. Barrick
Dr B. Baxter
J. Baxter
E. Birdsall
E.C. Campbell
J.G. Carruthers
M. Cassidy
Thomas Comer
Michael Conly
W.M. Connell
G.S. Cotter
A.A. Davis
Robert H. Davis
John Donaldson
J.H. Donnelly
Thom. Doyle
J.D. Edgar
G. Ellis
C.W. Evans
John Farmer
John Farrell
J.E. Fissette
J.G. Foote
J. Francis
Wm. G. Gibbins
G.A. Gibson
J.M. Gifford
A.K. Goodman
Geo. L. Goodrow
W.A.D. Grant
J.L. Jeffries
John A. Jennings

*Names which are illegible on the original are not included here

William Kerr
A. M. Kerry
J. Kohler
G. Lishman
M. McClung
Alesd. McFarlane
D. McFarlane
Peter J. McMullin
James Mitchell
J.A. Murphy
P. Murphy
James Murray
R. Mussen
J. Nagel
A.P. Parsons
W.J. Quinsey
A.J. Rebbetoy
E.L. Rigg
John H. Rogers
L.E. Russell
Ed. T. Seaton
J.M. Sheppard
Annie Sider
T. Snider
J.E. Steele
E. Storkton
Andrew T. Thompson
D. Thompson
M.C. Upton
Jno. Walsh
Thomas Walsh
E. Waters
George Waters
Richard Weir
F.W. Wintermute
A.Y. Young

CHEAPSIDE
W.S. Buckley

DUNN
John H. Baker

William G. Brennan
George Buckmaster
Robert E. Duffy
John Hamilton
John McFarel
Ed Nickerson
Witham Patton
Jas. G. Ramsey

DUNNVILLE
E.J. Aikens
John Arderlay
T. Arderlay
Matthew Armour
J.J. Asher
W.A. Bailey
A. Barker
Norman H. Beebe
Albert Bell
Robert Bennett
E.F. Benson
M.M. Billy
F. Blott
John Bolger
R. Bradley
Wm. N. Braund
William Bromley
S.W. Brown
M.S. Brunt
William Bullock
Wilson Bullock
J.L. Burgess
J.F. Carmody
John L. Chapman
J.B. Clark
Daniel Clemo
Wm. Clemo
Louis A. Congdon
Archibald Cooper
C.N. Crawford
Hary Crayston
John Crick
E.J. Crumb

E.L. Crumb
Mrs. Currey
A.T. Deake
Geo. B. Docker
Miss Dunham
S. Dunham
H. Eaton
James Edgar
Bert Ell
W.H. Ford
Lewis Fox
H. Fralick
Miss Fry
B. Fryer
Melvin Gayman
Rev. James Gourlay
John Green
W.J. Griffith
John Hamilton
E.J. Haney
James F. Haney
John Happell
R.A. Harrison
S. Hays
William Henry
Charles Herring
Jacob Hind
Wm. Hindson
W.W. Hines
John A. Honsberger
Paul Honsberger
W.R. Jackson
H.C. Killins
R.M. Killins
F.W. Klingender
William Kohler
Charles Krick
W.W. Krick
F.R. Lalor
E.J. Lasalle
Wm. H. Latimer
R.F. Lattimore
Geo. Lint

David Logan
Mark Logan
Chas. L. Longham
A. T. Pringle, M.D.
N. Hopkins M.D.
G.M. Marshall
J. Marshall
John D. Martin
Charles May
Alfred McDonald
D. McDonald
George McGraw
I.A. McIndoe
W. R. McIndoe
M. McLean
John Miller
Geo. A. Montague
P. Montague
T. Montague
W. Montague
J.T. Moore
Jno. Moote
P.C. Moote
W.S. Moote
A. Nash
Richard Neuman
Sarah J. Nichol
William Nicholson
John Norris
Wm. Oakes
F.G. Orme
G.H. Orme
W.D. Patterson
F.J. Perry
John Phippel
F.J. Ramsey
A.C. Rastrick
Bruce Reed
W.H. Rhora
John Riddell
Jas. R. Robb
G.W. Robinson
James Rolston

L.G. Rolston
A.A. Root
John Root
N.J. Root
Fergus Scholfield
Frank Scholfield
Jas. Shand
Halton A. Sheehan
Harry Sheehan
J.B. Sheehan
Issac Sherbek
Philip Sibbert
Peter I. Sime
D. Simpson
George Smith
George R. Smith
J.H. Smith
F.P. Smithers
R.A. Smithers
George Spence
H.L. Spence
George Spraling
I. Steel
A. Steele
Allen Stevens
Charles Stevens
Jno A. Stevens
Walter Stone
Isaac Strohm
A.S. Swayze
S. Swazye
R.H. Sweet
John Taylor
Wesley Teller
A.W. Thewlis
Thomas L.M. Tipton
Thos. A. Tipton
Charles Trimble
J.J. Vankeuren
Robert Wait
W.F. Wardell
Daniel Warner
N.L. Weatherby

Geo. H. Werner
J.B. Werner
D. Westcott
Chas. Widerick
M.D. Winslow
D. Wismer
Levi Wismer
John K. Woods
C.C. Yocom
W. Young
Ed Zimmerman

FISHERVILLE
Levi Drehmer
Nicholas Last
George Nablo
John H. Nauman
Gordon Paterson
Jas. G. Paterson
Albert Reicheld
Edward Reicheld
Henry Reichheld
Jacob Rohrback
Henrcy Schneider
Lillian Schneider
Ernest Walker

GALT
D. Patterson

HAGERSVILLE
W.D. Aiken
W.J. Anderson
Walker C. Anderson
Andrew Burbidge
F. Donly
W.A. Flack
Alex Fleming
J.H. Forman
H. Gallagher
John Graham
Mr. James Harkins
Mrs. James Harkins

Chas. Harris
Thomas Harris
William Hopper
J.S. Kelly
Benjamin Kinsley
Daniel J. Lynch
J. Lynch
J. M. McBride
Jarvis McBride
Robt. McBride
Samuel C. McBride
A. McDonald
Robert McDonald
Daniel McNaughton
H.C. Morrow
Charles Smelser
Wm. Swayze
Wm. Trotter
John Walker

HAMILTON
James Hall
M.J. O'Reilly

MOULTON
William Aikin
Samuel Allen
Joshua Boughner
James T. Burger
Jacob Burtch
James H. Cameron
Daniel Clifford
Martin Dolan
David Ecker
A.W. Emerson
R.C. Glaves
John Jones
Viola Jones
Geo. Van Keuren
Francis Kinney
George Lambier
Alex Mcdonald
Alex McGregor

Wm. McQuillan
Joseph Mossip
Henry Smith
James Sullivan
John W. Teft
Jas. S. Waddell
Frank Waines

NANTICOKE
William Walker

NORTH CAYUGA
J.A. Chrysler
Mrs. R. N. Chrysler
W. A. Chrysler
T.A. Gifford
Frank Hammond
Simeon Honsberger
Peter Mclaren
George Mills
Mrs. L. Mino
George W. Parsons
Mrs. G. Parsons
Geo C. Sevenpiper
Wm. Walters
John Wardell
Mrs. J. Wardell
Ida Williamson
Maggie Williamson
Mark Williamson
Sarah Williamson

ONEIDA
R. John O'Reilly

PORT MAITLAND
Charles Ross

RAINHAM
Michael Arnold
Ethel Badley
Mrs. Badley
William Bessey

Mrs. P.A. Raichelt
Nicholas Nablo
Alex Cronk
Tillman Dennis
Frederick Drecker
Edward Evans
G. H. Evans
Wesley Evans
David Featherston
G.E. Fitzgerald
F.I. Fitzpatrick
Abraham Gee
J.B. Harrison
R.A. Havill
Fred Held
John High
Lorraine High
Rosell High
Samuel Honsberger
James Hoover
A. Kendrick
Hattie Kendrick
Libbie Kendrick
Mrs. A. Kendrick
Fred Makey
Delmar Middaugh
William Miller
Adam Nablo
Albert Neigh
Fidelia Nie
E.H. Overholt
Mary Overholt
Samuel Peacock
John H. Reichheld
Guy A. Reichel
Mary S. Reicheld
Nichoals Reicheld
Caroline Schier
Jacob Schier
Manford Schier
Nicholas Schier
Catherine Schneider
Charlotte Schneider

Felty Sitter
Mrs. Felty Sitter
Parker Tate
James Topp
Robert Ullman
J.A. Waldron
John Walker
Mrs. John Walker
Albert Weaver

SELKIRK
L.H. Brock
W.J. Brown
David Byers
S. Culp
G.C. Derby
M.F. Derby
J. H. Eckhardt
Nelson Edsall
Dr. J. Fry
Mrs. Fry
Mrs. George Gamble
Byron Gee
Jonathan Gee
W.O. Hahn
Albert Hedden
Geo. Y. Hedden
Chris Helka
Elias Hoover
J.D. Hoover
John Oscar Hoover
Mrs. John Hoover
Ben Hurst
Alfred Knisley
Esther Miller
B.E. Nablo
E.G. Overholt
N. Overholt
E.E. Phillips
David Ross
Sarah Ross
John Shaveleer
Mrs. Mary Shaveleer

Isaac W. Smith
Mrs. A. Steele
Peter W. Steele
Isaac Wardell
John Wardell
Mrs. T. Wardell
T. Wardell

SHERBROOKE
John Cumming
Nelson Kinnaird
T. McCallum

SOUTH CAYUGA
Celia S. Benner
George Benner
G.T. Culp
James Forbes
Eliza High
Ezra High
Joseph Hughes
Danford Krimberger
George Nie
Robert Overholt
Clara M. Raichell
Edward Raichelt
John Reichall
Herbert Sherk
Lizzie Sherk
John H. Stengel
Isaac G. Wismer

STROMNESS
Jno. Logan

WAINFLEET
Thomas Burgess
Geo. Cooke
E.M. Gleason
John McCallum
Bradford Moore
Hamilton Ricker

WALPOLE
Daniel Keyes
J. Marke
John Wardell
Walter T. Wardell

YORK
A.A. Bain
John Thompson

**PETITION
CIRCULATED IN
LINDSAY**

Mrs. Archambault
Mrs. Cathro
Mrs. W. Cathro
Miss V. McD. Coulter
Miss A.S. Dufferin
Mrs. Hughson
Miss A.E. Laidlaw
Cora Little
Mrs. Little
Mrs. W. M. McCarty
Mrs. Wm. McDonald
Mrs. Jno. Mitchell
Miss E.M. Perrin
Miss L. Perrin
Mrs. L. Perrin
Miss Porter
Mrs. Porter
Mrs. L. Smith
Mrs. A. Soames
Miss I.M. Welsh
Miss M. C. Windrum
Mrs. Wright

PETITIONS CIRCULATED IN TORONTO

W.F. Ardagh	319 Sherbourne St.
John Armstrong	67 Colborne St.
J.G. Ashworth	660 Euclid Avenue
W. Banks	579 Parliament St.
I. Bellick Bathurst	48 Gildersleeve Ave.
Frank Barnes	413 Spadina Ave.
T.W. Barton	32 Phoebe St.
Thomas Bell	437 Euclid Avenue
John Bengough	534 Church St.
F.H. Brown	37 Wood Street
J.R. Brown	14 Wood Street
Jno. S. Bruce	35 Walton St.
A.W. Campbell	Parliament Buildings
Henry Carter	142 Manning Ave.
W.H. Cathro	677 Queen St.
George Chamberlain	675 Queen West
John G. Chester	783 Queen St. East
N.J. Clark	120 Yorkville Avenue
Geo. Craig	595 Manning Avenue
Rebecca Cunningham	12 Ross St.
B.T. Cupplers	123 Berkely St.
Mabel Dalby	343 College St.
John Darrach	282 Avenue Road
M. Darwin	33 Arthur Street
Thos. Davidson	31 Hayden St.
John Davis	93 Euclid Avenue
R. Defoe	201 Jarvis
N.M. Devean	159 Yonge St.
I. Devline	47 Markham
D.J. O'Donoghue	95 D'Arcy Street
W.N. Douglas	14 Russell Rd.
A. Duncan	241 Chestnut
J. Dunlop	165 Elizabeth St.
E. Easton	181 Borden St.
Florence Harrison	Ont.Medi.Col./Women
A. Elvins	8 College Street
Edna Fallis	127 Spruce Street
K. Fallis	127 Spruce Street
Mrs. R. Fallis	127 Spruce Street
Edith Fisher	119 Indian Rd.
Geo. F. Forster	144 Macpherson Ave.

W.G. Forsyth	225 Victoria St.
Vincent P. Foyle	273 Landsdowne Ave.
K. Frawley	2 College St.
Jennie Frazier	40 Cecil St.
W.O. Galloway	632 Bathurst St.
D.P. Garrow	51 Ontario St.
R.C. Gavin	39 Adelaide East
R. Gibson	15 Toronto St.
Robert Glockling	55 Kensington Avnue
P.M. Grant	Toronto Junction
W. J. Gray	31 St. Andrew Street.
Thomas A. Gregg	392 Huron St.
M. Grupe	286 Parliament St.
A.E.H. Grupe	159 Yonge St.
Wm. Guthrie	12 Ross St.
Pauline Guthrie	12 Ross St.
Eliza L. Guthrie	12 Ross St.
Robert P. Hall	370 College St.
Ella Halstead	40 Cecil St.
R.B. Hamilton	236 Sherbourne St. S.
A.E. Harper	196 Sherbrooke St.
F.A. Harrington	345 Jarvis St.
A. Harris	702 Queen West
Ed Harris	365 Wellesley St.
John Hayward	452-1/2 Yonge St.
J. Henderson	50 Homewood Ave.
J. Henderson	30 Melbourne Avenue
F. Hewitt	8 Teranlay St.
Y. Hewitt	54 Brunswick
C.J. Higgins	Parliament Buildings
Robert Hodgins	60 Robinson St.
C.B. Hoggan	26 Alexander St.
Arthur W. Holmes	39 Northwest Avnue
E. Horwood	Technical School
E.N. Houghton	127 Clinton Street
A. Howell	316 Wellesley St.
N.A. Ingram	67 Confed. Life Bldg.
Wm. T. James	10 King St. West
C.H. Jenkins	157 Yonge St.
T.W. Johnstone	Islington
Mrs. Frank Jones	50 Regent Avenue
Frank Jones	50 Regent Avenue
William Jones	31 Jackney St.

M.H. Jones	108 Amelia Street
J.H. Jones	108 Amelia Stret
William Joyce	47 Ontario St.
A.F. Jury	19 Richmond St.
Wisdom Kennedy	232 Gerrard East
Geo. King	55 Kensington
H.A. Laurence	32 Church
Edw. C. Lean	423 Carlton St.
Mrs. T. LeBelle	39 Woolsely St.
W.R. Ledger	48 Melbourne Ave.
C. Levesque	16 Adelaide St. West
D.S. Macorquodale	214 Dovercourt Rd.
D. Macorquodale	214 Dovercourt Rd.
J. Macorquodale	214 Dovercourt Rd.
G. Macorquodale	214 Dovercourt Road
Mary McDonnell	"Sunnyside"
F.D. McEntee	40 Cecil St.
Thoms. McGillicudy	369 Givens Street
James McLaughlin	552 Adelaide West.
Flora MacDonald Merrill	205 Wellesly St.
A. Miller	8 Bellevue Rd.
S. Drury Monroe	632 Queen St.
J.A. Monson	135 Tecumseth St.
Mrs. I. Morton	282 Bathurst St.
G.E. Morton	282 Bathurst St.
A. Morton	282 Bathurst St.
Wm. G. Murray	31 Hayden St.
C.S. Myers	18 Borden St.
S. Nesbitt	138 Brunswick Avenue
A. Nurmberger	301 Jarvis St.
S. O'Brien	Parliament Buildings
Wm. O. Connor, M.A. M.D.	632 Queen St.
A. Oldfield	17 Wilton Crescent
W. B. Oxley	121 Brooklyn Avenue
W. Patterson	38 Wilton St.
Edward Perrin	77 Victoria St.
R.E. Port	20 Franklin Avenue
J.A. Radford	266 Church St.
John Randall	500 Queen St. W.
E. Rinsley	Hamilton
W.D. Robbins	127 Spruce Street
F. Robson	131 Claremount St.
J.A. Rosser	88 St. Patrick St.

L.W. Roy	295 Church St.
Wm. Scott	87 Beaconsfield Ave.
Sallim Elias Sherck	54 Edward St.
S.J. Sheridan	172 George St.
G.L. Simpson	214 Shaw St.
Chas. T. Sissons	77 Victoria St.
May Smith	269 Broadview Avenue
C.W. Snyder	189 McCaul Street
Thos. Southwaite	Parlt. Buildings
J.K. Stewart	45 Yorkville Avenue
J.E. Stewart	43 Wyndham St.
G. Taylor	770 Yonge St.
Robert L. Thomson	25 Gerrard St. W.
John Thompson	129 Spruce
L.B. Thompson	Shirley St. School
Wm. Thompson	12 Dean St.
Phillips Thompson	199 Indian Road
Jos. E. Thompson	13 Regent St.
Clara Thompson	119 Indian Road
F.E. Titus	25 King St. W.
R.T.A. Titus	81 Oxford St.
Geo. B. Towers	444 Shaw Street
James R.H. Warren	Trinity College
A.P. Watts	10 College St.
Alfred Watson	Trinity Medical College
Ernest Webb	109 Seaton St.
A. White	200 Seaton
H.B. Willwood	164 Yonge St.
Wm. Wilson	47 Mailtand St.
John Wilson	139 Yonge Street
Madam Wiren	69 Shuter St.
Frank A. Wood	47 Adelaide St.E.
W.Wood	722 Dufferin St.
M.E. Youmans	752 Dufferin St.

BIBLIOGRAPHY

BOOKS

Adam, G. Mercer. *Toronto Old and New.* (Facsimile.) Toronto: Coles Publishing Company, 1972.

Anderson, Frank. W. *Hanging in Canada.* Aldergrove, B.C.: Frontier Publishing Ltd., 1973.

—————. *Canadian Women On the Gallows.* Saskatoon: 1987.

Boyd, Neil. *The Last Dance: Murder in Canada.* Prentice Hall Canada Inc. 1988.

Campbell, Marjorie F. *A Century of Crime: The development of Crime Detection Methods in Canada.*

Canadian Legal Directory, ed. Henry J. Morgan. Toronto: R. Carswell, 1878.

Cayuga-North Cayuga Centennial History 1867-1967. Cayuga: 1967

Cayuga United Church Historical Booklet 1969. Cayuga: 1969.

Clark, S.D. *The Social Development of Canada.* Toronto: University of Toronto Press, 1942.

Charlesworth, Hector. *Candid Chronicles.* Toronto: The Macmillan Company of Canada Limited, 1925.

—————. *More Candid Chronicles.*

A Cyclopedia of Canadian Biography, being Chiefly Men of the Time. Toronto: Rose Publishing Company, 1898.

Crime and Insurance. 1903.

Dictionary of Canadian Biography. Volumes XII and XIII. Toronto: University of Toronto Press.

Dunn, Walter S. *History of Erie County 1870-1970.* Buffalo: The Buffalo and Erie County Historical Society, 1971.

Eberle, Scott & Grande, Joseph A. *Second Looks: A Pictorial History of Buffalo and Erie County.* Norfolk, Virginia: The Donning Company, 1987.

Friedland, Martin L. *The Case of Valentine Shortis*. Toronto: University of Toronto Press, 1986.

Habenstein, Robert W. and William M. Lamers. *The History of American Funeral Directing*. Milwaukee: Bulfin Printers, Inc. 1955.

Hassard, Albert R. *Famous Canadian Trials*. Toronto: The Carswell Company, Limited, 1924.

Hamilton, James Cleland. *Osgoode Hall: Reminiscences of the Bench and Bar*. Toronto: Carswell Co. Ltd. 1904.

A History of the City of Buffalo, Its Men and Institutions. Biographical Sketches of Leading Citizens. Buffalo: nd.

History of Erie County.

History of the Bench and Bar of Erie Co. Buffalo: The Genealogical Publishing Company, 1909.

History of Welland County, nd., np.

James, Marquis. *The Metropolitan Life*. New York: Arno Press, 1976.

McDougall, Bruce. *John Wilson Murray*. Toronto: Fitzhenry & Whiteside Limited, 1980.

McGrath, W.T. (editor). *Crime and Its Treatment in Canada* (Second Edition). Toronto: Macmillan of Canada, 1976.

Middleton, Jesse Edgar. *The Municipality of Toronto, A History* (Vol.II) Toronto: The Dominion Publishing Company, 1923.

Morgan, Henry James. *The Canadian Men and Women of the Time*. Toronto: William Briggs, 1898.

Morton, Desmond. *The Queen vs. Louis Riel*. Toronto: University of Toronto Press, 1974.

Murray, John Wilson. *Memoirs of a Great Detective*. London: Heinemann, 1904.

Nelles, Robert Bertram. *County of Haldimand in Days of Auld Lang Syne*. Port Hope: The Hamlyn Press Book Printers, 1905.

Official Report of the Debates of the House of Commons of the Domininon of Canada, 3rd Session, 8th parliament, Vol. XLVI. Ottawa: Queen's Printer, 1898.

Selkirk 1792-1985. Selkirk Public Library and North Erie Shore Historical Society: 1985.

Sitting, Marshall. *Handbook of Toxic and Hazardous Chemicals.* Park Ridge: Noyes Publications, 1981.

Thomson, William A.R., M.D. *Black's Medical Dicitionary,* 31st edition. Rome & London: Buller & Tanner Ltd. 1976.

Thorwald, Jurgen. *The Century of the Detective.* New York: Harcourt, Brace and World Inc. 1965.

Toronto the Prosperous. Toronto: Mail & Empire, 1906.

Waite, P.R. *Macdonald, His Life and World.* Toronto: McGraw–Hill Ryerson, 1975.

Wallace, W. Stewart., ed. *The Macmillan Dictionary of Canadian Biography.* (Fourth Ed.) Macmillan of Canada, Toronto, 1978.

Who's Who in Canada 1922. B.M. Green, Editor, Toronto, International Press Ltd.

NEWSPAPERS

Buffalo Evening News
Buffalo Morning Express
Daily Mail and Empire
Dunnville Chronicle
Dunnville Gazette
Evening Tribune (Welland)
Globe (Toronto)
Haldimand Advocate (Cayuga)
Hamilton Evening Times
Hamilton Spectator
Mail & Empire
Ottawa Citizen
Simcoe Reformer

MAGAZINES and JOURNALS

The Embalmers Monthly. January 1896.

——————. June 1897.

Dubinsky, Karen and Franca Iacoveta. "Murder, Womanly Virtue and Motherhood: The Case of Angelina Naplitano, 1911–1922" in *The Canadian Historical Review*, LXII 4, 1991.

Hassard, Albert R. "Famous Canadian Orators: Britton Bath Osler" in *The Canadian Magazine*, February 1920.

Mitchell, Tom. "Blood with the Taint of Cain": Immigrant Labouring Children, Manitoba Politics, and the Execution of Emily Hilda Blake. *Journal of Canadian Studies*, Vol. 28, No. 4 (Winter 1993–94).

Star Weekly, May 15, 1915.

Strange, Carolyn, "Wounded Womanhood and Dead Men: Chivalry and the Trials of Clara Ford and Carrie Davies," in *Gender Conflicts: New Essays in Women's History*. Toronto: University of Toronto Press, 1992.

DOCUMENTS

Cayuga Methodist New Connexion Church, Session Minutes, Vol. 1, 1886–1910. United Church Archives, Toronto.

Chipman Family Tree.

Congregational Minute Book, Cayuga Methodist Church, 1862–1896. United Church Archives, Toronto.

Genealogy and general files, Haldimand County Museum Archives, Cayuga.

Haldimand County Council Minutes, North Erie Shore Historical Society, Selkirk.

Methodist Church Hamilton Conference Minutes, 1921. United Church Archives, Toronto.

Minutes of Trustee Board, Cayuga Methodist New Connection Circuit, 1889–1923. United Church Archives, Toronto.

Minutes of Cayuga Methodist New Connexion Circuit, Quarterly Board, 1843–1926, Vol. 2.

Keifer, Freida, "History of Fisherville." Typescript, 1979. North Erie Shore Historical Society Collection, Selkirk,Ontario.

The Matthews Northup Co's New Map of the City of Buffalo, 1895.

Rainham Township Census 1871.

Rainham Township Census 1881.

Sternaman Case. National Archives of Canada RG 13, Volume 1431, File 286A.

Sternaman File, Haldimand County Museum Archives.

Toronto Public Library Scrapbook Biographies of Men.

ENDNOTES

Prologue

Page 11,	Line 5*	Strictly speaking, Haldimand County no longer exists, having been absorbed by the Regional Municipality of Haldimand–Norfolk in 1974.

Suspicious Deaths

Page 21,	Lines 7–9	Transcript, p. 215.
	Lines 10–11	Ibid.
	Lines 17	Ibid.
Page 24–25,	Lines 43	Hamilton Spectator, Nov. 14, 1896.
Page 25,	Lines 7–27	Exhibit – Trial Documents.
Page 27,	Lines 8–10	Globe, November 19, 1897.
Page 27,	Lines 21–26	Transcript, p. 194.
Page 28,	Lines 36–43	Transcript – Page 63.
Page 29,	Lines 1–2	Ibid.
	Lines 11–18	Hamilton Spectator, Sept. 30, 1896.
	Lines 34–36	Hamilton Spectator, Nov. 18, 1896.
Page 30,	Line 2	Hamilton Spectator, Sept. 30, 1896.
	Line 36–43	Exhibit – Trial Documents.
Page 31,	Lines 1–11	Ibid.
	Lines 17–21	Transcript, p. 245.
	Lines 35–36	Hamilton Spectator, Sept. 30, 1896.
	41	Ibid.
Page 32,	Lines 39–43	Hamilton Spectator, Sept. 2, 1897.
Page 34,	Lines 15–27	Transcript, p. 89–90.
	Lines 32–33	Montreal Medical Journal, 1894.
Page 35,	Lines 7–21	Transcript, p. 93–4.
Page 36,	Lines 8–21	Transcript, p. 96.
	27–28	Ibid.
Page 37,	Line 43	Transcript, p. 97.
Page 38,	Lines 10–15	Ibid. p. 98.
	Line 43	Ibid.
Page 39,	Lines 9	Hamilton Spectator, November 18, 1896.
Page 40,	Lines 3–8	Hamilton Evening Times, Sept. 3, 1897.
	19–25	Ibid.
Page 40,	Lines 22–40	Transcript, p. 100–101.

Inquest and Extradition

Page 42,	Lines 28	Transcript, p. 169–70.
Page 43,	Line 18	Transcript, p. 195.
Page 44,	Line 4	Transcript, p. 199.
Page 45,	Lines 35–38	Transcript, p. 251.

*Line numbers refer to Lines in standard typeface.

Page 46,	Line 43	Transcript, p. 252.
	Lines 1–7	Ibid.
	Lines 33–34	Transcript, p. 103.
Page 47,	Lines 25–30	Transcript, p. 102.
	Lines 31–33	Ibid.
Page 48,	Lines 5–9	Hamilton Spectator, Sept. 30, 1896.
	Lines 15–22	Ibid., October 2, 1896.
Page 49,	Line 8	John Wilson Murray's background and exploits are legendary, although there is evidence that he fabricated portions of his colorful career. Nevertheless, at the time of Olive's trial, he was a celebrated figure, described by an 1870 writer as "Strong as a bull, quick as a cat, rather a silent fellow, slow to anger and plenteous in vengeance once he was aroused. He feared neither man, gun nor belaying pin. He was a faithful friend and relentless foe. He was the last to pick a quarrel, but once it was picked he was the last to drop it. His associates liked him. He was a silent, sturdy, self-contained man, with a remarkable gift for gaining the confidence of other men."
Page 49,	Lines 29–30	Ibid.
Page 50,	Lines 1–5	Hamilton Spectator, October 28, 1896.
	Lines 27–34	Buffalo Evening News, Oct. 28, 1896, 5th edition.
	Lines 39–40	Ibid.
Page 51,	Lines 10–15	Ibid., 6th edition.
	Lines 20–25	Dunnville Chronicle, Oct. 30, 1896.
Page 52,	Lines 30–37	Hamilton Spectator, Nov. 14, 1896.
	Lines 40–53	Dunnville Chronicle, Nov. 13, 1896
Page 54,	Lines 8–9	Ibid.
Page 55,	Lines 12–16	Ibid.
	Lines 17–43	Hamilton Spectator, Nov. 13, 1896.
Page 56,	Lines 6	Ibid.
	Lines 13–14	Ibid.
	Lines 20–30	Dunnville Chronicle, Nov. 20, 1896.
Page 57,	Line 5	Buffalo Evening News, Nov. 13, 1896.
	Lines 13–14	Dunnville Chronicle, Nov. 20, 1896.
	Lines 35–43	Buffalo Evening News, Nov. 13, 1896.
Page 58,	Lines 1–15	Ibid.
Page 59,	Lines 27–43	Buffalo Evening News, Nov. 14, 1896.
Page 60,	Lines 7–11	Buffalo Evening News, Nov. 18, 1896.
Page 61,	Lines 5–7	Ibid.
	Lines 30–35	Ibid.
Page 64,	Lines 5–10	Buffalo Evening News, Nov. 24, 1896.
	Lines 29–43	Hamilton Spectator, Nov. 25, 1896.
	45–51	Ibid., December 4, 1896.

Page 66,	Lines 3–5	Federal Reporter, p. 597.
Page 66,	Lines 21–43	Buffalo Evening News, Dec. 24, 1896
Page 68,	Lines 18–31	Buffalo Evening News, Dec. 26, 1896.
	Lines 35–43	Ibid.
Page 69,	Lines 36–38	Federal Reporter, p. 690

Trial for Murder

Page 70,	Lines 36–38	Robert Bertram Nelles, County of Haldimand in Days of Auld Lang Syne p. 96.
Page 71,	Lines 24–25	County Council Minutes, January 1897.
Page 72,	Line 18	Obituary, Feb. 21, 1907, Haldimand County Museum.
	Lines 28–43	Hamilton Spectator, Sept. 2, 1897.
Page 73,	Lines 1–14	Ibid.
	Lines 36–43	Hamilton Evening Times, Sept. 3, 1897.
Page 74,	Lines 1–3	Ibid.
	Lines 28–43	Ibid., Nov. 17, 1897.
Page 76,	Line 20	Osler's first venture into business came when he realized that school boys had an insatiable appetite for candies, he laid in a supply and sold them to his chums on allowance day, making a small profit from the venture. Although his career was brilliant, his personal life was tragic: his face was badly scarred from burns received while rescuing his wife from a house fire. She remained an invalid for the rest of her life, and Brick often spent nights keeping her company when she was unable to sleep. A widower at the time of Olive's trial, Brick was planning a second marriage.
Page 77,	Lines 19–28	Hassard, Albert R., "Great Canadian Orators – VII. Britton Bath Osler," in The Canadian Magazine, February 1920, p. 356
Page 79,	Lines 17–19	Hamilton Evening Times, Nov. 17, 1897.
Page 80,	Lines 10–17	Ibid., Nov. 18, 1897.
Page 81,	Lines 1–8	Daily Mail & Empire, November 18, 1897.
Page 82,	Lines 26–27	Transcript, p. 8
Page 83,	Lines 1–9	Ibid.
	Lines 11–16	Ibid., p. 16.
	Lines 23–24	Ibid., p. 18.
Page 84,	Line 18–21	Ibid., p. 27.
	Lines 31–42	Ibid., p. 38.
Page 85,	Lines 6–7 1	Ibid., p. 38–39.
	Lines 8–15	Ibid., p. 39.
	Lines 21–41	Ibid.
Page 86,	Lines 4–11	Ibid., p. 39–40.
	Lines 24–31	Ibid., p. 41.

Page 124,	Lines 1–4	Ibid.
	Lines 9–23	Ibid., p. 236.
	Lines 26–27	Ibid., p. 238.
	Lines 29–43	Ibid.
Page 125,	Lines 1–34	Ibid., p. 239.
Page 126,	Lines 33–43	Ibid., p. 241.
Page 127,	Lines 1–25	Ibid., p. 241–242.
	Lines 32–34	Ibid., p. 247.
Page 128,	Lines 3–23	Ibid., p. 248.
	Lines 28	Ibid., p. 252.
	Lines 33–34	Ibid., p. 256–257.
Page 129,	Lines 1–7	Ibid., p. 257.
	Lines 33–43	Ibid., p. 276.
Page 130,	Lines 2–7	Ibid., p. 278.
	Lines 10–15	Ibid., p. 279.
	Lines 19–23	Ibid., p. 281.
	Lines 31–37	Ibid., p. 283–284.
Page 131,	Lines 3–13	Ibid., p. 288.
	Line 16	Ibid.
	Lines 23–30	Ibid., p. 295.
	Lines 34–35	Ibid., p. 301.
	Lines 40–43	Ibid., p. 302.
Page 132,	Lines 1–25	Ibid.
	Lines 30–41	Ibid., p. 303.
Page 133,	Lines 5–7	Ibid., p. 305.
	Lines 16–24	Ibid., p. 307.
	Lines 27–29	Ibid., p. 309.
	Lines 30–32	Ibid., p. 310.
	Line 43	Ibid., p. 313–314.
Page 134,	Lines 1–15	Ibid., p. 314.
Page 134,	Lines 36–41	Ibid.
Page 135,	Lines 7–14	Ibid., p. 317.
	Lines 22–26	Ibid.
	Lines 35–37	Ibid., p.324.
	Lines 41–43	Ibid.
Page 136,	Lines 1–10	Ibid.
	Lines 11–21	Ibid., p. 326
	Lines 25–33	Ibid.
	Lines 37–42	Ibid., p. 330.
Page 137,	Lines 5–15	Ibid., p. 331–332.
	Lines 23–42	Ibid., p. 332
Page 138	Lines 17–26	Ibid., p. 343.
	Lines 40–43	Ibid., p. 343–344.
Page 139,	Lines 1–7	Ibid., p. 344.
	Lines 12–22	Ibid.
	Lines 27–32	Ibid., p. 346.
	Lines 35–41	Ibid., p. 349.

Page 140,	Lines 10–15	Ibid.
	Lines 20–23	Ibid.
	Lines 28–40	Ibid., p. 352–353.
Page 141,	Lines 1–10	Ibid., p. 353.
	Lines 42–43	Ibid.
Page 142	Lines 1–4	Ibid.
	Lines 15–42	Ibid., p. 355
Page 143,	Lines 1–3	Ibid.
Page 143,	Lines 14–24	Daily Mail & Empire, November 22, 1897.

In the Shadow of the Gallows

Page 144,   Lines 5–10   Toronto Star, n.d.

Lines 11–21   Quoted in Hamilton Evening Times,
November 26, 1897.

Lines 26–34   Ibid.

Page 145,   Line 12   Anderson, p. 241. Workman despite
repeated beatings from her husband James, had
raised his two children as her own. Often, when
he was in a drunken rage, Elizabeth took refuge
with neighbours. A devout church goer, she
practised the Christian philosophy of turning the
other cheek for many years, until October, 1872.
Then, unwilling to endure another beating, she
turned on her husband and beat him to death
with a club. A guilty verdict was a foregone conclusion, since there was little doubt that Elizabeth
was responsible for her husband's death. Given
the circumstances, however, most people believed she would be given life imprisonment. No
commutation order ever came; in May 1873,
clutching a white handkerchief in one hand and
a bunch of white flowers in the other, she walked
calmly to the gallows.

Although public hangings were still considered entertainment, few spectators had gathered.
The execution was a clean one—Workman died in
seconds, of a broken neck. Out of respect, her
body dangled for only twenty minutes, rather
than the traditional sixty, then was cut down,
placed in a waiting coffin, and buried beneath the
scaffold.

Angeline Poulin, condemned at Bathurst, New
Brunswick, for complicity in the axe murder of
her husband Xavier, was sentenced to death.
Pregnant at the time of the trial, she was given a
reprieve of several months, during which time
her lover was hanged. A short time later, on

December 22, 1874, Angeline's sentence was changed to life imprisonment. After serving more than ten years at the Dorchester Penitentiary, she was pardoned and released into the care of one of her married daughters.

A year after Angeline Poulin's death sentence was changed, another woman was on trial for her life in Toronto. Alice Davis, wife of a Toronto abortionist who practised medicine without a license, was convicted for her part in the death of Jane Vaughn Gilmour, a young Scottish immigrant. When the pair were sentenced to hang on December 8, 1875, Alice became the first Toronto women to receive the death penalty. Again, there was no recommendation of mercy, although newspaper reporters portrayed Alice as the less guilty of the two. As one reporter commented, "It is a woman's ambition to marry well, and she, as a farmer's daughter from the state of New York no doubt thought she was doing well to marry Dr. Davis." Despite public condemnation of abortion, the government took a less severe view of the crime, and, on November 30, commuted both sentences to life imprisonment. Alice Davis served just five years in Kingston Penitentiary before receiving her parole.

Susan Kennedy emigrated from Leeds, England and settled in Griffintown, a poorer section of Montreal. Although she was married to an Irishman, Jacob Mears, Susan worked as a prostitute. Although tall and well-built, she was exceptionally bad tempered. Often, she would sit at her open window and shout insults at passersby until the police were called in.

On June 27, 1879, Susan, a client named Michael Flanagan, and another prostitute, Mary Gallagher, were drinking in Susan's rented apartment. Sometime around noon, while Flanagan was sleeping off the effects of whisky, Susan killed Mary with a small meat axe, chopped off her head and dumped it in a pail, leaving the body on the kitchen floor. It was discovered several hours later by Jacob Mears.

Initially, Susan and both the men were suspected of the crime. However, Mears was not indicted, and Flanagan was acquitted at the murder trial. Although there were strong indications that

Susan was not in her right mind, she was found
guilty and sentenced to death. The sentence was
later commuted life imprisonment in Kingston
Penitentiary, where Susan died two years later.

	Lines 36–43	Affidavit, December 3, 1897, National Archives (NA) RG 13, Vol. 1431, File 286A
	Lines 20–40	Daily Mail and Empire, December 6, 1897.
Page 147,	Line 14	Thomas Phillips Thompson as a special reporter covering Ireland, he became something of an expert on the question of home rule for that country, as well as a sympathizer. Nevertheless he was well liked for his excellent sense of humor, which he shared through hilarious public speeches. Thompson, recovering from the recent loss of his wife, was at a particularly vulnerable stage of life.
	Lines 25–43	Globe, December 11, 1897.
Page 148,	Lines 1–42	Ibid.
Page 149,	Lines 6–16	Ibid.
	Lines 21–43	Ibid., December 18, 1897.
Page 150,	Lines 5–27	Ibid.
	Lines 34–43	Ibid.
Page 151,	Lines 1–4	Ibid.
	Lines 14–28	A.A. Davis to Mills, December 10, 1897, NA.
	Lines 36–43	Globe, December 25, 1897.
Page 152,	Lines 14–30	Mail and Empire, undated clipping, NA.
	Line 41	Ibid.
Page 153,	Lines 1–16	Ibid.
Page 154,	Lines 1–43	Thayer to Mills, January 1, 1898, NA.
Page 155,	Lines 1–43	Ibid.
Page 156,	Lines 1–30	Ibid.
Page 157,	Line 5	Ibid.
	Lines 20–35	Daily Mail and Empire, January 8, 1898.
Page 158,	Lines 1–43	Ibid.
Page 159,	Lines 16–25	Globe, January 8, 1898.
Page 160,	Lines 1–41	Thayer to Mills, January 4, 1898, NA.
Page 161,	Lines 26–36	Charlton to Mills,January 5, 1898, NA.
Page 162,	Lines 1–35	Mills to Charlton, January 7, 1898, NA.
Page 163,	Lines 5–35	Foote to Mills, January 5, 1898, NA.
	Line 43	Phillips Thompson to Mills, January 8, 1898, NA.
Page 164,	Lines 1–11	Ibid.
	Lines 20–43	Various petitions. NA.
Page 165,	Lines 43–43	Cayuga area petition, ibid.
Page 166,	Lines 10–15	Ibid.
	Lines 18–43	Thayer to Mills, January 13, 1898, NA.
Page 167,	Lines 1–43	Ibid.

Page 168,	Lines 1–12	Ibid.
	Lines 23–43	Armour to Mills, January 14, 1898, NA.
Page 169,	Lines 1–11	Ibid.
	Lines 18–36	Hamilton Spectator, January 20, 1898.
Page 170,	Lines 5–9	Ottawa Citizen, November 18, 1897.
	Lines 15–19	Ibid., January 18, 1897.
	Lines 26–43	Buffalo Morning Express, January 19, 1898.
Page 171,	Lines 1–5	Ibid.
	Line 22	When he was not carrying out an execution, Radclive worked as a steward at the Sunnyside Boating Club in Toronto, at least until one of the guests, an office in the Northwest Mounted Police, recognized him and complained that he would not be served by a "common hangman." Radclive was fired. Newspapers referred to him as something of a mystery man. He tried to keep his private life separate from his professional one, although his notoriety eventually led to the break–up of his marriage. His domestic situation might also have been exacerbated by his own attitude towards the job. Radclive was bore no ill–will towards condemned prisoners, but nevertheless believed he was serving justice. However, he was no cold–blooded functionary, and the executions sometimes weighed heavily on his mind. For one thing, he had to face the censure of crowds who objected to capital punishment, or to the execution of a particular individual. And sometimes he was appalled by the vindictiveness of officials. Once, when an elderly murderer in Ste–Scholastique, Quebec, died of a heart attack on the gallows, the sheriff insisted that Radclive hang the corpse. Following this travesty, Radclive, who had long relied on alcohol for comfort after performing his grim duty, began drinking heavily.
Page 172,	Lines 11–12	Charlesworth, Candid Chronicles, p. 216–217.
Page 173,	Lines 6–9	NA.
	Lines 20–25	Hamilton Evening Times, January 19, 1898
	Lines 30–40	Hamilton Spectator, January 19, 1898
Page 174,	Lines 7–31	Regina vs. Sternaman, statement by Mills, singed January 19, 1898, NA.

The Power of Public Opinion

Page 176,	Lines 15–21	W.A. Mackey's letter in Toronto World, reprinted in Dunnville Chronicle, January 28,

		1898.
	Line 27	Ibid.
Page 177,	Lines 11–22	Dunnville Chronicle, February 18, 1898.
	Lines 17–25	Ibid., March 18, 1898.
	Lines 30–31	Ibid.
Page 178,	Lines 27–43	Ibid.
Page 179,	Lines 1–25	Ibid., April 8, 1898.
Page 180,	Lines 1–43	Ibid.
Page 181,	Lines 1–16	Ibid.
	Lines 27–28	Official Report of the Debates of the House of Commons of the Dominion of Canada, 3rd Session, 8th Parliament, Vol. XLVI, March 10, 1898. Ironically, Nicholas Flood Davin had a political connection with Haldimand County, having unsuccessfully run for election there in the 1870s.
	Lines 35–40	Dunnville Chronicle, April 22, 1898.
Page 182,	Lines 1–25	Ibid.
	Lines 33–43	Ibid., May 6, 1898.
Page 183,	Lines 1–36	Ibid.
Page 184,	Lines 1–41	Ibid.
Page 185,	Lines 1–10	Ibid.
	Line 30	Charlesworth, Candid Chronicles, p. 262.
	Lines 41–43	Charlesworth, More Candid Chronicles, p. 232.
Page 186,	Lines 6–30	Ibid. p, 233–234.
Page 187,	Line 32	Hamilton Spectator, May 5, 1898.
Page 188,	Line 11	Ibid.
Page 190,	Lines 23–39	Charlesworth, Candid Chronicles.
Page 191,	Lines 3–18	Dunnville Chronicle, May 13, 1890.
Page 193,	Lines 22–38	Hamilton Spectator, May 9, 1898.
Page 194,	Lines 2–14	Ibid.

Aftermath

Page 196,	Line 8	Hamilton Spectator, June 30, 1898.
	Lines 25–34	Dunnville Chronicle, June 10, 1898.
Page 197,	Lines 10–16	Hamilton Spectator, June 30, 1898.
Page 198,	Lines 2–11	Charlesworth, More Candid Chronicles, p. 262.
	Lines 35–38	Haldimand Advocate, March 6, 1902.
Page 199,	Lines 36–39	Transcript, p. 55.
Page 201,	Lines 28–35	Ibid., p. 353.
	Line 43	Ibid., p. 349.
Page 202,	Lines 1–5	Ibid.
Page 203,	Line 38	Ibid., p. 90.

INDEX

THE AUTHOR

Although Cheryl MacDonald has written on subjects ranging from peanut farming to time management, her first love is history. Since moving to rural Nanticoke, Ontario in 1981, she has written extensively on Canadian and local history. Previous books include *Adelaide Hoodless: Domestic Crusader*; *Emma Albani: Victorian Diva*; *A View in Verse* (a collection of folk poetry from Haldimand–Norfolk); and a history of the Norfolk County Fair, *Splendor in the Fall.*

A graduate of the University of Waterloo, Cheryl has also written articles for the 1992 best seller *Chronicle of Canada*, *Horizon Canada* and *The Beaver*. She is active in several heritage groups and is currently preparing another book with a Haldimand connection–a biography of poet Wilson MacDonald.